IMPROVING
EDUCATIONAL QUALITY

IMPROVING EDUCATIONAL QUALITY

A GLOBAL PERSPECTIVE

Edited by
David W. Chapman
and
Carol A. Carrier

Contributions to the Study of Education, Number 35

GREENWOOD PRESS
New York • Westport, Connecticut • London

Library of Congress Cataloging-in-Publication Data

Improving educational quality : a global perspective / edited by David
  W. Chapman and Carol A. Carrier.
    p.   cm.—(Contributions to the study of education, ISSN
  0196–707X ; no. 35)
    Includes bibliographical references.
    ISBN 0–313–26623–9 (lib. bdg. : alk. paper)
    1. School improvement programs—Developing countries.
  2. Education—Developing countries.   I. Chapman, David W.
  II. Carrier, Carol A.   III. Series.
  LB2822.84.D44I48   1990
  370'.9172'4—dc20   89–37317

British Library Cataloguing in Publication Data is available.

Library of Congress Catalog Card Number: 89–37317
ISBN: 0–313–26623–9
ISSN: 0196–707X

First published in 1990

Greenwood Press, Inc.
88 Post Road West, Westport, Connecticut   06881

Printed in the United States of America

The paper used in this book complies with the
Permanent Paper Standard issued by the National
Information Standards Organization (Z39.48–1984).

10 9 8 7 6 5 4 3 2 1

Contents

Illustrations

Part One

IMPROVING EDUCATIONAL QUALITY

1

Introduction: Improving Educational Quality in Developing Countries

David W. Chapman and Carol A. Carrier

One of the most severe challenges facing education systems in most countries today is how to meet demands for higher quality public education within increasingly severe national economic and fiscal constraints. Faced with severe economic pressures, many countries must find new fiscal resources (an economically unrealistic alternative), accept quality deterioration and continued inequity in access (a politically and ethnically unacceptable solution), or increase the efficiency with which educational resources are applied to the problems of instructional quality and equity of access (Windham & Wang, 1986; Chapman & Windham, 1986).

This book examines national-level strategy for improving the quality of education. It identifies and analyzes key interventions to improve educational quality. Strategies for selecting among those interventions are discussed and the major issues encountered in implementing those interventions are analyzed. The major thesis of the book is that a systems approach, as exemplified in instructional systems design technology, offers the most effective and efficient intervention for improving educational quality. A systems-based approach can work, however, only if sufficient attention is given to the motivation, knowledge, and behavior of the individuals within those systems on whose actions success of any intervention ultimately depends. Instructional systems design is based on a systems approach that recognizes that subsystems are interrelated and that changes to any one subsystem have consequences that impact on other subsystems. Effective interventions are those that anticipate and simultaneously address key issues across several subsystems.

Many interventions intended to improve education quality have focused on improving a particular dimension of the educational experience—for example, teacher training, facilities construction, instructional supervision, or the provision of instructional materials. These interventions often fail because they do not recognize or address the interacting nature of these components. Specific components are treated as if they were disconnected from the larger context of interwoven pressures that characterize complex social systems. Other interventions have tried to address the multiple interacting factors, only to get bogged down in complex political, logistical, and coordination issues beyond the ability or resources of the project to address. The critical challenges for educators and program planners in implementing a systems approach is to identify the key subsystems that must be addressed and design programs that, on one hand, are feasible within the available resources and, on the other hand, can respond to the shifting and interrelated contexts in which such programs must necessarily operate.

Particular attention is given to the issues confronting educational quality improvement in the developing world. This focus is of particular importance since:

1. there is substantial evidence of serious declines in educational quality in many developing countries even at a time when massive donor assistance has been directed toward educational improvement;

2. developing countries are the focus of many of the large-scale instructional improvement activities. These large-scale projects often try to implement strategies for quality improvement that have not been fully tested on a large scale in more industrialized countries;

3. the volatility of social, economic, and political environments that characterize developing countries makes education quality improvement efforts a particularly complex challenge;

4. lessons from developing countries' experiences often have direct relevance for more developed countries. However, inadequate attention has been given to documenting those lessons as they have occurred in developing country contexts; and

5. the transfer of instructional systems design technology from developed to developing countries has fallen short of expectations because insufficient attention has been paid to contextual differences.

AUDIENCE

This book is designed for instructional designers, program planners, administrators, evaluators, and supervisory personnel who are concerned with the design and implementation of programmatic interventions in education, particularly in international settings. It also is intended as a text for graduate students preparing for these types of positions; it is appropriate as a textbook for a variety of graduate-level international education courses. The book offers a global perspective—the principles and strategies discussed have wide application in both industrialized and developing countries.

OVERVIEW OF CHAPTERS

The book is composed of 14 chapters organized in two parts. Part One, consisting of 5 chapters, provides a general framework for formulating educational interventions to improve educational quality. Included in this section are discussions of investments that lead to student achievement, the use of efficiency as a criterion to judge the effects of educational investments, the ways in which instructional systems models enhance efficiency and educational quality, and the role that donors play in efforts to improve educational quality in developing countries. Part Two, consisting of 9 chapters, discusses a series of issues more specifically concerned with program implementation. These are addressed in three categories: (1) the teachers' role in quality improvement; (2) monitoring, evaluation, and data management; and (3) instructional delivery.

PART ONE: IMPROVING EDUCATIONAL QUALITY

In Chapter 1 the editors introduce the book, discuss the recent pressures on educational quality and the evidence of quality decline in both industrialized and developing countries, offer an overview of the chapters, and synthesize seven themes that emerge across the chapters.

In Chapter 2, Bruce Fuller reviews recent research on the factors related to student achievement in the Third World and draws a set of conclusions about what investments in education contribute to student learning. Evidence suggests that schools may exert a greater influence on achievement within developing countries compared to industrialized nations, after accounting for the effect of pupil background. However, much of the research on developing countries remains focused on material inputs. Less attention has been given to how material ingredients are actually mobilized and organized within schools and classrooms. He concludes that the provision of well-designed curricula and materials can be one of the most powerful interventions to improve students' achievement. At the same time, he argues for paying more attention to how teachers actually implement these materials in their individual classrooms. Fuller's chapter sets up the argument for the book by (a) identifying the range of interventions that have been advocated as improving instructional quality, and (b) critically reviewing the research on the contribution of these interventions to student learning in developing countries.

In Chapter 3, Douglas M. Windham argues the growing importance of efficiency as a criterion in selecting and designing strategy to improve education. One of Windham's conclusions is that systematic instructional design can be a cost-effective intervention, given a series of considerations that he identifies. In building his argument, Windham addresses four areas that have often been the subject of disagreement between instructional design specialists and economists. First is the extent to which instructional costs and effects can be measured. He addresses the concern of many educators that economic analysis does not provide a sufficiently sensitive means for evaluating nonmonetary costs or subjective benefits. Second, he examines the transferability of instructional systems across the countries. Given the existence of a variety of successful instructional systems, can a country justify the expenditure of scarce funds for design of a new system unique to a particular cultural environment? Third, he examines the application of four forms of efficiency analysis to instructional development activities and concludes that cost-effectiveness analysis offers an efficiency measure that both instructional development specialists and economists can accept. Finally, Windham suggests a management approach that incorporates economists and instructional development specialists in a collaborative manner to help ensure that the contributions of both are provided in a timely and constructive way.

Robert M. Morgan, in Chapter 4, describes instructional systems design (ISD) as an efficient strategy for improving educational quality. His argument is that meaningful interventions must be addressed from a systems perspective, in which multiple interacting factors are simultaneously addressed. He traces the adoption of systems analysis as a planning and management tool in education and its eventual application to instructional development. Morgan suggests that the use of ISD in planning and developing educational programs can result in efficiency improvements that can fully justify the time and investment required. Equally important, he suggests that ISD provides a mechanism whereby efforts of developing countries to upgrade their educational program can be tailored to the special needs and resources of those countries, thereby avoiding unreflective duplication of educational patterns (and problems) from more industrialized nations.

Given the financial constraints being experienced by most developing countries, many of the resources for education quality improvement activities are provided by international donors. Many countries, particularly in Africa, show little or no development of their education system despite massive infusions of donor aid to education over the last 20 years. In Chapter 5, Joan M. Claffey examines this problem and suggests potential solutions. She reviews the reasons donors invest in educational development and, more specifically, the donor role in instructional improvement activities. Her analysis examines the problems experienced by recipient governments in planning, targeting, and managing donor assistance activities and, secondly, the problems experienced in coordination among donor agencies working in the same country. Lack of coordination can lead to a piecemeal and noncumulative—even competitive—approach. Where this has occurred, it has led to redundant or unnecessary investments in some areas and unmet needs in others. The pressures on both donor and recipient countries that lead to lack of coordination are important to understand if such competition is to be reduced.

Donor assistance may be misplaced because of the lack of a comprehensive national educational policy to provide a context for new programs. Even where donor assistance is well targeted, however, its impact has been too often wasted for lack of a workable implementation plan and inadequate attention to the capacity of the recipient country to sustain the initiative as external monies end. Claffey argues that these are considerations that can and should be addressed at the project planning stage. She argues that the donor investment strategy in education needs to emphasize greater donor–government and donor–donor collaboration, more appropriate forms of assistance, more attention to implementation strategy, and greater sustainability if meaningful educational improvements are to follow from external assistance to education.

PART TWO: ISSUES IN IMPLEMENTING QUALITY IMPROVEMENT PROGRAMS

The Teacher's Role in Quality Improvement

Regardless of the specific focus of an educational intervention, teachers are a factor in its success because they manage classrooms and interact with students on a day-to-day basis.

The teachers' role in large-scale quality enhancement activities is examined from three perspectives. First, Sivasailam Thiagarajan, in Chapter 6, argues that traditional interventions aimed at group-oriented teacher training programs to upgrade pedagogical and content expertise have been expensive, required complex logistics, and been largely unsuccessful. He challenges a series of assumptions commonly made about the recruitment and training of new teachers as an appropriate solution to the low quality of education. The causes of poor teacher performance, he suggests, can be attributed to deficits in organizational support, job design, facilities, motivation, and teacher skills and knowledge. Not all of these can be addressed effectively through more teacher training. Rather, improved teacher performance requires the integration of training with other types of support. Thiagarajan uses the Improved Efficiency of Learning Project in Liberia to illustrate how such an integrated system can work.

Frances Kemmerer, in Chapter 7, explores ways of designing and managing teacher incentives. She treats teacher incentives as part of a larger resource allocation problem. The ability of many countries to meaningfully alter monetary incentives is severely limited by economic and fiscal constraints that are not expected to improve in the foreseeable future. With direct monetary incentives limited by larger economic and fiscal constraints, many countries will need to make better use of indirect monetary and nonmonetary incentives.

Kemmerer presents a model to outline choices among teacher incentives and offers criteria for selecting an efficient combination of incentives. Using the model, she examines typical problems encountered in the operation of central and local-level incentive systems in developing countries. Finally, she explores the political constraints to reform of incentive systems in developing countries.

Improving instructional quality always involves change at the classroom level of instruction. Conrad Wesley Snyder, Jr., in Chapter 8, suggests that an important dimension of instructional improvement efforts too frequently overlooked is that instructional interventions, in altering the activities of the classroom, may seriously impinge on the worklife of the teacher. Unless teachers' affective environment is given adequate consideration, good ideas and interventions may falter from teacher neglect and avoidance.

He argues that to have a sustainable impact, instructional interventions must attend to implicit social and cultural conditions that comprise the context of implementation. Interventions in schools can be enacted only if the teachers understand the intervention and are willing participants in the change process. Second, he suggests that teacher receptivity to the innovation can be anticipated in advance of implementation and used as a basis for altering the intervention to accommodate the local affective environment. In discussing this, he introduces the concept of "assimilation resistance."

Teachers develop certain means–ends cognitive structures to deal with the enactment of teaching. These schemes provide psychological balance for the individual's actions and serve to test new events and information. Initially, teachers will try to assimilate an instructional intervention into their perceptual and conceptual context. If this succeeds, the teachers adopt the innovation as a "good idea" within their own experience and understanding of the local situation. When this happens, it is referred to as assimilation. If they cannot reconcile the characteristics and demands of the intervention with their situation, they may resist the innovation. The degree to which assimilation fails and accommodation is necessary is referred to as assimilation resistance.

Snyder reports two studies that examine the structure of teacher affect in Botswana. He interprets the results to show that such information can be used to help reduce assimilation resistance.

Monitoring, Evaluation, and Data Management

The last several decades have been marked by increased demand for responsible use of public monies. One expression of the increased public demand for accountability has been the mandating of evaluation. Yet the evaluation of educational programs faces several challenges: (1) social and educational programs go to the heart of the value system of a society and have complex impacts that go well beyond the obvious; and (2) education is a multi-input, multi-output system with a poorly defined process of production. Understanding the multiple impacts of such programs is important in project planning and administration and is a critical part of evaluation.

Carol A. Carrier, in Chapter 9, describes these factors. While ISD models prescribe ongoing evaluation throughout the planning, design, and implementation of new programs, certain factors inhibit the straightforward application of these procedures within developing countries. She argues that stakeholder groups have unequal amounts of power so not all priorities are weighted the same. Traditional summative evaluation models may call for comparative data across programs, but such data are meaningless in developing countries because conventional programs lack even modest amounts of material, trained teachers, or consistent teaching approaches. The collection of data is hindered by poor communication systems and the inaccessibility of schools during certain seasons. The need to identify and train individuals with no experience to collect data can also negatively impact the quality of the data.

Planning can reduce these constraints, especially when evaluators systematically attend to six components within the instructional environment: the context for the new program, the treatments to be administered, the outcomes to be assessed, the learners and their characteristics, the nature of the teachers and principals involved, and the subject matter to be taught. Considering the context, for example, a new program is embedded within extant political, cultural, and social conditions that affect how much resistance will be encountered. Instructional treatments that challenge existing norms can threaten schools and communities. The selection of criteria that define a successful program vary by stakeholder group and determine the choice of outcomes that will be assessed. Participants in the instructional program, including students, teachers, and principals, have personal characteristics that affect their receptivity and capacity to participate in the program. Host country administrators believe that the subject matter of new programs should be consistent with national curriculum goals, but such goals may not be feasible. Evaluation designs that call for monitoring each of these components and the interplay among them will provide decision makers with comprehensive information to assist in large-scale implementation.

Evaluations of large-scale education programs frequently find no immediately observable effects. One reason for this experience may be that the intended education treatments never occurred or were inappropriately delivered. As a result, potentially effective programs may be discredited by negative results derived not from the ineffectiveness of the program concept, but from a failure to consider whether the treatment was ever delivered at all. The failure of program managers to monitor program implementation may help explain the poor results of what started out as promising educational interventions. In Chapter 10, David W. Chapman argues the importance of monitoring implementation, identifies six purposes that monitoring implementation can serve in program management and evaluation, and presents a model of the influences affecting the implementation of large-scale educational programs. The model identifies 10 organizational, individual, and program factors that influence implementation and that should be examined as part of an implementation monitoring activity.

Chapman, in Chapter 11, examines the role of information management in educational quality enhancement efforts. One of the highest priority issues in many international education development projects is the improvement of the collection, analysis, and use of quantitative data in decision making. This priority emerges from the convergence of five trends: (1) the explosive growth of the education system in many countries; (2) the increased complexity of education systems as ministries of education have undertaken more complex programs and pursued multiple objectives; (3) the increased financial pressures experienced by many governments, which has created pressure for more efficient resource allocation procedures; (4) increased donor demand for quantitative data to meet their own pressures for accountability; and (5) the availability of low-cost technology for handling large amounts of data. The response to the need for better data has been the widespread implementation of computer-based management information systems, massive national data collections, and a flurry of analysis. What is less clear is the extent to which these efforts to improve information have resulted in improved decision making or enhanced educational quality.

Chapman suggests ways that management information systems can contribute to improving educational quality. However, his review of

Third World experience with educational management information systems (EMIS) suggests that, despite the potential for contributing to quality enhancement, the EMIS record has been mixed. Key components of
an EMIS are then discussed, with particular attention to problems encountered in specifying data needs and selecting appropriate indicators.
Chapman argues that a narrow (versus a broad) spectrum data system
is the most appropriate design for an EMIS in a developing country
setting, but it should incorporate a series of techniques for expanding
the information utility, including the use of derived indicators and common coding schemes. He argues that effective education information
systems should be developed from a realistic assessment of what types
of decisions can be based on objective criteria. Having education data
does not improve education unless the data are linked to specific strategies, resources, and commitments.

Even when trial projects are evaluated and judged to be successful,
they may encounter unanticipated difficulties when they are adopted
for larger-scale implementation. In Chapter 12, Frances Kemmerer addresses the issue of "going to scale" and examines why seemingly successful instructional development projects fail to be adopted.

Project success is likely to vary both with the stage of the project
(identification, design, development, evaluation, diffusion) and a person's relationship to the project (host country representative, donor,
technical assistant, participant). Even if host country representatives and
the donor begin a project with an identical goal—to increase student
learning—political, economic, and logistical pressures may force their
interests to diverge as the project moves from one stage of development
to the next.

Kemmerer suggests that successful pilot projects are difficult to replicate during larger-scale implementation because of the bureaucratic
nature of educational systems and the relatively poor observability of
short-run results of many education projects. Successful projects may
fail at the point of full-scale implementation either because project personnel ignore warning signals that delivery systems and other types of
infrastructure support are inadequate or because little attempt is made
to market the innovation. The need for structural change and the relatively poor observability of the results of instructional technologies in
the short run suggest that either extraordinary incentives must be provided for system reform or more attention paid to the social marketing
of the implementation.

Instructional Delivery

Chapters 13 and 14 focus on unique concerns that confront the delivery
of instructional interventions in developing countries. The diversity of

languages within countries poses a practical constraint on the design and selection of instructional materials. Similarly, while technology can be a powerful means of delivering education, limitations on equipment, facilities, and personnel demand careful and realistic planning.

In Chapter 13, Jerry L. Messec examines the implications of national language policy on educational development. In particular, he draws attention to the problems posed by "language switching" on efforts to design and implement instructional improvement activities. For example, in Liberia, national-level implementation of a primary education curriculum involved students from 16 language backgrounds, for whom entry into formal schooling was the first time many of them had to speak English. In Somalia, depending on a student's academic track, students may use Somali in primary school, English at the secondary level, and Italian at the local university. Messec argues that a country's choice among national, international, and vernacular languages has meaningful consequences for the efficiency of the educational system. He concludes by offering a scale of language use that reflects the impact of national language choices on the efficiency of educational development.

John K. Mayo, in Chapter 14, examines the role of selected technologies as instructional delivery systems. In the last two decades, politicians and planners have marshalled a growing variety of communication media in an attempt to accommodate increasing enrollments and to raise the quality of instruction at all levels. The performance of educational radio and television are reevaluated here in terms of their original promise to (1) enrich classroom teaching, (2) provide direct instruction, (3) stimulate system-wide reforms, and (4) extend distance learning opportunities. While the broadcast media have succeeded in reaching millions of new learners in and out of school, their record in raising student achievement is uneven at best. Furthermore, some of the most innovative media-based teaching programs, such as interactive radio instruction, have failed to sustain institutional support once their pilot phases concluded. Mayo argues for more comprehensive approaches to the design of multi-media systems as well as implementation policies more closely attuned to the opportunities and constraints facing learners and teachers at the local level.

Seven themes emerge from the author's analyses. First, the factors that affect educational improvement efforts often come from outside the education system. Understanding how to structure and present content in an interesting way, at an appropriate level of difficulty, and in the optimal sequence are the heart of good instructional improvement interventions—but they are not enough. As a sole strategy for improving educational quality, attention to content and pedagogy alone is naive. Long-term improvements to educational quality grow only out of an understanding of how such interventions fit into the larger cultural, political, and economic contexts. Those committed to improving educational quality cannot be interested only in education, but must be responsive to the impacts of the programs and materials they introduce on a larger set of individuals and institutions, some of whom have little directly to do with students, classrooms, or schools.

Second, improving educational quality in any large-scale way depends ultimately on affecting the day-to-day instructional transactions of students. In both developing and more industrialized nations, these transactions generally occur in classrooms, usually facilitated by teachers, and sometimes supported by educational materials. While none of these conditions are necessary or sufficient, the combination enjoys a long tradition and widespread credibility. Even when the system appears to be failing, there is a tendency to preserve the structure—sometimes from a belief that even in its failure the structure offers the best mechanism for an intervention, sometimes because the structure yields a series of secondary benefits (other than student learning)—such as employment generation—that policy makers are reluctant to forgo.

Third, when educational change threatens conventional educational symbols, signs, or images, resistance is inevitable but may be surmountable. Ingrained in the psyche of a culture are the symbols of its institutions, be it family, religion, government, or education. In education, although these symbols may bear little relationship to the actual quality of instruction, they are strongly associated with the meaning and value attributed to schooling in the minds of students, teachers, and the public in general. Textbooks, school uniforms, homework, and classroom configurations are examples of some of these universal symbols. When innovations in the school may diminish or eliminate these symbols, the worth of the total innovation may be questioned. Whether an innovation can be sustained in the schools will depend in part on whether those involved can adopt new symbols and embrace new images of schooling.

Fourth, those interested in improving instruction certainly must understand the societal and economic forces that buffet new ideas and programs. But, they also must understand how to translate their interventions to a level at which individuals can relate and engage. Implementation requires attention to the needs of individuals within complex systems. Discussing change as a clash among systems may be sociologically satisfying, but it misses the heart of the issue. Improving educational quality requires attention to the real incentives that operate during the processes of adoption and implementation, attention to the affective environment into which a new program is being introduced, and adequate marketing of the successes that are achieved. The challenge, then, is to translate good ideas and large-scale projects into changes that policy makers want to support and in which teachers want to participate.

Fifth, the criteria for judging the success of an educational project must be broadly interpreted in developing countries. Although there can be no argument that enhanced achievement and efficiency are appropriate criteria of improved educational quality, other outcomes may be equally important to the participants and supporters of the program. Programs that broaden access to schooling, promote equity, or reduce attrition are significant in countries where a low percentage of children begin school or remain enrolled past the first few grades. Schools that "look like schools" may be a source of pride for a community and result in a deepened commitment to education in general. The worth of an educational program is based not only on the perceptions of those who fund or administer the program, but on those who participate in it on a day-to-day basis, those who send their children to engage in it, and those who live with the program in their communities long after the program originators have moved on.

Sixth, good and successful projects are not always implemented, even in the face of clearly demonstrated need and overwhelming evidence of project effectiveness. This occurs not because the program was poorly conceived, but because its merits were not marketed properly and incentives for adoption and implementation provided by the project were not fully understood. Promising benefits in terms of student learning seldom are enough. There also have to be discernable benefits to the teachers, policy makers, and others directly and indirectly involved in determining a project's fate.

Seventh, improving instructional quality always means change—new ways of doing things and different patterns of relationships. Resistance to change is not because people are lazy or malevolent. Often it reflects a wisdom and insight into the incentive systems within which participants live and operate. They recognize that changed ways of doing things may alter patterns of relationship they value and patterns of exchange from which they benefit. What is good for a country in the long run is not necessarily good for individual participants in the short run. Even when the positive short-term benefits outweigh the negative, a new program will not necessarily be simultaneously good for everyone. The incentive value of participating in, supporting, or just tolerating a new project varies across groups. Those seeking to improve educational quality, whether from host or donor country, must operate from an equation that incorporates these factors.

The risks to investments in large-scale educational quality improvement efforts are substantial. Good ideas can falter for failure to give sufficient attention to individual motivation and behavior, for failure to consider the incentive systems that operate, and for failure to anticipate the rippling effect of each system change on other parts of the system. Projects falter because they were not fully implemented, or were implemented incorrectly. Even demonstrably successful projects can fail when program managers do not publicize and market the success a project does achieve or when the infrastructure necessary to support a successful pilot is not available at a level that can support larger scale implementation. On the other hand, when large-scale interventions do succeed, the payoff can be substantial. Formal education is recognized as one of the most important ingredients in the economic, social, and political development of a nation.

REFERENCES

Chapman, D. W., & Windham, D. M. (1986). *The evaluation of efficiency in educational development activities.* Tallahassee: Florida State University, Improving the Efficiency of Education Systems Project.

Windham, D. M., & Wang, W. L. (1986, June). *Fiscal capacity constraints in quality/quantity trade-offs in educational development.* Paper prepared for the Conference on Economics of Education, University of Dijon, Dijon, France.

2

What Investments Raise Achievement in the Third World?

Bruce Fuller

Looking back in time, the collapse was so predictable.

Since 1950 the proportion of children entering and persisting through Third World schools has inched up steadily—even exceeding explosive growth in child populations. Yet, since the early 1970s, many developing countries have been buffeted by damaging economic forces, especially falling prices for critical exports like farm commodities and oil, as well as burgeoning debt burdens that eat into governments' own domestic spending.

The eagerness of Third World governments to expand schooling, and the social opportunity it signals, continues unabated. But budget resources—necessary for erecting more classrooms, training more teachers, and producing more books—have leveled off or declined in the case of Africa, south Asia, and much of Latin America. The devastating effect of these conflicting trends are that fixed resources are being stretched over rapidly rising numbers of pupils. The resulting collapse in school quality diminishes the school's capacity to raise even basic literacy of young children. This erosion in school quality is apparent in many places.

In the African nation of Malawi, the pupil–teacher ratio in primary schools has climbed from 41:1 to 63:1 since 1970. Per-pupil spending has declined 4.1 percent each year in real terms. Only 50 cents is now spent annually per pupil on textbooks, writing pads, and other instructional supplies.

In Nepal, one-third of all teachers have no more than a primary school education. Education spending has remained stagnant over the past decade—equalling $11 per pupil. Less than one-third of all children reach the fifth grade (Government of Nepal, 1988).

In relatively affluent Latin America, the foreign debt crisis has decimated governments' capacity to support basic education. Per-pupil spending at the primary level has fallen by 40 percent in Mexico since 1980. In northeast Brazil, one-third of all teachers have completed just four years of schooling or less (Armitage, Batista, Harbison, Holsinger, & Helio, 1986).

In Somalia, one-fourth of the teaching force quits the profession each year. The number of textbooks printed last year equalled one-fifth the number published a decade ago. The absolute number of pupils enrolled has fallen by 27 percent since 1980 (Smyth, 1987).

Inferences about educational quality stem not only from such information on material resources (or inputs) available to schools but also from evidence on pupil performance. Findings from the first international evaluation of achievement, for instance, revealed that just 1 out of 10 Third World students at age 14 was as literate in their native language as the average pupil from an industrialized country (Thorndike, 1973). Average reading scores in developing countries, such as Chile and India, were half the level found within industrialized nations. We must be sensitive to cultural differences in how curricula are organized and achievement is measured; yet schools around the world are charged with imparting these basic literacy skills.

EFFICIENT STRATEGIES FOR BOOSTING ACHIEVEMENT

Governments and international agencies now are pursuing more balanced investment strategies: focusing on the maintenance, even improvement of primary school quality while recognizing that pressures to expand enrollments remain intense.

The question then arises, What policy and spending strategies can most efficiently impart basic literacy and raise pupil achievement? Such strategies may involve policy reforms that shift limited resources to the most effective school inputs, improvements in the form of curricula and textbooks, or local interventions into how headmasters manage and how teachers teach. In each case, projects are mounted that presumably address those facets of the school institution that yield the most cost-effective return (in terms of higher achievement). A major barrier to proceeding so rationally is our ignorance regarding what points of intervention work best, why, and under what conditions.

This lack of knowledge is costly. It is relatively easy to symbolically raise the "quality" of schools. Education ministries commonly move to fund textbooks with color pictures, install science laboratories, or convince a willing donor to spruce up the architecture of new schools. Governments presume that these factors raise pupil achievement (or at least boost the state's own popular legitimacy). But if these facets of school quality have no influence on pupils' acquisition of literacy, then governments and aid agencies are squandering scarce resources. Thus we have recently seen a growing concern with pinpointing those material inputs and social processes within schools that most efficiently boost achievement.

This chapter begins with a summary of what we know about the school's overall influence on children's literacy, net the influence of family background and community conditions. Second, a brief review is provided of the past 15 years of empirical research on school factors that efficaciously (or ineffectively) boost student achievement. Many of the findings on this latter question come from studies originally designed to answer the first query: Do Third World schools really make a difference in boosting literacy? As we look inside the school to see what facets are most effective, we must remind ourselves of the school's context. We must keep asking, about external forces, that is, how does the demand for children's labor, their nutritional status, and parents' views of modern schooling influence pupils' school performance? Third, this chapter reports on initial research that looks inside Third World classrooms at the lives of teachers, their pedagogical practices, their forms of interactions with children, and their perceptions of the schooling process. This emerging area of inquiry reveals how the teacher mobilizes instructional materials and sets the social rules that govern the instructional process.

DO THIRD WORLD SCHOOLS MAKE A DIFFERENCE?

Third World research on school effects has focused on one basic question: Do schools raise achievement after taking into account pupils' family background? The survey or experimental designs of most studies also yield findings on the *relative effectiveness* of different school or classroom factors. But researchers remain primarily concerned with the aggregate achievement effect of school. Heyneman and Loxley's (1983) findings are particularly important here. They examined the influence of family background and school factors on pupils' science achievement from 16 developing and 13 industrialized countries. Various school attributes (such as the availability of textbooks and school libraries, teachers' school attainment, and length of the instructional program) were analyzed as a block of school qualities. Science achievement scores were then regressed on indicators of pupils' social class (e.g., parents' occupational and educational status) and the block of school factors.[1]

For industrialized countries, variation in school factors explained small portions of variance in achievement, after controlling for parents' social class. However, in developing countries the block of school factors explained significant portions of the variance in achievement. For instance, 27 percent of the variance in achievement among East Indian children was explained by differing levels of school quality; social class background explained just 3 percent. In Thailand, school factors explained 25 percent of the variance in achievement, versus 6 percent that was attributable to family background. Among the 29 countries included in the study, a significant correlation was observed between a nation's wealth (GNP per capita) and the amount of variance explained by school factors (r = .66).[2] One should note that these findings apply only to science achievement, a subject that is distant from indigenous forms of language and knowledge in most Third World countries. In fact, school factors tend to be weaker relative to pupil background when achievement in reading is used as the dependent variable.

To observe the school's aggregate effect one can also look across the 60 school effects studies that have been completed in Third World countries. Table 2.1 summarizes the types of school factors investigated. The body of empirical evidence is reviewed in detail below. However, two general points are useful here. First, the majority of these multivariate studies have found significant achievement effects from school factors, net the influence of pupils' social class background. Very few investigators have reported effect sizes, elasticities, or an apportioning of variance explained. So reports on the *magnitude* of the school's effect are rare; the Heyneman and Loxley (1983) paper is a notable exception. But in general these studies consistently find that school factors do influence achievement (at statistically significant levels).

Second, material school inputs are related to achievement in the Third World. Very few studies from the United States or Great Britain find effects from the level of material inputs. Effects from the school's social organization and teaching practices appear to be stronger (Barr & Dreeben, 1983; Fuller, 1986a). In developing countries, however, simple inputs—especially those directly related to the instructional process—are consistently associated with higher achievement. For instance, of the 24 multivariate studies that have looked at the number of textbooks available in classrooms, 16 have found significant achievement effects (again, controlling for the influence of pupils' social class). Qualities of Third World teachers are related to achievement, particularly years of tertiary and teacher training. The teacher's own social class background and verbal proficiency also are associated with higher student performance.

The evidence summarized in Table 2.1 suggests that some costly inputs are *not* related to higher levels of achievement, including class size, teacher salary levels, and science laboratories (at the secondary level).

Table 2.1
School Factors and Achievement in the Third World

School Quality Indicators	Expected Direction of Relationship	Total Number of Analyses	Number of Analyses Confirming Effect
School Expenditures			
1. Expenditures per pupil	+	11	6
2. Total school expenditures	+	5	2
Specific Material Inputs			
3. Class size	--	21	5
4. School size	+	9	4
5. Instructional materials			
Texts and reading materials	+	24	16
Desks	+	3	3
6. Instructional media (radio)	+	3	3
7. School building quality	+	3	2
8. Library size and activity	+	18	15
9. Science laboratories	+	11	4
10. Nutrition and feeding programs	+	6	5
Teacher Quality			
11. Teacher's length of schooling			
Total years of teacher's schooling	+	26	12
Years of tertiary & teacher training	+	31	22
12. In-service teacher training	+	6	5
13. Teacher's length of experience	+	23	10
14. Teacher's verbal proficiency	+	2	2
15. Teacher's salary level	+	14	5
16. Teacher's social class background	+	10	7
17. School's percentage of full-time teachers	+	2	1
18. Teachers punctuality & (low) absenteeism	+	2	0
Teaching Practices/Classroom Organization			
19. Length of instructional program	+	14	12
20. Homework frequency	+	8	6
21. Active learning by students	+	3	1
22. Teacher's expectation of pupil performance	+	3	3
23. Teacher's time spent on class preparation	+	5	4
School Management			
24. Quality of principal	+	7	4
25. Multiple shifts of classes each day	--	3	1
26. Student boarding	+	4	3
27. Student repetition of grade	+	5	1

Source: Fuller, B. (1987). What school factors raise achievement in the Third World? *Review of Educational Research, 57* (3), 255–292.

A recent longitudinal study of primary school pupils in rural Brazil provides excellent evidence backing the claim that the quality of physical facilities is not related to higher achievement. Armitage, et al. (1986), tracking 4,902 pupils over two years, found that teacher quality and instructional materials exerted significant influence, while the character of school buildings did not.[3]

SCOPE AND LIMITS OF THE EMPIRICAL LITERATURE

Shortly I will summarize findings from these 60 empirical studies conducted in the Third World. A detailed review of this work also appears in Fuller (1987). I begin with a statement of how studies were selected for inclusion in the review. Selecting studies of adequate quality immediately prompts questions regarding how achievement models are specified, including how pupil background is measured and the consistency with which school factors are specified across models. Only studies that used some form of control for pupils' social class were included here. Class is typically measured in terms of parents' occupational status or educational attainment. Most studies involve surveys of large numbers of schools and students. Typically data were collected on a variety of pupil characteristics and attributes of schools and teachers. Multivariate regressions or production-functions were then built to estimate school effects, net the influence of pupils' social class. Only two experimental studies have been done with matched control groups (detailed below). A few studies have employed log-linear production-functions, which allow for easier interpretation of elasticities to assess the magnitude of effects from specific school factors. Very few researchers report on the level of between-school differences in achievement (employing Analysis of Variance (ANOVA) designs or dummy variables within an ordinary least squares (OLS) model). This would inform us on the proportion of variance explained by measured factors versus the total variance among schools. In general, most investigators have collected cross-sectional data and have applied OLS regressions to control on pupils' social class characteristics. In this review when a "significant effect" is reported in the text or tables, this means that the relevant statistic (t- or f-value) was significant at $p < .05$ or stronger.[4]

SPECIFYING PUPIL BACKGROUND IN THE THIRD WORLD

Have pupil background factors been specified adequately in achievement models? If they have not, then the school's discrete effect may be overstated. Most studies reviewed below have confirmed Heyneman and Loxley's (1983) finding that pupils' social class affects achievement less in the Third World than within industrialized nations. However, in the poorest countries, social class structures are not as stratified as they are within industrialized nations. Therefore, Western measures of class may not vary substantially. This does not rule out the possibility that socioeconomic factors significantly determine the mean level of achievement nationwide; yet because of the lack of variation, traditional constructs of class would simply not be strongly associated with *variation* in achievement around the mean.

This issue of constrained variance is especially important when interpreting models of pupils' secondary school performance. In many developing countries only a small fraction of children enter secondary schools. Such high selectivity certainly implies restricted variance in pupil samples at the secondary level. Few researchers have explicitly addressed the basic issue of constrained variance in conventional measures of social class. Many researchers have drawn heterogeneous pupil samples, including schools that are located in rural and urban areas. Here variability in pupils' social class would likely be greater.

Another model specification issue is whether to control on pupil "ability." Only two studies were found that attempted to do so (Heyneman & Jamison, 1980, in Uganda; Jamison & Lockheed, 1985, in Nepal). The construct of ability is difficult to measure within developing countries, given that many tests rely on vocabulary and concepts from the West. I found only one study that regressed post-test achievement scores on pre-test scores, family background, and school factors (in Thailand; Lockheed, Vail, & Fuller, 1986). Experimental interventions with matched control schools provided longitudinal data from the Philippines (Heyneman, Jamison, & Montenegro, 1983) and from Nicaragua (Jamison, Searle, Galda, & Heyneman, 1981). Only these three studies effectively controlled on prior levels of pupil achievement.

Almost no work in the Third World has focused on levels of early cognitive development. Evidence does exist indicating that the child's long-run nutritional status, and whether his or her growth has been stunted, are related to later school performance (e.g., Balderston, Wilson, Freire, & Simonen, 1981; Hartley & Swanson, 1984). Parents also influence the child's early cognitive development, and some behaviors and beliefs of parents vary independent of the material facets of social class. For example, in both Japan and the United States, pupils' later academic performance is higher when their parents encourage them to achieve, expect earlier mastery of developmental skills, and ask children questions rather than prescribe action (Hess, Kashiwagi, Azuma, Price, & Dickson, 1980; Holloway & Hess, 1985).

However, few investigators have inquired into parents' influence within the Third World. We do know, for instance, that Mexican mothers possess child-rearing beliefs that may not encourage later school performance. Holloway, Gorman, and Fuller (1987) report that mothers, in contrast to teachers, emphasize the importance of learning to obey (not to act independently) and expect later mastery of basic social skills. But we do not know whether these parenting beliefs and behaviors actually influence school achievement. The basic point remains as follows: Given that these social antecedents to early cognitive development are left out of Third World achievement models, are we overstating the school's aggregate influence? Parenthetically, this is not a specification problem limited only to school effects research in developing countries; it also limits the validity of current models within industrialized nations.

SCHOOL EFFECTIVENESS VERSUS SCHOOL EFFICIENCY

To date, research in developing countries continues to focus on testing the basic Coleman (Coleman et al., 1966) finding that schools make little difference. Therefore, the relative magnitude of effects from different school factors has been explored only rarely. This is unfortunate. As seen in Table 2.1, we can discriminate, to some extent, between those material inputs and social practices that have a consistent achievement effect and those that do not. However, we know very little about the efficiency with which school factors raise or lower achievement. The following review highlights the few studies that have emphasized effect sizes or the efficiency with which a particular school factor boosts achievement.

Next, specific studies are reviewed within the five major types of school factors indicated in Table 2.1: Overall school expenditures, specific material inputs, teacher quality, teaching practices and classroom organization, and school management. I will elaborate on the limitations of achievement models specified in the existing literature—regarding identification of family background factors and specification of how material school inputs are organized and used in classrooms. Notwithstanding these weaknesses, this body of work does narrow the range of school factors that should receive more (or less) attention in future research.

RESEARCH REVIEW

School Expenditures

A slim majority of studies have found a positive relationship between school expenditures per pupil and achievement. The influence of this factor is strong in some analyses. For example, in a Columbian study of academic achievement (4,233 secondary school pupils), the influence of per-pupil expenditures was exceeded only by children's verbal ability. The influence of this factor was also significant for achievement in the commercial curriculum. This study found more moderate but significant achievement effects in Tanzania (2,803 secondary pupils; Psacharopoulos & Loxley, 1986).

The magnitude of the achievement effect from per-pupil expenditures was thoroughly examined in an early study of primary and secondary school students in Kenya (Thias & Carnoy, 1973). No significant effect was found at the primary school level. At the secondary level, per-pupil expenditures did influence achievement. The authors estimated the magnitude of this effect. Second, they identified the strength of the relationship between higher national test scores (their indicator of achievement) and future earnings. Thias and Carnoy estimated that raising national exam scores among secondary students by 5 percent would require a 50 percent boost in expenditures per pupil. The rate of return to this investment in terms of increased income would be significant (6 percent), but only for low-achieving students. For high-achieving students, income benefits gained from higher achievement were entirely offset by the cost of raising achievement.

The second set of school factors include discrete material inputs that operate more closely to the instructional process. Third World findings on possible achievement effects from smaller class size are quite similar to evidence from industrialized nations. Within normal ranges, the presence of fewer students per classroom has held no consistent effect on achievement in 11 of 21 analyses. In 5 additional studies, students working within larger classes actually performed at higher levels. I should quickly point out that "normal ranges" are often exceeded in the poorest developing countries, given that the mean national ratio of primary school pupils to each teacher equals 44 within the poorest nations (Fuller, 1986b). In addition, achievement effects for specific ranges of class size have not been investigated in the Third World.

Yet, given the existing evidence, substantial reductions in class size would be necessary to raise achievement. In contrast, incremental increases in class size would free up resources while not diminishing overall student achievement. Just one study has found that smaller classes at the primary level are significantly related to higher achievement. This report comes from an analysis of science achievement among 837 urban students in Colombia (Arriagada, 1981). Most studies simply report no effect from variation in class size.

Two studies have examined the magnitude of the class size effect. First, the Malaysian study of 89 secondary schools found a significant effect of smaller class size on pupils with respect to language achievement (Beebout, 1972). The researcher then estimated the marginal (achievement) product associated with spending one additional dollar to lower class size. Raising student achievement by just 1 percent would cost an additional $50 per student if allocated to help lower class size. In contrast, this same gain in student achievement could be accomplished at one-third the cost if resources were allocated to teacher training. Cost data used for these estimates are admittedly rough. But this method for comparing the cost-effectiveness of alternative school factors is instructive.

The positive impact of instructional materials—especially those directly related to reading and writing—is consistent across several studies. The availability and use of textbooks (measured, for instance, in terms of number of textbooks available per student) have been looked at in 24 analyses. Significant effects were observed in 16. Early research in the 1970s relied on survey instruments developed by the International Association for the Evaluation of Educational Achievement (IEA). These questionnaires asked students and teachers about the availability of textbooks in classrooms (Comber & Keeves, 1973; Purves, 1973). This factor was statistically significant in many Latin American countries that employed these measures. Actual counts of textbooks in Uganda also revealed a significant influence on pupil achievement (Heyneman & Jamison, 1980).

This research indicates a moderate effect of textbooks and instructional materials on achievement. In Uganda, for instance, textbook availability strongly influenced achievement in English, dwarfing the effects of the child's social class (based on 1,907 students in 61 primary schools). However, aggregating test scores across curriculum areas, the influence of textbooks was smaller than social class, preschool competence, pupil health, and the teacher's verbal (English) proficiency. In Malaysia (Beebout, 1972) and Chile (Schiefelbein & Farrell, 1973), textbook availability was related to higher achievement. But the correlation between these two variables was less than .20 in both studies, before controlling for the effects of student background and other school factors. In the Chilean study, textbooks explained about 4 percent of the variance in achievement.

The influence of textbooks appears to be stronger within rural schools and among students from lower-income families. In rural Brazil, for instance, students with parents who had received no schooling were almost 3 times as likely to pass primary school if they had used two or more books (67 percent graduating), compared to students in this same group who had no textbooks in school (only 24 percent graduating). Among students with parents who had completed primary school, 73 percent of all pupils were at least two books passed primary school, versus 61 percent of those with no books (the total sample equaled 1,006 primary school students; Wolff, 1970). Similarly, the study of 6,056 young Malaysians found that the availability of books in school was more strongly related to achievement among lower-income children from Chinese and Indian ethnic groups.

Clearer evidence on the magnitude of textbooks' effect comes from more recent studies that have employed experimental research designs—thereby holding constant student background and other school factors. For instance, a controlled experiment in the Philippines provided textbooks to 2,295 first- and second-grade pupils in 52 schools (Heyneman et al., 1983). A control group of similar schools also was selected. Books were then introduced at ratios of two pupils per book and one pupil per book in alternate classrooms. Achievement gains resulting from the intervention were substantial. In first-grade science, performance was .51 of a standard deviation higher in the experimental classrooms, .30 of a standard deviation higher in mathematics, and .32 higher in Phillipino. In this study, the .51 standard deviation change indicated that the mean score achieved by 50 percent of all students was obtained by 69 percent of those students in the treatment group. This improvement was twice the impact of what would be gained by lowering class size from 40 to 10 students (using evidence from the Philippines on textbooks and from the United States on class size). The influence of the textbook program on achievement was greater for children with parents who had received less schooling.

Very little research has been conducted on how, and the conditions under which, textbooks shape achievement. An important exception is a recent longitudinal study of 4,030 grade 8 pupils in Thailand (Lockheed et al., 1986). The relative influence and interaction of textbook availability, teacher training levels, and curriculum content was assessed. Pupils of teachers who use textbooks scored one-half point higher on the math post-test, controlling for pre-test score and pupil background characteristics (or one-sixth of the average gain for the academic year). Interestingly, textbook use did not interact with the teacher's training level; in fact, textbooks could be substituted for training, and the effect size for textbooks was considerably greater. Textbook use also was colinear with curriculum content. In general, teachers reporting more frequent use of math textbooks also reported that they covered more math concepts during the academic year. In this way, textbooks in Thailand helped to deliver a more structured curriculum.

Desks in classrooms represent another material input to the instructional process. All three analyses of this factor have found significant achievement effects. For instance, a recent study of 324 sixth-grade students in Peru discovered that the percentage of children with classroom desks was more strongly related to reading achievement than was the influence of social class background (Arriagada, 1983). As with textbooks, the availability of a desk is easily measured, and observed achievement effects appear to be significant. But we know little about how children's classroom time is structured, particularly how the material desk fits into opportunities to read and write. In some instances, the desk may hold more utility as a symbol of constructing a "modern school." Whether teachers structure lessons to encourage even simple use of desks is a separate issue. Pushing students to write may be more important than reading, from the standpoint of motivation, in that writing is a productive form of literacy.

The early IEA surveys included questions asking schools about the use of classroom laboratories in the teaching of science. This particular material input remains controversial. Governments and development agencies have invested sizable resources in building school laboratories and in financing the purchase of laboratory equipment. Whether this investment is paying off in higher levels of achievement remains an unanswered question. The early IEA investigators asked school staff about the presence and utilization of classroom laboratories. These measures were related to higher achievement in three of the four developing countries (India, Thailand, and Iran) included in the study. Two indicators of laboratory use—number of students in laboratory classes and time spent in laboratory classrooms—were related to achievement. However, the subsequent Latin American survey used these same items and found no significant relationship with pupil performance (Heyneman & Loxley, 1983).

School feeding programs have received limited attention from researchers. More is known about the effects of poor health, malnutrition, and hunger on children's school achievement than on the ameliorative effects of school feeding initiatives. The effects of poor health can be dramatic. In a study of 3,699 primary school students and dropouts in Egypt, health status was one of the strongest predictors of academic achievement. For instance, children who had suffered from a serious illness in the preceding year scored 20 percent lower on the literacy test and 10 percent lower on the numeracy exam. Children who had a major physical disability or suffered from malnutrition also achieved at significantly lower levels (Hartley & Swanson, 1984).

The earlier study in 61 Ugandan primary schools provided similar results (Heyneman & Jamison, 1980). Multiple measures were used, asking children whether they had suffered from malnutrition, how often they had chills or a fever, how often they had stayed in a clinic overnight, and whether they had seen blood in their stools. Among the 1,907 surveyed, 74 percent reported having suffered from malaria; 37 percent answered that they had stayed overnight in a clinic or hospital; 12 percent had seen blood in their stools; 5 percent claimed that they had been treated for malnutrition. This latter 5 percent of children performed a quarter of a standard deviation below all other students on an achievement test. Controlling for family background and other school quality elements, pupil health (an overall index) contributed significantly to academic achievement.

Teacher Quality

Thus far, only material school inputs have been discussed. But how well are material resources managed by the teacher within instructional activities? One way to approach this question is to look at individual characteristics of teachers. Because most school effects research in the Third World has relied on large-scale surveys, easily measured proxies for teacher quality have been used most often. For instance, many studies have asked about teachers' qualifications in terms of their total length of schooling or their amount of postsecondary teacher training. Whether and how these proxies are related to the teacher's proficiency in organizing instruction and in motivating children remains quite cloudy.

Yet even rough measures of teacher quality are related to higher levels of student achievement. Findings are mixed on the effect of the teacher's length of schooling. A significant relationship was found in 12 of these studies. The strength of this relationship is moderate in a few analyses. The IEA survey of literature achievement in Chile included 103 schools and 1,311 students (Husen, Saha, & Noonan, 1978). A moderate correlation between teachers' school attainment and pupil performance was observed ($r = .34$); the significance of this factor remained after controlling for student background and other school factors. An early study of school quality in Puerto Rico found that teachers' schooling level was most strongly related to the achievement of primary school students and among pupils from lower-income families. No significant relationship was found for secondary school students (Carnoy, 1971).

Teacher schooling effects have been negligible in several other studies. For example, a study of more than 27,000 Thai primary school students found a statistically significant, yet small association ($r = .11$). This low level of magnitude is troubling from a policy viewpoint (Fuller & Chantavanich, 1976). Allocating additional resources to increase teacher candidates' total length of schooling may be an inefficient strategy for raising pupil achievement. One analysis based on IEA data for Chile and India found that moving the average length of teachers' schooling to the 75th percentile (of the teacher schooling level previously found in these countries) would boost pupils' reading scores by 10 percent. But the cost of such an improvement would be extraordinary (Comber & Keeves, 1973).

In contrast, achievement effects are more consistent for teachers' length of postsecondary schooling and for the number of teacher training courses completed. The first IEA survey included items on both of these areas; identical measures were used in the subsequent Latin American survey. Either the original IEA research group or Heyneman and Loxley (1983) found significant effects from at least one of these factors in each of 11 countries. Independent work in 10 other countries has revealed significant effects. In total, 22 of 31 studies have found a significant achievement effect from teachers' general university or specific teacher training.

Only a few studies have examined how a teacher's skills relate to pupil achievement. Proxies such as the teacher's level of schooling or in-service training assume that additional competencies are obtained that subsequently increase pupils' achievement levels. More direct assessment of actual skills related to the teacher's effectiveness is very rare. The school effects literature from industrialized countries, for instance, emphasizes the strength of teachers' verbal competence in boosting pupil performance. Researchers in the Third World are beginning to examine teacher attributes more carefully. For instance, the previously mentioned study of 1,907 primary school students in Uganda (Heyneman & Jamison, 1980) found consistent and strong achievement effects from teachers' English proficiency on pupils' achievement in both language and mathematics achievement. This factor influenced pupil performance more strongly than did students' social class background, preschool ability, and two other school factors included in the model. The teacher's achievement level (on a secondary school leaving exam) was correlated with pupils' performance in a study of 797 second-grade students in Iran. The bivariate association was weak for the student sample overall ($r = .14$). However, in a multivariate analysis of students from rural or poor backgrounds, the teacher's achievement level more strongly influenced their pupils' subsequent achievement (Ryan, 1973).

Two alleged indicators of teacher quality hold little influence on achievement. Teacher experience did appear to make a significant difference in the early IEA survey, at least for reading teachers in Chile, India, and Iran. However, research since the IEA study has yielded more pessimistic findings. The recent study of 37 primary schools in Botswana found that the influence of teachers' experience rivaled the influence of father's occupation (used as a background control variable; Loxley, 1984). A second study from Malaysia found that length of teachers' experience was associated with pupil achievement, but only among teachers receiving more preservice training courses (Beebout, 1972). In sum, 13 of 23 studies that have looked at teacher experience have found *no* significant achievement effect. Similarly, teacher salary levels are *not* consistently related to pupil performance. Two recent analyses from Tanzania (2,803 secondary students) and Colombia (4,233 secondary students) found that higher-achieving vocational students actually were taught by lower-paid teachers (Psacharopoulos & Loxley, 1986). The negative influence of teacher salaries in Colombia was strong, exceeding the achievement effect of students' social class background and other school factors.

Teaching Practices and Classroom Organization

Despite the burgeoning literature in industrialized countries on how teachers manage instructional resources and organize their classrooms (Gage & Berliner 1975; Rutter, 1983), very little work has occurred in developing countries. Length of instruction stands out as a consistent predictor of student achievement among the 14 studies of this factor conducted in the Third World. This important school factor, however, suffers from inconsistent definition and the use of various measures. Indicators range from the number of days in the school year to how many hours science is taught during the school week.

The amount or length of instruction offered by schools is bounded, in part, by available material resources. Yet in many settings, the length of the school day, time spent on particular curricular areas, and the efficient use of instructional time within classrooms is more strongly determined by management practices than by material inputs. Classrooms vary enormously in the amount of time actually spent on instructional tasks rather than keeping order, checking each student's homework, or arranging lessons. Efficient use of classroom time is related to pupil performance in industrialized nations (for review, see Karweit, 1985). Considerable progress on this potential source of school efficiency could be made in the Third World by sharpening classroom management and teaching skills within constrained levels of material inputs.

In Brazil, the early study of primary school achievement (1,006 pupils) included a question for teachers on the length of their school day (Wolff, 1970). This simple measure was significantly related to achievement in rural but not urban schools. The influence of this indicator was modest, though similar to the magnitude of pupils' family background. Arriagada (1981), working in Colombian primary schools (826 sixth-grade pupils), found that the hours of class offered per year moderately influenced reading achievement. This factor's strength was comparable to the significant influence of students' social class background. This same measure of instructional time also significantly affected reading achievement in a subsequent study of 324 grade 6 pupils in Peru (Arriagada, 1983). And the recent studies of secondary school achievement in Tanzania (922 students) and Colombia (4,233 students) found that the number of class periods spent in academic or vocational courses helped estimate performance on corresponding achievement exams. The strength of these instructional time measures usually exceeded the influence of pupils' social class background and was comparable in magnitude to other school factors (Psacharopoulos & Loxley, 1986).

Heyneman and Loxley's (1983) analysis found science achievement effects for different measures of instructional time. For instance, the number of hours of instruction spent per year on general science was significantly associated with achievement in India, Thailand, and Iran. Hours of instruction in reading also helped predict science achievement in Chile and India. The authors did not estimate the magnitude of these instructional time effects, but the consistency of positive findings across different indicators and countries should be highlighted.

The assignment of homework—a second aspect of the organization of instruction—also shows promise in raising student achievement. The first IEA survey accounts for two analyses, where positive findings were reported for Chile and Iran (but not for India and Thailand; Thorndike, 1973). The magnitude of effect was small, although multivariate models simultaneously tested for possible effects of many school factors. One modest study of 83 urban Tunisian students found that reported conditions at home for studying were related to language achievement. This measure is not an indicator of teaching practices. But the variable's strength is notable, exceeding the effects of school factors and approximating the influence of pupils' social class.

Other teaching practices have received only slight attention from researchers working in developing countries. Three studies have examined the extent to which active learning roles are created for students in classrooms. Self-reports by teachers on the amount of time they spent explaining academic material to students held no relationship to reading or math achievement in Peruvian primary schools (Arrigada, 1983). The recent study of pupil performance in rural Brazil found a consistent effect for the number and variety of instructional activities reported by teachers. Teachers were asked whether they employed nine different activities, including small work groups, dramatic reading, manual work, and storytelling. The total number of activities helped to explain pupil achievement (Armitage et al., 1986). The recent study in Botswana found no relationship between the frequency of classroom discussions reported by teachers and achievement on national reading and math exams (Loxley, 1984).

School Management and Structure

Management of the entire school also includes an important set of school factors. The school's organizational structure, in part, drives the efficiency with which school inputs are managed. The first four sets of school factors—expenditures per pupil, specific material inputs, teacher quality, and teaching practices—apply to various types of schools. Once a society decides to formalize the socialization and training of their children, these four sets of factors are important in improving diverse types of schools. But the fifth area—management and organizational structure—raises issues that at times are pertinent to particular kinds of schools. For instance, the structure of vocational schools may differ substantially from the organization of basic education in a rural primary school. In addition, the social rules that define management practices often are tied to the local culture or grow from social norms within the government. A hierarchical style of school management would be viewed as desirable in some national contexts; a more participatory and professional school structure would be normative in other cultural settings.

Research on management practices of headmasters is blossoming in industrialized nations (for review, see Leithwood & Montgomery, 1982). Unfortunately, very little is known about how headmasters in the Third World act to improve the school's instructional program. Researchers in the Third World have largely employed proxies that indicate the quality of a school's headmaster. For example, Heyneman & Loxley (1983) found that in Egypt (60 primary schools) students performed better in schools with principals who had attended more training courses and had longer teaching experience before becoming principals. This finding also appeared for science achievement among primary and secondary school students in Paraguay. The magnitude of these effects was not reported.

Stronger findings came from the Indonesian study of 124 secondary schools (Sembiring & Livingstone, 1981). Two characteristics of headmasters were among the three strongest school factors associated with pupil achievement levels. The authors found moderately high associations between pupil performance with both the headmaster's salary level ($r = .50$) and the headmaster's length of teaching experience ($r = .33$). Both factors remained strongly associated in a large model that estimated pupil achievement from 13 student background factors and 17 other school factors. The magnitude of these headmaster effects exceeded the influence of most pupil background variables. The analysis failed, however, to explore whether these characteristics of headmasters were acting as proxies for other school qualities or for other headmaster attributes. The headmaster's salary level holds no logical relationship to pupil achievement. Yet salary could be acting as a proxy for length of training or experience. This work does encourage deeper research into an important issue: What specific actions do headmasters engage in that directly affect student achievement?

In Bolivia, a study of 53 primary and secondary schools found a relationship between student achievement and the headmaster's length of postsecondary schooling. The magnitude of this factor was comparable to the influence of expenditures per pupil in a simple model that included just seven other school factors. Each of these two predictors of achievement was stronger than the students' social class background.

These results held only for urban, not rural, schools (Morales & Pinell-siles, 1977). The recent Botswana study (Loxley, 1984) found no effect from the headmaster's years of experience among standard grade 7 students.

Another area of school structure—repetition of grade levels by low-achieving students—also holds significant cost implications. Four analyses have examined whether repeating a grade improves performance in the long run. This is a difficult issue to model and study empirically. Positive effects have been observed in just one study (Fuller & Chantavanich, 1976). Hartley and Swanson's (1984) study of 8,570 primary students in Egypt found no effect from grade repetition on pupils' academic achievement. Nor did repetition lower the probability of eventually dropping out of school, holding constant pupils' prior achievement level.

FOCUSING ON TEACHER ACTION

Research to date has been limited in two ways. First, policy makers and scholars continue to be preoccupied with the large question: Do schools make a difference in boosting achievement after accounting for pupils' family background? Governments and aid agencies, facing criticism of the priority placed on education spending, continue to sponsor research that evidences the schools' sharp effect on literacy, and secondarily on economic outcomes and desirable demographic effects. Large surveys are mounted that focus on easily counted material inputs and yield generalizable findings.

Second, the schooling process is represented by the production-function metaphor. A variety of material and human "inputs" are tossed into the classroom where they magically coalesce into some kind of instructional process, resulting in varying levels of pupil achievement. A prominent, yet befuddled economist colleague still refers to this classroom process as "the mysterious black-box."

Sociologists and psychologists in the United States and Europe, of course, have been illuminating this black box for over two decades. But development economists are correct in the sense that we know little about the lives and actions of teachers within Third World classrooms. The teacher is the key actor who must manage and mobilize this variety of inputs that governments and donors throw at them. In the following section I briefly review early work, which to date simply describes the actions of teachers. I begin with a look at teacher observation studies in the United States. Comments are also put forward on how we cast and interpret knowledge coming from the West and from initial Third World studies.

Why Worry about Teacher Action? Functional versus Critical Studies

Political leaders become very nervous when they perceive that teachers are not meeting the state's ideals regarding the school's intended impact. Hoped-for effects speak both to the amount learned as well as the (overt or hidden) curriculum in terms of cognitive skills, normative behaviors, and attitudes. In the United States, for instance, recurring anxiety over low and declining pupil achievement (on standardized exams) has led to sharp administrative reforms and much research on how the school's influence over children can be deepened. Research on what teachers do in classrooms is driven by the state's and the broader public's concern that children are not learning enough. So researchers attempt to link certain teacher behaviors with higher test scores. The content and form of knowledge to be learned is not questioned; nor are the social rules examined within which the teacher imparts these codes. Desired achievement outcomes are simply passed down by school elders as sacred, unquestionable "social facts" (in Durkheim's vernacular). The researcher then engages in the instrumental technical task of trying to discover how teacher action in the classroom can raise orthodox forms of pupil virtue (measured by standard exams, which assess retention of vocabulary, grammar, arithmetic, or civics).

At a *functional* level, reports of teachers' classroom action have contributed important pieces of evidence. Early research in classrooms by Jane Stallings and colleagues in the United States revealed that many teachers spend an enormous amount of time simply organizing lessons, grading homework, and disciplining pupils—rather than actually delivering instruction (Stallings et al., 1978). For instance, one study found that pupils spend only about 38 percent of a typical school day actually engaged in academic tasks. A more recent study, also done in the United States, confirmed that some teachers spend less than half of each class period actually involved in instructional tasks (Karweit, 1985). Subsequent work both in Britain and the United States has documented that the amount of time teachers spend engaged in academic tasks does influence levels of pupil achievement (Rutter, Maughan, Mortimore, Ouston, and Smith, 1979). At least one state government now actually certifies new teachers based on observed proficiencies in "minimizing time spent on noninstructional activities, clarity of lesson structure, citing (behavioral) rules when students disobey them, and moving about the classroom and constantly scanning it" (Department of Education, 1986).

These observational studies focus exclusively on the technical link between teacher behavior and pupil achievement, given the sacred definition of "achievement." Rarely do analysts assume a critical posture and ask, As adoration for tighter teacher controls and routinization of lessons intensifies, what social rules and forms of intellectual action are being taught? Ignoring such normative issues leads to (almost) funny clashes between scientifically derived findings and a culture's own priorities. Psychologists Harold Stevenson and James Stigler, for instance, recently completed a technically exquisite study of teaching practices in the United States, Taiwan, and Japan. Similar to previous work, they estimated that North American teachers spent 19 hours per week, on average, engaging pupils in academic tasks (after subtracting time spent on classroom management, discipline, and pupil time spent goofing-off). In contrast, Japanese teachers had pupils working on academic tasks 40 hours per week. During this "time-on-task," Japanese teachers were leading the class 70 percent of the time, versus less than half the time in the United States. Forty-seven (47) percent of instructional time in the United States was spent with students individually working on seat-work with little interaction taking place (Stevenson et al., 1986).

Stevenson's et al. message is that Japanese teachers run tighter class-rooms, act more strongly in leading lessons, and demand greater attention from their pupils. If the state's goal is to deepen the school's effect—in terms of raising social conformity and the learning of simple pieces of knowledge—then this apparent Japanese strategy should be replicated in other nations. Ironically, however, these messages from U.S. re-searchers come at the precise time that many Japanese political leaders and scholars are encouraging greater creativity among pupils and a nar-rower role for classroom teachers (Fuller et al., 1986). In addition, other researchers argue that early schooling in Japan holds a deep effect due to the teacher's subtle practice of receding into the background and delegating authority to and expecting responsible action from cooper-ative work groups (Lewis, 1984).

Socialization in (and for) Mass Organization

Let's turn to *critical* studies of teachers' action. I have mentioned two key findings that come from functional studies of teacher behavior. First, both teachers and pupils spend a lot of time disengaged from instruc-tional tasks. Second, when teachers are placing academic demands on kids, "teaching" is usually defined either as (a) lecturing at pupils (with variable rates of asking questions of the entire class or to an individual child), or (b) assigning seat-work whereby pupils work silently on a uniform task. Importantly, these two patterns are particularly common in Third World settings. Recent studies in Nigeria and Thailand found that in over two-thirds of all classroom observations, teachers were sim-ply lecturing at children. In much of the remaining time, pupils were sitting alone (on the floor or at desks) working on assigned exercises.

When teachers spoke or queried pupils, these utterances were most often directed at the entire class, not spoken to an individual student. Teachers' questions usually demanded recall of a piece of information, rarely asking for more complex knowledge or pupils' own ideas (Anderson et al., 1987).

A third finding, emphasized by critical observers of teachers, is that lower-status pupils are treated differently than higher-status students. Researchers Jean Carew and Sarah Lawrence Lightfoot (1979), working in U.S. classrooms, found that teachers tend to interact less with ethnic minority youngsters compared with high-achieving or white children. When a teacher does interact with a low-status pupil, the teacher's communication is more often a directive linked to procedures rather than an inquiry related to academic subject matter or an elicitation of the student's own views. Looking at how pupils are arranged into curriculum tracks, Oakes (1982) found that they reflected different ways in which low- versus high-status pupils are socialized in mass schools. Based on classroom observations, she found that low-status pupils were less often engaged in academic tasks, messages from teachers were more often punitive in nature, and pupils reported higher levels of alienation from the teacher. Critical ethnographies elaborate the latter point, showing that working-class kids are far less integrated into the work and ideology of the classroom, often times actively resisting the teacher's socialization pressures (Everhart, 1983). Teachers' requests for support from parents—to help with homework or to attend school meetings—receive variable responses depending on parents' social class (manifest in their level of schooling), free time, and resources (Lareau, 1987).

Interpretive analysts emphasize how this differential treatment of children by teachers serves to reinforce class inequality. Within industrialized countries, middle-class children and offspring of the elite receive more attention from the teacher; they may be encouraged to work independently and think more creatively. Working-class kids come to school with less cultural capital, that is, their parents have fewer resources (linguistic consonance, social rules, and time) to assist their kids. The teacher then pushes these children to fit into classroom routines, while choosing to engage less frequently in substantive discourse or complex instructional tasks. Despite the modern school's rhetorical claim to lessen ascriptive determinants of status and success, teachers' practices may help reproduce class differences.

In the Third World, all children in mass schools may be treated like working-class kids of North America. An initial ethnographic study of classrooms in Botswana reveals a startling picture of children sitting passively while the teacher talks at them, asking occasionally for a choral response from the entire class to a closed-ended question. Researchers Robert Prophet and Patricia Rowell focused specifically on instruction of science over a 2-month period of observation. Children were not encouraged to conceptualize certain processes, say the reproduction of plants and flowers. Instead, the teacher insisted that pupil respondents utter the correct technical terms in English. Prophet (1988) concluded that primarily elite codes were being taught, including the teacher's modern authority to relay these facts and vocabulary. Pupils had no chance to think through underlying processes nor apply this knowledge to their own conditions.

Putting together these basic lessons from classroom-observation studies, a more fundamental point arises: The teacher, concerned with maintaining order among many children, must move toward bureaucratic forms of control—lecturing the class as one uniform batch of kids, spending time on administrative procedures, assigning seat-work to silent, isolated, individual pupils. Little evidence suggests that central state actors are directly manipulating teachers to engage in such bureaucratic, factory-like actions. Yet the state, in a less obtrusive manner, is creating and legitimating the mass conditions under which socialization unfolds in the classroom. This is particularly true within Third World political structures, comprised of elites anxious to build schools as a signal of mass participation and economic opportunity. Their emphasis is on rapid expansion of the mass school. Education ministries, however, often are impotent when it comes to enforcing compliance with central ideals: the curriculum is unclear or presented with varying levels of fidelity; instructional materials (beyond standardized textbooks) are scarce; teachers act from diverse ideologies about how children should be socialized and taught. Even within industrialized countries, the conditions of mass schooling are surprisingly similar across local areas: Large numbers of children enter classrooms where material resources are scarce, and the teacher relies on routine forms of instruction that serve to maintain control and reinforce his or her own authority. Third World states—by allocating high status and modern expectations to teachers—do help reinforce the social authority of local educators. But day to day, teachers must set classic bureaucratic social rules if order, authority, and modern social rules are to be reinforced.

In addition, most Western countries write "modern curriculum" that is foreign to indigenous forms of knowledge and that is broken into small, uniform pieces. The curriculum's fragmented and prescribed character fits nicely with bureaucratic social rules and practices. Much of this action is ritualistic, as sociologist John Meyer (1987) emphasizes. Teachers spend class time arranging lessons, talking at the pupil masses, and watching over students working on routine seat-work. Whether these teaching practices effectively impart literacy or higher-order cognitive skills is a question rarely asked. These actions are symbolically rich in maintaining order and expressing the teacher's authority within a modern, mass organization—the classroom. The teacher is acting out the behaviors and rules that are expected, following legitimate images of what is supposed to occur in the classroom. Such action also responds to the mass conditions established by the Western countries—whereby political leaders anxiously try to show that access to the school represents membership and opportunity within the formal polity. The schooling "treatment" displays a predictable character, whether it leads to significant achievement effects or not.

SUMMING UP

Almost two decades of empirical research in Third World schools have yielded a wealth of evidence. We now know that the school consistently contributes to the acquisition of basic literacy in most developing country settings, net the a priori influence of family background and community context. This line of school effectiveness research also points to specific material inputs and teacher characteristics that most efficiently boost achievement. Conversely this work suggests that investments in other school factors could be lowered with very little effect on pupil performance.

Three shortcomings of this work must be emphasized. First, production-function models point to efficacious school inputs. But we gain little sense of the social process within which such materials are embedded. Textbooks seem to make a great difference, for example. But how and through what teaching practices is this effect realized?

Second, the conventional research strategy yields little understanding of how principal school actors—the headmaster and teacher—organize and mobilize material inputs. We do know that teachers from higher social class backgrounds and with more schooling do a better job. Yet we do not understand why. Indeed even basic descriptions of what Third World teachers do and how they see their own work are just beginning to emerge. This is a huge area of ignorance that researchers should help lessen.

Third, the conventional line of research attempts to identify basic school inputs that may hold universal utility across very different developing countries. Inquiries are structured in this way largely because they are sponsored by international agencies that hunger for general prescriptions. But the most exciting work is getting us closer to the heart of the instructional process—focusing on the teacher's form of action within the classroom. This unavoidably involves us in normative issues of what teaching behaviors and social rules more effectively motivate children, and within what cultural situations. By focusing on books, desks, and general teacher characteristics, we have worked only on the safe technical task of relating these inputs to literacy and numeracy.

When we move into the pedagogical practices and social rules set by the classroom teacher we move into more culturally sensitive issues. Teachers may enforce strict hierarchical forms of control, or encourage active participation by students. Third World teachers may stress memorization of "facts" that are legitimized and handed down by the central government, or teachers may nudge children to look at different sides of issues. These pedagogical practices, though complex and often controversial, impact both on how material inputs are utilized and on achievement levels. Thus if we are truly concerned about boosting school effectiveness, we cannot shy away from the action, social rules, and perceptions of the institution's central actor—the teacher.

NOTES

This chapter has been supported by the World Bank and the U.S. Agency for International Development. Views expressed do not necessarily represent official policy. Portions of this chapter appeared earlier in 1987 in the *Review of Educational Research*, *57*(3), 255–292 and in 1989 with Stephen Heyneman in the *Educational Researcher*, *18*(2), 12–19. These sections are reprinted with the permission of these journals.

1. In addition to Simmons and Alexander's (1978) first review paper, Schiefelbein and Simmons (1981) later summarized 26 studies, including simple correlational analyses. Heyneman and Loxley (1983) reported original data on 16 developing nations, focusing on the differences between these Third World and 13 industrialized countries. This chapter summarizes 60 empirical studies, excluding most work that did not statistically control for pupil's background. Haddad (1978) published a more limited review of class size effects.

2. Interpreting the relative shares of variance explained is not a sound practice when the antecedents compared are colinear. However, Heyneman and Loxley (1983) did not find high correlations between the level of school quality and family background among students in most low-income countries included in their study.

3. The economic effect from gains in Third World school quality, another form of the school's aggregate influence, is just beginning to be studied (for an initial review, see Fuller, 1986b).

4. If a study reported a correlation matrix and no association was observed between a school factor and achievement, this lack of relationship is reported. This is the only time that a control on pupils' social class was not taken into account.

REFERENCES

Anderson, L., Ryan, D., & Shapiro, B. (1987). *The classroom environment study: Teaching for learning.* Draft manuscript, University of South Carolina, Columbia.

Armitage, J., Batista, J., Harbison, R. W., Holsinger, D. B., & Helio, R. (1986).

School quality and achievement in rural Brazil. Washington, D.C.: The World Bank, Education and Training Department.

Arriagada, A. (1981). *Determinants of sixth grade student achievement in Colombia.* Unpublished manuscript, The World Bank, Education Department, Washington, D.C.

Arriagada, A. (1983). *Determinants of sixth grade student achievement in Peru.* Unpublished manuscript, The World Bank, Education Department, Washington, D.C.

Balderston, J., Wilson, A., Freire, M., & Simonen, M. (1981). *Malnourished children of the rural poor.* Boston: Auburn House.

Barr, R., & Dreeben, R. (1983). *How schools work.* Chicago: University of Chicago Press.

Beebout, H. (1972). *The production surface for academic achievement: An economic study of the Malaysian secondary education.* Unpublished doctoral dissertation, University of Wisconsin, Madison.

Carew, J., & Lawrence Lightfoot, S. (1979). *Beyond bias: Perspectives on classrooms.* Cambridge, MA.: Harvard University Press.

Carnoy, M. (1971). *Family background, school inputs, and students' performance in school: The case of Puerto Rico.* Unpublished manuscript, Stanford University, Palo Alto, CA.

Coleman, J., Campbell, E., Hobson, C., McPartland, J., Mood, A., Weinfall, F., & York, R. (1966). *Equality of educational opportunity.* Washington, D.C.: Department of Health, Education, and Welfare.

Comber, L., & Keeves, J. (1973). *Science education in nineteen countries.* New York: Halstead.

Department of Education. (1986). *Beginning teacher assistance program: What are the competencies that teachers will be expected to demonstrate?* Richmond, VA: Department of Education, Division of Professional Development.

Everhart, R. (1983). *Reading, writing, and resistance.* Boston: Routledge.

Fuller, B. (1986a). Defining school quality. In J. Hannaway & M. Lockheed (Eds.), *The contributions of the social sciences to educational policy and practice: 1965–1985* (pp. 33–70). Berkeley, CA: McCutchan.

Fuller, B. (1986b). Is primary school quality eroding in the Third World? *Comparative Education Review, 30,* 491–507.

Fuller, B., Holloway, S. D., Azuma, H., Hess, R. D., & Kashiwagi, K. (1986). Contrasting achievement rules: Socialization of Japanese children at home and in school. In A. Kerckhoff (Ed.), *Research in sociology of education and socialization* (Vol. 6, pp. 165–202). Greenwich, CT: JAI Press.

Fuller, W., & Chantavanich, A. (1976). *A study of primary schooling in Thailand: Factors affecting scholastic achievement of the primary school pupils* (Report). Bangkok: Office of the National Education Commission.

Gage, N., & Berliner, D. (1975). *Educational psychology.* Chicago: Rand McNally.

Government of Nepal (1988). *Nepal education and human resources sector assessment* (Report). Kathmandu: Ministry of Education.

Haddad, W. (1978). *Educational effects of class size.* Washington, D.C.: The World Bank.

Hartley, M., & Swanson, E. (1984). *Achievement and wastage: An analysis of the retention of basic skills in primary education.* Draft manuscript, The World Bank, Washington, D.C.

Hess, R. D., Kashiwagi, K., Azuma, H., Price, G. G., & Dickson, W. P. (1980). Maternal expectations for mastery of developmental tasks in Japan and the United States. *International Journal of Psychology, 15,* 259–271.

Heyneman, S., & Jamison, D. (1980). Student learning in Uganda: Textbook availability and other factors. *Comparative Education Review, 24,* 206–220.

Heyneman, S., Jamison, D., & Montenegro, X. (1983). Textbooks in the Philippines: Evaluation of the pedagogical impact of the nationwide investment. *Educational Evaluation and Policy Analysis, 6*(2), 139–150.

Heyneman, S., & Loxley, W. (1983). The effect of primary-school quality on academic achievement across twenty-nine high- and low-income countries. *American Journal of Sociology, 88,* 1162–1194.

Holloway, S. D., Gorman, K. S., & Fuller, B. (1987). *Contrasting social structures and child rearing beliefs: Mothers and preschool teachers in Mexico.* Unpublished manuscript, University of Maryland, College Park.

Holloway, S. D., & Hess, R. D. (1985). Mothers' and teachers' attributions about children's math performance. In I. E. Sigal (Ed.), *Parental belief systems: Psychological consequences for children* (pp. 177–199). Hillsdale, NJ: Erlbaum.

Husen, T., Saha, L., & Noonan, R. (1978). *Teacher training and student achievement in less developed countries.* Washington, D.C.: The World Bank.

Jamison, D. T., & Lockheed, M. E. (1985). *Participation in schooling: Determinants and learning outcomes in Nepal.* Washington, D.C.: The World Bank, Education and Training Department.

Jamison, D., Searle, B., Galda, K., & Heyneman, S. (1981). Improving elementary mathematics education in Nicaragua: An experimental study of the impact of textbooks and radio on achievement. *Journal of Educational Psychology, 73*(4), 556–567.

Karweit, N. (1985). Should we lengthen the school term? *Educational Researcher, 14*(6), 9–15.

Lareau, A. (1987). Social class differences in family–school relationships: The importance of cultural capital. *Sociology of Education, 60,* 73–85.

Leithwood, K., & Montgomery, D. (1982). The role of the elementary school principal in program improvement. *Review of Educational Research, 52,* 309–339.

Lewis, C. (1984). Cooperation and control in Japanese nursery schools. *Comparative Education Review, 28,* 69–84.

Lockheed, M., Vail, S., & Fuller, B. (1986). How textbooks affect achievement in developing countries: Evidence from Thailand. *Educational Evaluation and Policy Analysis, 8,* 379–392.

Loxley, W. (1984, April). *Quality of schooling in the Kalahari.* Paper presented at the annual meeting of the Comparative and International Education Society, Houston, TX.

Meyer, J. (1987). Implications of an institutional view of education. In M. Halinan (Ed.), *The social organization of schools* (pp. 157–175). New York: Plenum.

Morales, J., & Pinellsiles, A. (1977). *The determinant factors and the costs of schooling in Bolivia* (Working Paper No. 4–77). LaPaz: Universidad Catolica Boliviana.

Oakes, J. (1982). Classroom social relationships: Exploring the Bowles and Gintis hypothesis. *Sociology of Education, 55,* 197–202.

Prophet, R. (1988). *Rhetoric and reality in science curriculum development in Botswana*. Gaborone: University of Botswana. Mimeo.

Psacharopoulos, G., & Loxley, W. (1986). *Diversified secondary education and development*. London: Oxford University Press.

Purves, A. (1973). *Literature education in ten countries*. Stockholm, Sweden: Almqvist & Wiksell.

Rutter, M. (1983). School effects on pupil progress: Research findings and policy implications. *Child Development, 54,* 1–29.

Rutter, M., Maughan, B., Mortimore, P., Ouston, J., & Smith, A. (1979). *Fifteen thousand hours: Secondary schools and their effects on children*. Cambridge, MA: Harvard University Press.

Ryan, J. (1973). *Educational resources and scholastic outcomes: A study of rural primary schooling in Iran*. Unpublished doctoral dissertation, Stanford University, Stanford, CA.

Schiefelbein, E., & Farrell, J. (1973). *Factors influencing academic performance among Chilean primary students*. Santiago: Centro de Investigaciones y Desarrollo de la Educacion.

Schiefelbein, E., & Simmons, J. (1981). *Determinants of school achievement: A review of research for developing countries*. Ottawa, Canada: International Development Research Centre.

Sembiring, R., & Livingstone, I. (1981). *National assessment of the quality of Indonesian education*. Jakarta: Ministry of Education and Culture.

Simmons, J., & Alexander, L. (1978). The determinants of school achievement in developing countries: A review of the research. *Economic Development and Cultural Change, 26,* 341–357.

Smyth, J. (1987). *Somalia: Preparation mission report*. Paris, France: Office of the Assistant Director-General. Mimeo.

Stallings, J., Cory, R., Fairweather, J., & Needels, M. (1978). *A study of basic reading skills taught in secondary schools*. Menlo Park, CA: SRI International.

Stevenson, H. W., Stigler, J. W., Lucker, G. W., Lee, S., Hsu, C. C., & Kitamura, S. (1987). Classroom behavior and achievement of Japanese, Chinese, and American children. In R. Glasser, (Ed.), *Advances in Instructional Psychology* (Vol. 3, pp. 153–204). Hillsdale, NJ: Erlbaum.

Thias, H., & Carnoy, M. (1973). *Cost benefit analysis in education: A case study in Kenya*. Baltimore, MD: Johns Hopkins Press.

Thorndike, R. (1973). *Reading comprehension in fifteen countries*. New York: Halsted.

Wolff, L. (1970). *Why children fail in first grade in Rio Grande do Sul: Implications for policy and research*. Washington, D.C.: U.S. Agency for International Development.

3

Economics, Instructional Development, and the Enhancement of Educational Efficiency

Douglas M. Windham

INTRODUCTION

Instructional development can have multiple goals and objectives, but it must be judged according to a single criterion—efficiency. The success or failure of instructional development efforts can only be judged to the extent that the efforts contribute to increased efficiency in the classroom and school. To assess the achievement of efficiency, two major steps are required—the specification of resources and effects, and the operationalization of their measurement. Because instructional development often occurs within the context of multiple effects and the uncertain quantification of resource inputs and processes, the use of efficiency criteria has been slow to occur, and the acceptance of efficiency standards has not won general acceptance among instructional development specialists. In this brief chapter the attempt will be made to suggest how efficiency criteria can be applied to instructional development efforts and to assert that instructional development activities offer one of the most promising means for promoting enhanced efficiency in educational institutions in the developing world.

This presentation is made by an economist, and thus two caveats must be stated. First, no assertion is made that the author is an expert in instructional development, although experience and study have helped produce what the author hopes is deemed an acceptable familiarity with the major components of instructional development. Second, the orientation of the chapter is one that gives priority consideration not just to the instructional effects but also to the need to be responsible in the use of resources—financial and human—and to the relevance of the skills and knowledge produced to labor market and other social requirements.

It should be noted that relations between instructional development specialists and educational economists have been and remain strained. Many of the instructional development specialists question the propriety of the encroachment of economists into their domain and challenge the value to be derived from the analysis of instructional development systems by individuals who themselves are unfamiliar with the basic tenets of the instructional development methodology. Unfortunately for these individuals in the instructional development community, the increased scarcity of fiscal resources and the greater demand for accountability of educational systems have left educational managers with no choice but to attempt to incorporate economic analysis, and economic analysts, into their decision-making systems.

The skepticism of many instructional development specialists toward economists has been reciprocated in many instances. The economists often feel that instructional development occurs as a phenomenological exercise conducted by evangelical advocates of particular methodologies, without appropriate concern for the specific fiscal and labor market environments within which the educational enterprise must operate, and with inadequate attention to the earlier lessons learned and the possible transferability of existing instructional systems.

In fact, the two major ideological points that may be seen to divide instructional developers and economists are the following: (1) the ability to quantify the costs and effects of instructional design exercises in such a manner that they are subject to efficiency comparison with other instructional alternatives, and (2) the uniqueness versus the generalizability of instructional development efforts across regions within a country and among individual countries. In the first example of ideological disagreement, economists have manifested a much greater hubris in their attempts to work with estimates and approximations of costs and effects and a greater intolerance of assertions of costs or effects that are purported to exist but are "unmeasurable" by the tools of economic analysis. In the second example of disagreement, the majority of learning design specialists are appalled at what they perceive as the cavalier suggestions by economists that new instructional development costs are not justified because "similar" instructional systems have been developed elsewhere.

These two major ideological differences are reflective of the nature of training in the two fields. Instructional development training is heavily rooted in cognitive psychology and places a premium on the perception of the individual and unique needs of the learner. The environment of greatest import to the instructional development specialist is—and ought to be—the immediate environment of the home and school and not that of the government's fiscal condition or of the labor market's absorptive capacity. In contrast, economists practice what they refer to as an "individualistic science" but one that is, in fact, dependent upon the law of large numbers of its validity. The application of economic analysis to education almost always is a stochastic one, that is, based upon probable behavior. As with any given probability, the applicative predictive value increases when the number of cases increases. Thus, the questions of measurability and of uniqueness underlie the gap that exists between those who develop instructional systems and those who increasingly are being asked to analyze them.

In the following discussion, the attempt will be made to clarify several points of disagreement related to this controversy:

1. To what extent can instructional costs and effects be measured, and what are the appropriate roles for subjective and objective forms of analysis?
2. Is there a definition of instructional efficiency that is mutually acceptable to both instructional designers and economists?
3. Can the divergence between claims of uniqueness and assertions of generalizability be reduced or eliminated?
4. What is the appropriate management structure for reconciling the educational decision maker's need for the expertise of both instructional development specialists and economists?

THE MEASUREMENT OF INSTRUCTIONAL COSTS AND EFFECTS

In the evaluation of the costs and effects of instructional activities, measurement problems may be discussed in terms of three categories: (1) the explicitly quantified effects, (2) the effects that are quantifiable by proxy measures, and (3) the purely subjective effects. In making a private decision, individuals can compare these different effects through the common metric of their utility or preference functions. Subjectively, the individual compares the expected gains and losses of utility (pleasure) from the various amounts and forms of costs and effects, and selects the alternative activity that is perceived as optimal. Therefore, although the preference for monetary versus nonmonetary effects from an instructional change may be expected to differ across individuals who face identical sets of monetary and nonmonetary results, this should not reduce the efficacy of the decision-making process.

The economist, recognizing that public investment decisions should be made on the basis of more objective and generalizable criteria for trading off alternative forms of costs and effects, often has found it valuable to use the monetary metric as a common numeraire. No unique political calculus exists that will allow policy makers to execute the types of interpersonal comparisons of utility that would be appropriate if either marginal utility or indifference function analysis were to be extended from the individual to the collective case. To understand how the use of the monetary metric as a common numeraire for economic effects is both valuable and inherently flawed, examples of the aforementioned three categories of costs and benefits will be presented. Following this clarification of the monetary versus nonmonetary dichotomy, there will be a discussion of the relevance of these concepts to the question of instructional development contributions to increasing educational efficiency.

Explicitly Quantifiable Effects

The most easily measured costs and effects of an instructional activity are those where a direct transfer of monies takes place. In the case of basic education, teachers' salaries, textbook costs, and construction charges often are cited as obvious costs and the increased earnings of graduates are seen as equally obvious effects. Since these costs and effects are easily recognizable and are already in monetary form, it is very easy to overlook the difficulties in interpretation that exist even here. First, teachers' salaries may not represent the full cost of teachers' services. In many communities in developing nations, parental and local community assistance may be of equal or even primary importance as an incentive for a teacher to continue teaching and many nonmonetary bureaucratic incentives may exist (Thiagarajan & Kemmerer, 1987). Textbook costs may not include distribution costs; this means that one may underestimate the cost of rural or remote instruction or, as is common, cost differences may not explain properly the differences in the actual dissemination of textbooks among schools and regions (Searle, 1985). Also, construction charges may include a variety of local or donor subsidies. However, a more important issue in regard to construction costs is the failure to budget adequately for maintenance. Many educational institutions in developing nations (and some in developed nations) increasingly must engage in "negative financing" because of their inability to prevent the deterioration of instructional facilities (Windham, 1987).

Rate of return analysis has led to many insights related to the possible pitfalls in the economist's use of increased earnings as a benefit measure. It is interesting to note that there is a longstanding controversy over whether the education–earnings correlation is not a matter of reverse or even coincident causality (Blaug, 1972; Psacharopoulos, 1985). The continuing complex debate over screening, veiling, certification, and credentialism has raised doubts about the extent to which education directly produces earnings. Obviously, estimates of the earnings effect at least must control for influences of individual ability differences and family environmental determinants.

An additional problem with the earnings measure is that it is not adjusted for equalizing differences (status, working conditions, and other perquisites) among specific jobs or even occupations, or for cost-of-living differences that make the purchasing power of any earnings geographically specific. In the case of basic education, the best that can be said for all of this is that for the "explicitly quantifiable" effects, ease of measurement may be more apparent than real. However, adjustments usually can be made to improve the specification of these effects (with the result that this first category of effects becomes very much like the following category).

Effects Quantifiable by Proxy Measures

In most instructional activities there exist costs and effects that, although not involving an explicit exchange of money, may be evaluated in monetary terms by the use of proxies. An example on the cost side of education would be the earnings foregone by students while in school. No direct financial exchange takes place in this case but the earnings foregone are a very real cost to the individual and the family. This point has become an important issue in the financing of education because even where financial assistance has become more readily available for the direct costs of education, the failure to provide prospective students from low-income homes with financial assistance to offset their foregone earnings acts as a potential barrier to access.

It was once assumed that foregone earnings in education could be estimated simply through use of the earnings of the group who did not pursue the next educational step. The foregone earnings of college students, therefore, were estimated from comparisons with the earnings of secondary school graduates. Attempts have been to adjust such estimates to take into account the different innate and environmental advantages the two groups possess, the idea being that college students—if they had stopped their education at the secondary school level—would have earned more than those who actually did stop there. Thus, a proper proxy measure of foregone earnings would increase the measured earnings of secondary school graduates when using these earnings as a foregone earnings measure.

One of the most commonly used proxy measures in instructional analysis is that of the teachers' credentials (Fuller, 1985). Normally, one is concerned with both formal academic and training in pedagogical skills. The difficulty with this proxy measure is that it has an uncertain correlation with actual instructional performance. The level and quality of academic and pedagogical preparation are assumed to be positively correlated with a teacher's knowledge of subject matter and instructional skills, but the correlation is likely to be extremely variable in reality in any group of teachers with similar credentials.

The problem is magnified when one converts the proxy measure into monetary terms by using teacher salaries as the proxy for teacher quality. This formulation requires two implicit assumptions: (1) that credentials are correlated with instructional effectiveness, and (2) that the progression rate of salaries by credential level is justified by the increased rate of effectiveness by credential level. There is little in the way of research evidence, logical argument, or intuitive insight to support faith in their concomitant incidence.

Purely Subjective Effects

The final category of costs and effects is the one with that the economist *cum* policy analyst must feel least comfortable. As much as some advocates of quantification may resist, there are instructional costs and effects that simply are not quantifiable with any reasonable precision even in proxy form. Attempts to quantify such subjective factors are themselves so arbitrary as often to confuse rather than to enlighten the debate. In education, one such effect is what is called the "psychic cost" of education. In addition to direct cash outlays and the estimates of foregone earnings, one cost of education to any participant is the disutility incurred in the education process itself. An intriguing and imaginative early piece by Edward Lazear (1974) suggested that for most participants, education exists as an economic "bad" rather than as an economic good. Unsurprisingly, the better the student, the less of a "bad" consumption effect education appears to have.

Some researchers would assert that even these psychic costs can be approximated through comparisons of rates of return under ceteris paribus conditions (the higher return representing an offset to the unpalatable nature of the activity). As in all such attempts to categorize residual effects, the result is primarily a labeling of ignorance and involves more an application of taxonomy than of theory.

On the effects side of education, no easily adaptable technique exists for estimating interpersonal differences in the utility derived from earnings. Robert Michael (1972, 1982) has greatly advanced the understanding of the relationship between education and patterns of consumption. This work has been interpreted to imply that an additional advantage of education is that it "improves" the educated person's ability to use his or her earnings and thus enhances the utility he or she derives from any given level of earnings. Michael's own view (1972) is as follows:

We observe that, holding total consumption expenditures fixed, differences in the education level of the head of the household are associated with shifts in the composition of the household's consumption bundle . . . in terms of the composition of their expenditures, households with more educated heads behave as if they have more real income.

Michael's work allows one to use certain elasticity estimates to adjust for education's consumption effects of this type. However, this area of research has not yet developed sufficiently so that one could make such adjustments without introducing new, uncertain, and possibly dangerously large biases into the analysis. The interpersonal utility differences would, even with a perfected methodology, only be *better* approximated by such estimates.

Other differences in the household production of goods and services, the handling of assets, and the timing of and investment in children are all probably related to education but exist as effects that cannot be readily converted into a common financial denominator. This is especially true if one desires to compare the satisfaction derived from each instructional activity by the students or their families.

The Importance of Nonmonetary Effects

What value is there in the three-way categorization of these instructional development effects? In the situation of individual decision making such a categorization is, in fact, an indulgence. Individuals will make their decisions based upon their perception of the effects, with no reason to be biased in favor of monetary over nonmonetary results. Since both are evaluated in a personal calculus with a common numeraire of subjective utility, there is no serious difficulty in comparing between monetary or nonmonetary effects of any of the types mentioned above.

Two problems that are claimed to exist have to do with "logic" and information. The first would criticize individuals for the failure to take into account all of the costs and benefits that learning theory has suggested to the analyst.[1] Many students may fail to cite foregone earnings or psychic disutility as a cost or the household production advantages as a benefit of their education. This apparent oversight is not a serious problem, however, since it would appear to be more a problem of proper labeling than of actual consideration. Also, too much criticism is leveled at parents, teachers, and students in developing nations for making "foolish" or "illogical" instructional choices. All parties will make internally "logical" decisions; the reason for divergence of instructional choices probably has more to do with different preferences and different amounts and quality of information than with different reasoning abilities.

The second factor, information, is an important reservation to the use of economic science to forecast educational behavior. The aforementioned law of large numbers acts as a protective device against the rare individual whose utilities are actually inverse to that of the standard. No similar device can guard against the predictive vagaries resulting from an unequal access and/or utilization of information. Thus, the difficulty in situations of individual choice is not caused by the three different types of effects that must be considered but by the possibility of "wrong" decisions being made by someone who decides logically but based on erroneous or incomplete information.

The importance of the tripartite specification of educational effects becomes crucial when the decision locus moves from the individual to the group. In any form of societal decision making that purports to take into account the net effects on different individuals (as opposed to a dictorial system where one individual's choices are the basis for the group's activities) some nonsubjective common measure must be used. Whether it is called systems, benefit/cost, cost-effectiveness, or rate of return analysis, all such "objective" analyses of social decision making have been forced to return to money as a common numeraire for the diverse monetary and nonmonetary effects. Because of the measurement difficulty with nonmonetary effects, many investment analyses have concentrated on the explicit monetary flows, although a warning is usually attached that draws attention to the fact that not all effects are included. Policy prescriptions usually follow, however, which are based solely on the monetary results and often ignore the analyst's own caveats.

Public investment analysis should be carried out in the following manner. Costs and effects of type one should be adjusted for such obvious biases as purchasing power differences and variance in work/leisure ratios. Costs and effects of type two should be estimated whenever such estimation is possible without the introduction of potentially large and uncertain biases. The investment criteria then can be analyzed resulting in a cost-effectiveness ratio, a rate of return, or a benefit/cost ratio based on the net costs and effects of types one and two.

Type three effects are not susceptible to similar treatment. They can be considered only within a decision framework involving individual choice or the voting of preferences. In the latter case, each member of the group can argue the case for their perception of type three effects. The actual voting procedure is a separate matter; the important point here is that type three effects are two uncertain to be quantifiable in an acceptable form through any objective consensus.

Thus, to summarize, the economic analysis will require recognition of the need to utilize monetary, or at least quantitative equivalents whenever possible so as to promote greater objectivity in decision making concerning instructional development. However, all parties should be willing to accept that not all costs and effects can be stated in monetary or even acceptable quantifiable terms, and thus an inherent margin of subjectivity must always exist in the analysis of instructional development costs and effects.

THE TRANSFERABILITY OF INSTRUCTIONAL SYSTEMS

As noted above, a second major area of dispute between instructional development specialists and economists concerns the emphasis to be placed on transferability of existing instructional systems. While it is possible to accept that each country, and even each major cultural subgroup, can benefit from having an instructional system developed to meet its specific needs, the practical policy issue is quite different. Given the existence of successful instructional systems, can one justify the expenditure of scarce development funds for design of new systems unique to a particular cultural environment?

First, one must recognize that real differences do exist in curricula and in the underlying cognitive structures and learning regimes. However, one should also realize that the xenophobic concerns with cultural imperialism, whatever their original merit, are now mitigated by the existence of learning systems developed to fit a variety of developing nation contexts. It is not necessary for a nation interested in developing a ninth-grade science curriculum to look only to the United States or Europe for models. Latin American, African, and Asian models of instructional development abound, and these can be considered for transfer or adaptation.

To the economist this issue appears largely to be one of fiscal capacity: Can the nation afford the full developmental cost of new instructional system initiatives or is some transfer or adaptation process a more realistic alternative? A few countries may have, from their own resources or from donor support, the funds adequate for the full range of instructional development activities (including needs assessment/task analysis, instructional design, materials production, evaluation, revision, and dissemination). At the other extreme, some countries may have to accept a full transfer of systems without the opportunity, at least initially, for adaptation. The majority of countries requiring new instructional systems may have to begin with at least a partial transfer of existing systems but can embark almost immediately on a phased adaptation of the technologies and the materials.

This phased adaptation will be most appropriate for those subject areas with the greatest cultural generalizability: the sciences and mathematics. Phased adaptation will be least advantageous in such culturally specific areas as history, local geography, and civics. The adaptation process can begin with the evaluation step; however, under an adaptive strategy the evaluation must be concomitant with a needs assessment/task analysis exercise to determine the extent to which the adopted system diverges from an indigenously developed one. Again, local fiscal capacity and/ or donor support will determine the extent and speed with which the transferred system can be adapted to the specific requirements of the receiving nation.

While economists have a role to play in assisting with the determination of the cost-effectiveness of the adaptation alternatives, only the instructional development specialists can specify the nature of the adaptation process. Since the primary value of instructional development is in its creation of a *system* that links learning needs with appropriate technologies of instruction and materials, though a developmental exercise, the process of adaptation must assure that the systemic advantages are not lost as parts of the original instructional system are altered to fit local conditions and needs. The economist's role in this process is to cost the relevant alternatives and to determine the affordability of initial developmental costs and the sustainability of the instructional system's recurrent cost implications.

The mediation of initial differences between instructional development specialists and economists over adaptation issues, as with the other differences concerning specification and measurement of instructional costs and effects, will require acceptance of a common definition of efficiency. In the next section a discussion will be presented of proposed definitions that should be acceptable to both groups. The need is to go beyond a common lexicon to a commitment of a shared conceptual framework; while such a goal will be difficult to realize, the benefits of achieving it in terms of instructional policy and practice are such that the effort should be made.

EFFICIENCY DEFINITIONS FOR INSTRUCTIONAL DEVELOPMENT

In Windham (1988a, b), a careful distinction is made between the concepts of effectiveness (how well an instructional system achieves its stated goals) and efficiency (which relates goal achievement to cost). As Windham makes clear, the effectiveness and cost concepts are subsumed within the efficiency concept.

It is possible to analyze instructional development solely on the basis of its effects. This often is done in instructional development as an initial means of comparing alternative instructional treatments or of comparing the results of the same treatment applied to different groups. Also, as excellently presented in Coombs and Hallak (1987), cost analysis, even in the absence of effectiveness data, can identify certain internal inefficiencies and test for the general fiscal feasibility of an instructional activity.

However, it is only when cost analysis and effectiveness analysis are brought together that one can truly make a definitive evaluation of an instructional development activity. The general definition of efficiency then is the maximization of effectiveness for a given level of cost or the minimization of costs for a given level of outputs. From this definition one can see the problems caused by the aforementioned conceptual disagreement between instructional development specialists and economists. If the effectiveness measure is unidimensional and both effects and costs are quantifiable in terms of monetary values, it is easy to construct a benefit/cost ratio. When benefits of an instructional development exercise are greater than the cost, efficiency is achieved. Since monetary values that occur over different time periods can be adjusted through discounting to a common time period value (Windham, 1988b, pp. 118–122), cost/benefit analysis is especially appropriate for educational investments, such as instructional development, that create immediate costs but generate effects whose incidence extends into the future.

Also, benefit/cost analysis can be adapted to deal with multidimensional effects as long as all of the effects are expressed, inherently or by proxy, in terms of monetary values. Sobel and Kaufman (1988) note that

unfortunately, many educational economists and some educators have resisted measuring the societal impacts of educational progress, options, and interventions because a reliable and valid metric did not exist for those consequences which could not be directly measured through a monetary nexus. . . . It should be understood that while any such metric will be both imperfect and controversial, we suggest that it is more desirable to attempt its development than to take the greater risk of pretending that one is not possible.

Where monetary proxies are not calculable or are not acceptable to the relevant decision makers, a second form of efficiency analysis called cost-effectiveness may be applied. In cost-effectiveness the cost side of the equation is still in monetary form but the effects side can be in any quantitative form. The most common effects measures used in cost-effectiveness analysis of instructional development activities are changes in enrollment, attendance, retention, achievement, graduation, and future academic or economic success. The normal effectiveness measure will use an indicator that incorporates the average effect for a group; more sophisticated analyses may extend this to measure of the distributional incidence of these effects.

In the debate over the convertibility of instructional development effects into monetary equivalents, it is too easy for one to forget the methodological controversy that attaches to the measurement of instructional effects, regardless of their form. Chapman and Windham (1986) are especially critical of the excessive confidence placed in the use of standardized achievement measures as summary indicators of instructional effectiveness. The point is that precision in measurement cannot be achieved in this area of analysis primarily because of the inherent complexity of the instructional enterprise itself, not just because of scarcity of funding, lack of effort, or methodological disagreement.

Cost-effectiveness analysis does offer an efficiency measure that both instructional development specialists and economists can accept. It is most useful, however, when two instructional systems or treatments have the same level of effect and different costs, or the same costs and different levels of effect. When a situation is encountered wherein a treatment is both more costly and more effective, the simple cost-effectiveness ratio will not be an appropriate measure of efficiency.

The reason for this is that one cannot compare a 10 percent increase in costs to a 10 percent increase in effect (e.g., average measured achievement or increase in graduation rate). Because costs and effects are stated in different metrics, the only means for interpreting these relative differences is in terms of subjective values. This has led to the use of what Levin (1983) calls cost-utility analysis.

In cost-utility analysis, the educational decision maker (who can be a student, parent, or education or political official) must equate the cost and effect results of an instructional intervention in terms of their personal utility, that is, their subjective relative valuation of the change in costs versus the change in instructional effect. In the abstract this poses no problem; however, in reality, there is a consistent tendency for individuals to attach greater credence to the cost rather than the effect side of the equation. The reasons for this are multiple: (1) costs appear to be more objectively determined that many effect measures; (2) costs are stated in a monetary form, which is a more easily interpretable metric than the statistical measures used in expressing most instructional effects; (3) costs are immediate results of a decision while instructional effects will occur over time; and (4) the costs of an instructional change must be financed from scarce revenue resources while foregone effects can be absorbed through reduced utility. In addition, many decision makers act as if the probability of cost incurrence is certain while the probability of the instructional effects is more uncertain. In fact, this is often the case; the problem is that there may be an unduly high discount of the effects probabilities leading to a consistent pattern of cost avoidance at the expense of instructional improvements that are economically efficient. In summary, cost-utility analysis to determine instructional development efficiency is acceptable in the abstract but has a potential negative bias in practical application. The tendency of many instructional program managers to avoid or postpone cost analysis of their work may be related directly to the concern that decision makers may give undue weight to the cost information at the expense of effects data.

The final efficiency measure used in the analysis of instructional development activities is the least-cost standard. In this analysis, the effects side is treated in a simplified form and may refer to the provision of educational inputs, to the creation of instructional processes, or to the outputs of the processes. The least-cost standard simply requires that, of the alternative means of providing inputs, creating processes, or producing outputs, the one selected be the least costly. Least-cost analysis may be understood to represent a point of tangency between efficiency analysis and cost analysis.

The application of least-cost analysis still leaves room for differences between instructional development specialists and economists. Specifically the definition of the inputs, processes, and outputs can be an issue, but a more common problem is the definition of a threshold level. Since under different instructional alternatives the actual levels of inputs, processes, or outputs may vary, the least-cost methodology requires standardized minimum levels of attainment for the instructional alternatives. Levels beyond these minima are treated in the analysis as having a zero marginal value. This approach provides problems for both instructional developers and for economists, although often for different reasons. The economist may be concerned about excessive generation of effects given the need to minimize costs, while the instructional developers would argue that the cost comparisons ignore the additional benefits that exist when effects are created above the threshold levels.

All four forms of efficiency analysis have application to instructional development activities. Agreement on the form of analysis to be used may differ depending upon the complexity of the instructional development activity to be analyzed. In the next section, a management approach will be suggested that incorporates economists with instructional development specialists in a collaborative manner. Specifically, the approach will suggest where the two analyst groups can cooperate (and which of the two should lead the analysis) and where the work of the instructional development specialist can take place in isolation of the economist.

The Economist's Role In Instructional Development

Instructional development normally is described as consisting of six major steps: needs analysis; task analysis; design; production; evaluation; revision.

In this section a discussion will be presented to the advantages to be gained from the joint participation of economists in the work of the instructional development specialists. The management structure most appropriate to this collaboration would be one wherein the economist serves in an advisory position to the instructional development specialist. Where instructional development activities are only part of a project initiative, both the instructional development specialist and the economist could serve in advisory roles to a team leader who would have general educational planning or educational management expertise.

Needs analysis. In the identification of learning needs the economist's role will be a minor one. Primarily the economist can function as a moderating influence to the enthusiasm of the educationalists by stipulating the cost implications related to changes in policies or practices needed to remediate certain needs. The economist also can contribute to the needs analysis process by reminding other personnel of the requirement to be aware continuously of fiscal limitations. However, the economist must understand that the major activities involved in analyzing the needs of learners are not activities that fall within the economist's areas of comparative advantage.

Task analysis. As the process proceeds from the assessment of general learning needs to the specification of instructional tasks, the role of the economist remains a minor one. In fact, the traditional exclusion of participation by economists in either of these steps has not posed a serious constraint on the quality or relevance of instructional development activities. Where task analysis is technically specific (how to identify the skills required by welders) the economist's competencies are not immediately advantageous. Where task analysis is more general (the identification of skills that lead someone to be a better citizen), the economist may have opinions that are as valid as anyone else's but their validity is not related to his or her disciplinary expertise.

Design. It is at the design stage that the greatest discrepancy exists between the role normally played by economists in instructional development and the optional contribution economists can make to the process. Cummings (1986), in a review of the development of low-cost primary instruction in six developing countries, notes that the failure to incorporate economic and cost analysis in the design phase of instructional development was one of the major constraints on eventual dissemination of the instructional experiments he studied. Additional support by non-economists for the role of economic analysis in the analysis of instructional activities may be found in Friend (1985) and Postlethwaite (1987).

The design process is described by Briggs (1975) as consisting of the establishment of behavioral objectives, the appraisal of resources and constraints, and the selection of media (Briggs includes goal definition and learning task analysis as part of the design process whereas here they are designated as predesign steps in the instructional development process). The contribution of the economist is most significant in costing the design alternatives and in appraisal of the ability of the costs to be financed (see Jamison, Klees, & Wells, 1978).

Instructional development costing takes place by means of the instructional development specialist working with the economist to identify the major cost components. Normally these are instructional personnel, facilities, equipment, materials, supervisory–administrative effects, training, and other support costs. While in some cases these instructional development costs are estimated in the abstract, the most useful analysis will be based on a comparison of costs under the existing instructional system and under the new instructional design.

For example, instructional personnel costs of a new design for primary education instruction should be analyzed in terms of the effect of the change in instructional design on the requirement for instructional personnel. The issue of personnel "requirement" is defined as including consideration of both the number of personnel and their cost. For example, a new design might reduce the number of personnel by allowing for a higher ratio of students per teacher; however, this cost saving can be offset if the instructional design requires teachers with greater qualifications, which are concomitant with higher salary obligations. It is interesting to note that many of the low-cost learning instructional designs are able to claim savings in both the quantity of personnel and in the salary requirements of personnel (Nichols, 1982; Thiagarajan, 1984, 1985).

The second major cost category is facilities. Again, it is not appropriate to impute existing facility expenses as a cost of the new instructional design. Rather, the cost question is whether the new instructional design requires a change in existing facilities or an addition to them. Reduced facilities demand can be included as a short-run cost saving to the extent that the now excess facilities are convertible to other uses; in the long run, reduced facilities demand may result in reduced demand for new facilities construction.

The issue with equipment costs is the same as that with facilities: Does the change in instructional design alter equipment demand in terms of quantity, quality, or type? One must be very careful in making these comparisons because the comparison must be with what is, not what should be. For example, an alternative science instructional design that uses inexpensive, locally available materials rather than expensive formal laboratory equipment (as in Zim-Sci, the Zimbabwean low-cost science instruction design), must be compared with the equipment that one realistically can expect to find in classrooms. If the alternative to the low-cost option is expensive laboratory equipment, then a savings exists; if the alternative is no equipment, then the "low-cost" learning design actually may imply a more expensive, albeit improved, form of education. This is one of the dramatic ironies in the dissemination of "low-cost" learning systems; the existing systems in the poorest developing nations are so deprived of resources that even the "low-cost" system may involve an increased financial burden. It is for this reason that Windham (1983) argues that justification of such instructional designs in many developing nations should emphasize the characteristics of enhanced achievement and future cost containment rather than argue the issue of immediate cost savings.

With a paucity of equipment in most schools in developing nations, any instructional design requiring extensive equipment provision will be at a cost disadvantage. In the area of instructional materials, however, the situation is quite different. The large number of local and donor-financed textbook programs in the last decade has greatly increased the production (if not always the effective dissemination) of textbooks in many developing agencies (Searle, 1985). The cost question here is whether the new instructional design requires new materials production and whether these new materials are complements or substitutes for existing textbooks and material. If they are complements (e.g., instructional guides or manuals designed to help teachers and students make better use of textbooks or materials that already exist in the classroom), then their justification must be in terms of enhanced achievement not cost savings.

If the new instructional materials are substitutes, then the relative cost of the new materials versus the old is the basis for estimating the marginal cost effect of the new design. It should be noted that in materials-based strategies such as programmed instruction and programmed learning, resistance has been encountered in terms of a reluctance to abandon traditional textbook materials even where significant achievement advantages can be shown for the new programmed materials. Also, one must be careful in costing the textbook alternative since the issues of initial costs (less expensive production technologies are evolving for textbooks), usable life, and textbook-per-student ratios are all variable among individual countries.

An often overlooked issue is the question of administration and supervision. The supervisory and inspectorate systems that exist in many developing nations are severely constrained by insufficient staffing, poor quality of training, and inadequate support costs (especially in the area of transportation). New instructional designs, such as the Improved Efficiency of Learning (IEL) System in Liberia, were questioned because they involved a higher level of supervision of and assistance to teachers than did the traditional instructional system. However, while this was appropriately viewed as a cost effect of the new instructional design, it was overlooked as a major increase in efficiency. The increase in efficiency came about because the new design improved the quality and effectiveness of administrative and supervisory activities. Since prior to the IEL project, large amounts were being spent on the supervisory system with little or no effect, the IEL instructional design deserved credit for making a potentially major improvement in instructional effectiveness with a relatively small additional cost. As we noted earlier, efficiency sometimes can be achieved simultaneously with increased cost. This is why the issues of efficiency enhancement and fiscal absorptive capacity are parallel concerns but not identical considerations.

Training costs attached to new instructional designs have separate implications depending on whether they are transitional or permanent effects. For example, if training costs are a one-time effect linked to initial design implementation, the major issue is affordability; often, such initial costs may be financed externally or amortized over the useful life of the training. However, most new designs require some permanent training reform. If this can be absorbed within the normal pre-service or in-service teacher training budget, the cost effect for the new design will be negligible. The training cost issue is significant only when substantial new training costs must be absorbed on a recurrent basis. When such training costs do occur, they must be rationalized in terms of either offsetting cost savings created by the new design in other cost categories or by compensating increases in measured instructional performance and student achievement.

Another area sometimes overlooked is that of the prerequisite or concomitant support costs related to introduction of the new instructional design. For example, if the design requires electricity, or special transportation, or an improved communication infrastructure, these new costs must be charged to introduction of the new design. However, to the extent that these new support systems have other beneficial effects (an addition of electrical supply to the school may allow the use of the facility for night classes, for example), the charges related to the support systems must be prorated over the various benefits. Only the proportion of charges directly related to the new instructional design should be charged to the instructional development expenses.

Thus, the economist should be a major, even if not equal, partner to the instructional development specialist during the design phase. This partnership will continue during the last three phases of instructional development.

Production. The production decisions interact with the design decisions in that the instructional development specialist may determine that certain production alternatives involve prohibitive immediate costs or excessive dependence on external or otherwise unstable sources of supply. Thus, the design may need to be modified to fit these production considerations.

It is the responsibility of the economists once again to assist the instructional development specialist with the costing of alternatives and the evaluation of these choices. However, only the instructional development specialist can make the final decision on the relationship of production media costs to the needs of the learners and to the cognitive objectives of overall cognitive strategy. While subordinate, the economist's role is essential as one moves from design to experimental dissemination to full-scale dissemination.

Evaluation. Once the instructional system is disseminated initially, it is necessary to conduct a formative evaluation of its efficiency. One of the four efficiency models discussed above may be used to establish the efficiency criteria for the evaluation. Too often in the past instructional development evaluations have been concerned only with the success of implementation or only with the learning effects and not with the efficiency (including issues of initial affordability and fiscal sustainability) of the full instructional intervention. This is one major reason why instructional development systems can be experimental "successes" and yet result in dissemination "failures."

The economist has both a specific and general task in evaluation. The economist should help in the specific measurement of costs and effects but also should participate in the general design of the evaluation analysis. The latter is necessary to assure that proper weight is given to the issues of cost, fiscal capacity, and relevance to external (especially labor market) requirements. Successful evaluation of instructional development activities would involve both the economists and instructional development specialists in subordinate roles to that of an external evaluation specialist. The use of an external evaluation specialist will promote objectively and provide needed evaluative expertise to a process easily biased by the commitments and advocacy of the participants who have developed the system under study.

Revision. Following the evaluation, the instructional development specialist must revise the system to fit the new information on costs, effects, affordability, and relevance. One of the most successful examples of a cooperative revision effort was that made in the Liberian IEL Project (Thiagarajan, 1983). Revision also may be stimulated, of course, by design issues other than those related to the economist's areas of interest. However, whatever the origins of the revisions, they once again must undergo the economist's analysis to determine the effect of potential dissemination on the issues of cost, affordability, and external relevance.

The design, production, evaluation, and revision phases are not a single, unidirectional process. Rather, they are phases in a recursive process that should continue even after a system is fully disseminated. In fact, the economist must be made to understand that instructional development is a continuing activity and not one that is abandoned once the textbooks or new teacher training program is instituted. If instructional development is to promote efficiency in education, it can do so only as a permanent part of the educational system's ongoing operations. And if instructional development itself is to be efficient, a common ground must be found on which the work of economists and instructional development specialists may be joined in a collaborative and mutually respectful manner.

NOTE

1. One could make the case for a "money illusion effect," that is, that monetary outcomes or costs dominate because they appear more real to the individual. It is difficult to separate money illusion biases from other preferences for money receipts (greater exchangeability) and opposition to money costs (must be financed by additional work rather than by sacrifice of leisure).

REFERENCES

Blaug, M. (1972). The correlation between education and earnings: What does it signify? *Higher Education, 1* (Winter), 53–76.

Briggs, L. J. (1975). *An overview of instructional systems design.* Tallahassee: Florida State University.

Chapman, D. W., & Windham, D. M. (1986). *The evaluation of efficiency in educational development activities.* Tallahassee: Florida State University, Improving the Efficiency of Educational Systems Project.

Coombs, P. H., & Hallak, J. (1987). *Cost analysis in education.* Washington, D.C.: The World Bank.

Cummings, W. K. (1986). *Low-cost primary education: Implementing an innovation in six nations.* Ottawa, Canada: International Development Research Centre.

Friend, J. (1985). *Classroom uses of the computer: A retrospective view with implications for developing nations.* Washington, D.C.: The World Bank, Education and Training Series.

Fuller, B. (1985). *Raising school quality in developing countries: What investments boost learning?* (Report No. 2). Washington, D.C.: The World Bank, Education and Training Series.

Jamison, D., Klees, S., & Wells, S. (1978). *The costs of educational media.* Beverly Hills, CA: Sage.

Lazear, E. (1974). *Education: Consumption or production.* Paper presented at the Workshop in Applications of Economics, University of Chicago, Chicago, IL.

Levin, H. M. (1983). *Cost-effectiveness: A primer.* Beverly Hills, CA: Sage.

Michael, R. (1972). *The effect of education on efficiency in consumption.* New York: Columbia University Press.

Michael, R. (1982). Measuring the non-monetary benefits of education. In W. W. Geske & T. Geske (Eds.), *Financing education: Overcoming inefficiency and inequity* (pp. 119–149). Urbana: University of Illinois Press.

Nichols, D. G. (1982). Low-cost learning systems: The general concept and some specific examples. *NSPI Journal, 4* (September), 4–8.

Postlethwaite, T. N. (1987). Comparative educational achievement research: Can it be improved? *Comparative Education Review, 31*(1), 150–158.

Psacharopoulos, G. (1985). Returns to education: A further international comparison. *Journal of Human Resources, 20*(4), 584–604.

Searle, B. (1985). *General operational review of textbooks.* Washington, D.C.: The World Bank, Education and Training Series.

Sobel, I., & Kaufman, R. (1988). *Toward a "hard" metric for educational utility.* Paper presented at the Conference on Societal Impact Indicators and Their Role in Predicting and Evaluating the Contributions of Vocational Programs, Florida State University, Tallahassee.

Thiagarajan, S. (1983). *A report on the IEL Materials Cost Reduction Project.* Gbarnga, Liberia: The Improved Efficiency of Learning Project.

Thiagarajan, S. (1984). *Appropriate educational technology for developing nations: Low cost learning systems.* Bloomington, IN: Institute for International Research.

Thiagarajan, S. (1985). *Instructional system design for improved learning.* Gabarone, Botswana: Institute for Educational Research.

Thiagarajan, S., & Kemmerer, F. (1987). *How to improve teacher incentive systems.* Tallahassee: Florida State University, Improving the Efficiency of Educational Systems Project.

Windham, D. M. (1983, January). *Cost issues in the Liberian Improved Efficiency of Learning (IEL) Project* (Report No. 1). Monrovia, Liberia: Ministry of Education.

Windham, D. M. (1987). *Internal efficiency and the African school.* Washington, D.C.: The World Bank.

Windham, D. M. (1988a). Effectiveness indicators in the economic analysis of educational activities. *International Journal of Educational Research, 12*(6), 575–665.

Windham, D. M. (1988b). *Indicators of educational effectiveness and efficiency.* Tallahassee: Florida State University, Improving the Efficiency of Educational Systems Project.

4

Systems Design and Educational Improvement

Robert M. Morgan

Perhaps the most significant contribution of management science in the past 4 decades has been the concept and technology of *systems analysis*. Systems analysis was born of necessity during World War II when the planning and logistical requirements for the Allied invasion of Europe greatly exceeded the conventional management tools available at that time. The enormity of this task and its concentration in time and space demanded that new approaches to management planning had to be developed. In the postwar years, systems analysis strategies were found to be useful for a wide range of corporate and governmental activities, and the systems approach became fundamental to modern management.

Systems analysis is a logical and systematic way of organizing the conduct of any task, though it is most often utilized in the planning and performance of large, complex activities. Simply described, systems analysis requires that before starting a task, the intended outcomes of that task must be operationally defined, so that one can observe and know that success has been achieved. It also requires that all possible variables that may affect the successful completion of the task are identified, and that their contribution—positive or negative—is planned for. In the planning stages, the systems analyst will examine alternative ways of arranging resources in order to predict which combination and sequence of resources are likely to lead to task accomplishment in the least time and with the least cost (Churchman, 1964, 1965). Systems analysis tools, like Program Evaluation and Review Technique (PERT), have been developed to allow the graphic display of sequenced enabling tasks, resource requirements, and potentially contributing or interfering variables. The PERT display identifies all critical activities and functions essential to completion of the job, places them in the order in which they must occur, and shows the dependency between subtasks. An important feature of systems analysis is the estimation of time required for each subtask, which permits the entire project to be placed in a time frame with specification of a fairly precise schedule from start-up to completion (Weiner, 1948).

Applications of systems analysis range from planning and construction of supersonic aircraft to the determination of the optimum location of a new gasoline filling station in a community. Several years ago, a new community college was authorized in the state of Virginia and the managers of this development utilized the systems approach in the planning and development of the college. Land had to be purchased for the campus; a curriculum had to be planned; buildings had to be constructed; furniture and equipment had to be purchased; administrative and management procedures had to be established; students had to be recruited and admitted; and on and on. Moreover, all of these things—buildings, personnel, materials, and so on—had to come together when the school was ready to open, but not before. Using systems analysis the school was able to open a full year earlier than was normally required for such a development.

THE ADVENT OF INSTRUCTIONAL SYSTEMS

As with most new products and processes, the educational community was slow to adopt systems analysis as a planning and management tool, and its application to instructional development might never have occurred except for a fortuitous happening in the late 1950s. This important event was the introduction of the concept of programmed instruction by Professor B. F. Skinner of Harvard University (Skinner, 1968). Skinner, a leader in the psychology of learning, was dismayed at how little use was made in the conventional classroom of learning principles, whose criticality in the human learning process had been clearly demonstrated by empirical laboratory research. He set about designing a process of instruction that would effectively employ these learning principles. He was, perhaps, most concerned about the difficulty, in traditional instruction, of accommodating the variable aptitude for learning that is a universal characteristic of groups of learners. There are wide divergences in student backgrounds, intelligence, and motivation, and the failure of instruction to accommodate these individual differences significantly reduces the effectiveness of classroom instruction. In order for instruction to be effective it should be properly sequenced, going from the elemental to the complex. It should be meaningful to the learner and the learning steps shouldn't be larger than the student can manage. The instruction should require active participation from the learner with frequent and periodic responses made to the instructional stimuli. The instruction should be designed so that each learner can progress with success, with later learning building upon earlier learning. Finally, the student should receive continuing and frequent reinforcement of his or her correct responses, and corrective feedback when wrong responses are made.

Programmed instruction was designed to incorporate these instructional characteristics. The advance definition of the learning outcomes in the form of instructional objectives was an important feature of programmed instruction. These objectives served as the specifications against which the instruction was designed, and as the learning milestones against which the student's learning progress was assessed.

In the decade of the sixties, many world educators were experimenting with programmed instruction. When programmed instruction was carefully and empirically developed it would typically provide instruction that was measurably superior to conventional classroom instruction, for which the success criteria was required time for learning and terminal achievement. Since the early credo of programmed instruction was that it should successfully teach every student for whom it had been designed, the empirical development of the programs was essential. Empirical development means that after the learning objectives have been defined and the instructional sequences have been developed, the programs are tried out with students drawn from the learner population for whom the programs are intended. Using the success and failure feedback from these trial students the programs are then revised. The iterative process of tryout and revision is followed until the programs are of demonstrable teaching effectiveness. When these developmental steps were followed, programmed instruction usually resulted in significantly higher mean achievement and less learning time than was obtained with conventional instruction.

As experiments were being conducted with programmed instruction, researchers encountered many practical problems. Since the earliest forms of programmed instruction were of a self-instructional nature, students finished instruction at different times, creating logistical and scheduling problems for teachers. Also, programmed instruction at this time was almost always in print format, which meant that any teaching that needed graphics, sound, or motion was excluded. Finally, it occurred to some of the professionals working with programmed instruction that the basic principles of learning and the systematic, empirical design processes could probably be applied to many different modalities of instruction, not just print. To others, who encountered the administrative and logistical constraints on the classroom use of programmed instruction, it seemed essential to examine the classroom and school as a total system of learning, with attention given in the design process to the many variables potentially contributing to or interfering with effective learning. It was at about this point that educational developers began to be aware of the parallels between the work they were doing with programmed instruction and the work of the systems analysts in private industry and the government (Banathy, 1969).

INSTRUCTIONAL SYSTEMS DESIGN

In the ensuing 25 years, Instructional Systems Design (ISD), as an application of systems analysis concepts, has evolved as a serious academic discipline. More than 60 universities in the United States now offer masters or doctoral degrees in this field. These include such institutions as Florida State University, Syracuse University, Indiana University, the University of Texas, and many more. ISD now has several scholarly journals dedicated to the dissemination of its research findings. Hundreds of ISD graduates are now employed in training and educational development activities throughout the world (Bass & Dills, 1984). However, it should probably be noted that far more application of ISD is being made today in government, military, and industrial training than in formal education. Formal education has been historically one of the slowest sectors to adopt innovations.

Instructional systems design is grounded in both research and developmental application, and in addition to the influence of systems analysis its evolution has also been affected by three other disciplines (Morgan, 1978). In some respects, ISD represents a convergence of management science, communications, and the behavioral sciences, and it has drawn heavily on the research, knowledge, and philosophical foundations of these three disciplines. Researchers and practitioners of ISD, working in different environments on different problems of education and training, have developed a variety of models. Some 40 different ISD models were examined and compared by Andrews and Goodson (1980). Others have argued that there are too many models, suggesting that a single, all-purpose model should suffice (Montemerlo & Tennyson, 1976; Thiagarajan, 1976). Branson points out that while virtually all of the models are adaptations of one another, differing models are called for because of the highly varied situations of education and training (Branson, 1988). Branson, one of the pioneers of ISD, and his colleagues, developed one of the first and most comprehensive ISD models for the U.S. Department of Defense (Branson et al., 1976). This model, referred to as the Interservice Procedures for Instructional Systems Development (IPISD) will be described here because it is highly generalizable across educational settings and is a completely modular input–output model.

An adaptation of the model is shown in Figure 4.1. In this model there are five conceptual functions: Analyze, Design, Develop, Implement, and Control. Virtually all of the several ISD models currently in use are based on these same five functions. This model identifies the sequence of activities that are essential in the ISD approach and it is readily apparent that a great deal of work precedes and follows the development phase. This is in marked contrast with the way that educational programs and materials are traditionally developed, where almost all of the developer's attention is given to writing and production. It is the front-end analysis and design, and the implementation, evaluation, and control activities that truly differentiates ISD from conventional approaches to curriculum development.

Analyze. The analysis phase is crucial to successful application of the ISD approach. It is in this step that decisions are made as to what is to be taught, to whom, and why. For vocational or industrial training, the job for which the person is being trained is analyzed and all critical tasks are identified. For education, the course or block of instruction is analyzed. Is the course consistent with the goals and purposes that have been set for the educational system? What are the prerequisite educational attainments and prior knowledge requirements that are assumed for a student entering this course? Does the course content, with its beginning and end, articulate with what comes before and after it in the curriculum? What are the personal characteristics of the students for whom the instruction is being designed? What should the goals of the instruction be? What knowledge, skills, and attitudes are intended to be taught by the course? How will the student's progress in successfully achieving the course objectives be measured? Where will the course be taught and what will the physical conditions be in the instructional setting? How responsive is the existing course to these conditions and variables? What parts of the existing course can be retained and what parts should be abandoned or modified?

The power and quality of the instruction ultimately developed will be limited by the degree to which these questions are fully and accurately answered. Yet it is the analysis phase that is usually given the least attention in educational development. The analysis activities will almost always require the participation of several representatives of the educational system, and when broad educational goals are being reviewed, members of the community should probably be involved as well. While much of the analysis is necessarily a subjective process, it can still be informed and systematic.

Design. Beginning with Phase II, the ISD model is concerned with designing instruction using the information obtained in the analysis phase. The first step is the conversion of the subject matter selected for instruction into terminal learning objectives. Each terminal objective is

Figure 4.1
A Model for Instructional Systems Development

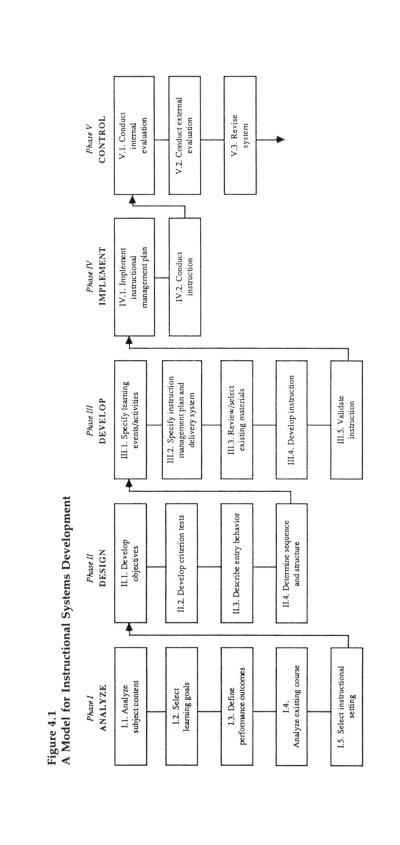

then analyzed to determine the intermediate objectives and learning steps necessary for mastery of each terminal learning objective. Test items are designed to match the learning objectives, so that their attainment or nonattainment can be reliably determined. A sample of learners drawn from the population for which the instruction is being developed is then tested to ensure that the student's entry behaviors meet the prerequisite levels derived from the earlier learning analysis. Finally, sequences of instruction are specified for the learning objectives.

Develop. In Phase III the actual development of the instruction is done. The first step is to classify the instructional objectives into types of learning. There are several classification systems of learning objectives, the most widely used of which were developed by Benjamin Bloom and his associates, and Robert Gagne (Bloom, Englehart, Furst, Hill, & Krathwohl, 1956; Gagne, 1977). A simple classification scheme that has been useful in ISD work is to differentiate objectives into: information, skills, process behaviors, and attitudes. Information is the knowledge-building part of learning, and probably represents the largest share of learning outcomes intended for achievement in schools. Skills are "doing" kinds of objectives—the student learns to conjugate a verb or complete an arithmetic exercise. Most skills depend, for successful completion, upon at least some basic information. Process behaviors are the competencies of analysis, synthesis, and problem solving. They usually require the prior attainment of certain information and skills. Attitudes are the beliefs and values that the society wishes its schools to impart. Knowing what types of learning are involved in the instruction is critical for the design of the optimal learning experiences.

Determining how instruction is to be packaged and presented to the student is accomplished through a media selection process that takes into account such factors as learning category, media characteristics, training setting, success criteria, logistics, and costs. Useful guidelines for media selection decisions have been developed by Briggs, and by Gagne and Reiser (Briggs, Campeau, Gagne, & May, 1967; Reiser & Gagne, 1983). At this point decisions are made whether to buy or make the instructional materials. The earlier analysis should have indicated the availability and suitability of teaching resources for the learning objectives. Most often for the standard blocks of school instruction there will be some materials, such as textbooks and workbooks, that will be satisfactory for teaching some of the objectives. However, the depth and rigor of subject matter analysis undertaken in an ISD approach will generally reveal important learning objectives for which no adequate instructional materials are commercially available. In this event it will be necessary to develop materials that are tailored to the objectives and the target student group.

It is almost always less expensive to purchase existing materials than to develop them, and development cost must be a major consideration in the decision as to which alternative to pursue. On the other hand, an educational program can be no better than the instructional resources—teachers and materials—that are dedicated to it.

Finally, instructional management plans are developed to allocate and manage all resources for conducting the instruction. Teachers are trained in the use of the instructional materials that have been selected and developed. Any new teaching processes or requirements are identified and provided for and the new instructional program will be tried out in pilot schools and classrooms and be revised and modified as necessary. When the instruction has been validated on the basis of empirical data obtained from these small-scale tryouts, it is ready for system-wide implementation.

Implement. Staff training of both teachers and administrators will be required for the implementation of the instructional management plan and the instruction. Some key personnel must be trained to be managers according to the needs specified in the management plan. The instructional staff must be trained to conduct the instruction and collect evaluative data on all the key components. At the completion of each teaching cycle, the management staff of the school should be able to use the collected information to improve the instructional system.

Control. A sine qua non of ISD is that the instruction will be of demonstrable effectiveness, that is, it will result in a specified group of students reaching predictable levels of achievement in an established time frame. Careful evaluation and revision of the instructional programs are critical to the success of the ISD approach. Preferably the evaluation and revision of the instruction will be carried out by personnel who are neither instructors nor managers of the course under study. The first activity (internal evaluation) is the analysis of learner performance in the course to determine instances of deficient or irrelevant instruction. The evaluation team then suggests solutions for the problems. In the external evaluation, the learners' performance after the instruction is evaluated (Tuckman, 1979). Has the student been prepared for a job, appropriate adult roles, or for successful entry into the next level of education? All collected data, internal and external, can be used as a quality control on the instruction and as input to any phase of the system for purposes of continuing revision and improvement (Morgan & Jeon, 1979).

WHEN TO USE ISD

Even a brief review of the ISD model suggests that it is a complex and involved set of procedures. In its full-scale application this is true. The time and resources required to undertake an ISD approach to educational development indicate that it is not an exercise to be entered into lightly. Branson has argued that educational programs, at least in developed countries, are performing at near maximum effectiveness as they are presently configured (Branson, 1988). He uses the analogy of the airplane to make his point, observing that by the late 1940s, the propeller-driven aircraft was performing at the peak of its effectiveness in terms of speed, payload, and fuel efficiency. This condition could not be changed until a fundamental change was made in airplane design with the invention of jet engines. With this innovation, there was a major breakthrough in efficiency and effectiveness.

There is some evidence, which will be examined presently, that the use of ISD in planning and developing educational programs can result in efficiency improvements that fully justify the time and investment required. In reality, ISD can be applied to single, small blocks of instruction or it can be used for planning and developing an entire national educational program. Clearly, large efforts where materials and programs are being developed for several years of use by thousands or even millions of learners allow for a much more comprehensive effort (Branson, 1981). Conversely, it has been demonstrated that a single classroom teacher can accomplish improved instruction by using the same basic principles of ISD. A teacher can analyze the content of the course he or she is teaching. A teacher can define the instructional objectives for the course and determine whether they are complete and in the appropriate order. It is also possible for the individual teacher to develop student tests that can be administered to yield feedback as to the effectiveness of the instruction, and to modify the instruction to improve student learning. It is very difficult for the teacher to develop any significant amount of new instructional materials and, with normal heavy teaching loads, it is difficult for the teacher to do many of the other things as well. Thus, the payoff in instructional improvement for the isolated teacher who uses ISD is positive but small.

While the share of educational budget dedicated to teacher training and materials acquisition is relatively small, usually no more than 2 to 5 percent, through time it adds up to quite a lot of money. An investment in an ISD-type revision of a national educational program can have a marked effect on overall student achievement, often without significant increases in the recurring operational budget. The initial development costs may be high, and there will be the extra costs of installing a new instructional system, but if these front-end investments yield significant gains in educational output, without corresponding increases in operational costs, the investment will have been prudent.

It seems characteristic of developing nations, in their attempts to upgrade their educational programs, to replicate the traditional teacher-centered systems of the industrialized nations. If the educational systems of the industrialized nations are at the asymptote of their efficiency, as Branson suggests, and are still not sufficient to these countries' needs, it would seem wise to avoid their duplication in developing states. It would be far more sensible, using the systems analysis tools described here, to arrive at the optimum deployment of resources available to education, which maximizes the accomplishment of the educational goals the nation has set for its schools (Windham, 1988).

It is beyond the limited scope of this chapter to inform the reader on the operational processes of ISD, however, a considerable body of literature is available on virtually every aspect of ISD (Gagne, 1987). Mager's guidelines on the development of instructional objectives, Dick and Carey's handbook on the systematic design of instruction, and Reiser and Gagne's book on instructional media selection are only a few of the excellent works available to the professional working in ISD (Mager, 1962; Dick & Carey, 1978). The work of an educational development team wishing to apply the tools of ISD would doubtless be facilitated by the inclusion of an experienced specialist in ISD. However, it is possible, with the use of existing resource material, for the team to teach itself during the process of doing the development work.

SYSTEMS AND TECHNOLOGY

In the development phase of ISD many different modalities of instruction had been tried out. In the conventional classroom the instructional resources have historically been limited to the classroom teacher, text and workbooks, the chalk board, and occasionally, audiovisual presentations, with the teacher as the principle means of managing and delivering the instruction. The pragmatic ISD specialist does not assume that the adult human teacher is the only, nor even the best, mode of delivering all types of instruction. Some things may be taught more effectively, less expensively, or both, using media of instruction other than the live teacher. Programmed instruction was met with some resistance in its early days, because some teachers thought they might be replaced by it. Given the self-instructional nature and the teaching effectiveness of programmed instruction, this threat was probably not entirely misplaced. It can be argued that there are some things that only a live teacher can do with students. Managing the teaching/learning environment, diagnosing learning problems of individual students, and providing motivation and tutorial support are only a few of these things. However, serving as the repository and disseminator of highly varied and large, complex forms of information is often not as well done by the ordinary teacher as it is by other forms of media.

In their search for increased efficiency and effectiveness of instruction, ISD researchers have generated many teaching by-products that show considerable promise for education. Programmed instruction has already been described. Radio, television, microcomputers, and videodiscs are some of these technological developments (Branson & Foster, 1978). These media are some of the more familiar applications of educational technology, though as with any other form of instruction, their teaching power is a function of how well their software or programs are designed. Those that have proved most effective have had programs that were developed following ISD procedures. For some educators the term educational technology connotes instructional hardware or equipment, though the most common usage in the profession treats educational technology and instructional systems design as nearly synonymous.

The various forms of instructional delivery modes differ in many respects. Some are geared to increasing the quality of learning. Some may be used to teach things that could not otherwise be taught in the classroom, for example a film to dramatically show the devastation of an earthquake. Others may be used simply to reduce the cost of mass instruction, such as the radio. Some—the videodisc and the computer, for example—are too costly at the present for widespread use even in industrialized countries. Most educational developers seem to be occupied with qualitative improvement of instruction. From the national perspective, however, the efficiency with which educational resources are used must be an additional consideration.

ISD AND IMPROVED EFFICIENCY

If an educational planner is working with an educational system in which improving access and equity are ambitions of the system (and where is it not?), then he or she will need to be concerned with the cost of instruction—how much is spent per student and what are the constituent parts of this cost (Coombs, 1970; Harbison & Myers, 1964)? If means can be found to reduce unit cost, then larger numbers of students can be enrolled within existing national educational budgets. Instituting larger student/teacher ratios is one way to reduce unit costs, as is simply paying teachers lower salaries. Though both of these means have been commonly employed, the former has been less acceptable to the public than the latter. An alternative to reducing per-pupil costs, when improved access and equity is desired, is to raise the overall level of funding for education within the state or nation. This has not been a realistic alternative for the last 3 decades, however, and in many nations educational budgets have not kept pace with inflation.

A worthy challenge for the planner is to reduce per-pupil costs and simultaneously raise the measurable quality of the instruction (Morgan, 1979). Instructional technologies, such as individualized and mastery learning, and communications media, such as radio, television, and computers, are promising means of increasing educational cost efficiencies.

There haven't been many empirical studies comparing cost efficiencies of alternative instructional approaches and the difficulty of controlling extraneous variables limits the generalizability of the findings. However, there do appear to be some consistent trends that may provide useful information for the educational developer. Lockheed and Hanushek of the World Bank have recently summarized a number of studies that have reported effects of differing instructional approaches (Lockheed & Hanushek, 1988). Instructional radio was used to teach basic English to primary students in Kenya, and mathematics at the primary level in Nicaragua and Thailand (Oxford, Clark, Hermansen, Christensen, & Imhoff, 1986; Searle & Galda, 1980; Friend, Galda, & Searle, 1986). The effects of variable uses of textbooks in Brazil, Nicaragua, the Philippines, and Thailand were described, and special teacher training programs in Brazil and Thailand were examined. According to the analysis of Lockheed and Hanushek, where comparisons were possible, investments in textbooks and radio appeared to be more cost-effective than investments in teacher education. In comparing students using textbooks to students for whom no texts were available, achievement differences ranging from 10 to 15 percent in favor of the group that had texts were reported (Heyneman, Jamison, & Montenegro, 1983).

Given the historical proclivity of educational decision makers to focus improvement efforts on upgrading teacher skills, the findings of these studies is a bit disquieting. That having textbooks is better in effecting student achievement than not having textbooks should not be surprising. Nor is the instructional effectiveness of radio a novel finding. However, the inferior cost-effectiveness of teacher training compared to the use of texts or radio is noteworthy. Persuasive arguments have been made that investments in in-service teacher training do not effect student learning in the long term as much as the same level of investment in well-developed instructional materials and other teaching interventions.

Programmed Learning and Teaching

Perhaps the strongest incentive in the developing world for trying out innovative instructional products and processes as alternatives to traditional instruction has been the shortage or absence of formally qualified classroom teachers. One of the earliest and largest applications of the systems approach to instructional development, mounted in the early seventies, was Project IMPACT (Instructional Management by Parents, Community, and Teachers). IMPACT is important for a number of reasons but particularly so because its conceptualization grew out of a regional organization chartered specifically for the development of innovational educational practices (Regional Centre for Educational Innovation and Technology, INNOTECH), and because it was eventually tried out in varying forms in several different countries—the Philippines, Indonesia, Malaysia, Jamaica, Liberia, and Bangladesh. An excellent historical review of the development and implementation of the IMPACT-type programs has been done by Cummings (Cummings, 1986).

The six national applications of the IMPACT concept varied according to the needs of the individual countries, but basically all were attempts to respond to rapidly growing school enrollments and limited educational resources. From the outset one principle aim of IMPACT was to change the ratio of students to teachers from the usual 30- or 35-to–1 to 150-to–1—without any reduction in accomplished learning. The Indonesian version of IMPACT, called Project PAMONG (Pendidikan Anak oleh Masyarakat, Orang tua Murid, dan Guru), was developed over a several-year period, and intended particularly to respond to an anticipated serious shortage of primary-level teachers (Nielsen, 1982a, 1982b). The instructional materials in Project PAMONG were similar in many respects to programmed instruction, which was developed in the United States in the late sixties. Learning objectives were operationally defined in terms of observable learning outcomes. Instructional sequences were developed for these objectives and tried out with samples of learners drawn from the population of intended users. The materials were accompanied by self-administered learning progress tests that provided feedback to the students and their teachers. The materials and teaching strategies were revised based on learning data until satisfactory and predictable achievement levels were obtained. Unlike conventional programmed instruction, the PAMONG lessons were generally used by small groups of students rather than in an individualized modality. In any case, the teaching/learning process was student centered and was not greatly dependent upon the continuous intervention of the teacher. Both the development processes and the instruction were logical and systematic, and equally important, were empirical.

Evaluations demonstrated the effectiveness of the PAMONG approach (Pappagianis, Klees, & Bickel, 1982). Children's learning in the PAMONG school compared favorably with learning in conventional schools, and teachers were able to handle larger than usual numbers in their classrooms. It was not unusual for classes to be as large as 50 or 60 students of varying grade levels to one teacher, though the projected 150-to–1 ratios were not realized. Even so, there was clear evidence that efficiency had been improved with no loss in quality (Nielsen & Bernard, 1983). However, during the several years of the PAMONG development effort, the significant shortage of teachers in Indonesia did not materialize. Growth in the teacher training programs and improved teacher recruitment effectively obviated this problem, with the consequence that the operational use of the PAMONG program has been pretty much restricted to the remote rural areas of Indonesia. Presently, several hundred such schools are using the PAMONG approach to teaching.

In 1979 the Liberian Ministry of Education decided to mount its own version of Project IMPACT with assistance from the U.S. Agency for International Development. In Liberia the project was called "Improved Efficiency for Learning" (IEL). As in Indonesia the IMPACT approach was modified to be more responsive to the Liberian situation. For the first two and a half years of primary school the programs were designed to be teacher presented, but in a programmed instruction format. In the instructional situation the teacher presented oral instruction from highly structured guidelines that required a great deal of student response, with the teacher providing feedback to the group. In the remaining primary grades, and after the students had acquired functional reading skills, learning took place in small groups led by a designated student leader. Again the instruction was logically organized in a programmed format. The IEL programs were designed against specific learning objectives in each course of instruction, and were tested with groups of students and revised according to need. The IEL programs were evaluated both during and after the development phase (Harrison & Morgan, 1982; Kelly, 1984a, 1984b). Generally, the evaluators found the IEL approach to be instructionally effective and more efficient than the traditional classroom approach. Perhaps the single greatest advantage of IEL was its reduction of dependency on the qualifications of the classroom teacher, which was of significant value in Liberia given the large numbers of underqualified teachers in the national system.

Given the level of projected enrollments and breadth of use of the IEL programs in Liberian schools, Windham predicted a cost-efficient use of IEL (Windham, 1983a-e). By 1985 the development phase of IEL was essentially completed and the government faced questions relating to the operational implementation of the programs. Their decision was confounded by a parallel development effort, which the government had undertaken with support from the World Bank, that involved the acquisition of textbooks for primary school use. Some Liberian educators believed the IEL approach was incompatible with the use of conventional texts and, indeed, IEL had been designed to "stand alone," without depending upon other instructional materials. The national implementation phase of IEL was delayed pending a resolution of this apparent incompatibility, and in 1986 an independent study was mounted to determine the feasibility of integrating IEL programmed learning with the texts and other elements of conventional instruction (Morgan, Adams, Cooper, Kraft, & Vinton, 1986). The study team concluded that the integration of IEL and the textbooks was not only possible but highly desirable and recommended a series of steps to accomplish the integration. These recommendations were accepted by the government and this work is presently underway.

Korean Elementary School Improvement

Perhaps the first large-scale system analysis and planning effort, where major improvements in educational efficiency was the intent, was undertaken by the Republic of Korea in 1970 (Morgan & Chadwick, 1971). Korea, confronted with a rapidly expanding and diversifying economy and a supply of trained workers insufficient to sustain the expansion, needed to modernize and expand its educational program. The country was already devoting 20 percent of its national budget to education and, given the military defense posture it needed to maintain, could not increase the overall funding for public education. An interdisciplinary team of specialists from Florida State University was invited to conduct a comprehensive analysis of Korea's total education program, to see if means could be found to increase the efficiency of the educational system enough so that enrollments could be expanded without increasing the total expenditure. Analysis and planning professionals involved in the effort included specialists in instructional systems design, teacher training, educational administration, economics, manpower planning, and educational technology. The analysis and planning effort took 7 months—3 months gathering information about the national system and 4 months analyzing these data and developing recommendations and a plan of action for the Korean government. The elementary and middle schools were recommended as the targets for major improvement and enrollment expansion. A new instructional delivery system was described, which was predicted by the team to be qualitatively equal to the existing program and capable of reducing unit costs by enough to permit the enrollment of all children in the elementary- and middle-school age cohorts. This would result in an enrollment increase of nearly a million children at the middle-school level. Korea had already attained nearly universal enrollment at the elementary level.

Included in the team's report was a plan for a development project utilizing the ISD approach for the design and tryout of the new curriculum. The plan estimated the costs for developing and demonstrating the new program, and the costs of implementing and operating it on a nationwide basis, if it were to be successfully demonstrated. Also specified were the time and resource requirements for the project, and specifications for a national educational development institute, which would have the responsibility for developing and testing the proposed instructional delivery system. The government created the Korean Educational Development Institute in 1971, and work began on the project as the institute was being developed (Morgan, 1979).

As parts of the new program were developed, they were tested in schools and then revised, based upon feedback from the learners. Through time these parts were aggregated into larger blocks of instruction, and teacher training programs were developed. By 1978 the entire elementary curriculum had been developed and was ready for a full test. It was implemented for a complete academic year in a number of representative schools through the nation, including nearly a quarter of a million children. The results, shown in Table 4.1, were highly favorable, with the children in the experimental curriculum significantly surpassing in achievement those children in the control schools in every subject and grade (Shin, Chang, & Park, 1984).

The overall difference between the mean achievement of the two groups was nearly 20 percent in favor of children taught with the new curriculum. During the life of the project the focus was deliberately shifted by the Korean developers away from reduced unit cost to an emphasis on qualitative improvement, though in the final analysis the annual per-student cost of the new program was no more than for students in conventional schools. More than a decade has passed since this project was completed, and in the ensuing years the national curriculum has undergone more updating and revision using the instructional design approaches that proved to be so effective in the late seventies.

In 1981 a comprehensive evaluation of the Korean project was mounted by the U.S. Agency for International Development in cooperation with the Government of Korea to determine the long-term impact of this development effort. The study reported that significant and enduring improvement had resulted from the project, and with reference to the use of the ISD approach to the development of the new curriculum the authors stated the following:

The power of ISD has been amply demonstrated. However, prior to this project it had never been applied to large-scale educational problems in a developing country. KEDI's successful use of this technology and the results achieved suggest that a wider use of ISD is in order. ISD should have utility in sectors such as health, agriculture, or industry, and in other countries. The technology of ISD is fairly intricate to learn and use. The products of ISD—new instructional materials and processes—should be inexpensive and simple to implement. The value of generalizing this "soft" technology to other developing countries should be evident. (Witherell, Morgan, Yoon, Kim, & Lee, 1981)

IEES—IMPROVING THE EFFICIENCY OF EDUCATIONAL SYSTEMS

The U.S. Agency for International Development (USAID), the World Bank, other international donor agencies, and many countries are now employing a refinement of the systems approach used in Korea, called

Table 4.1

Fifth Large-Scale Tryout (1978–79): Comparison of Students' Final Achievement in all Subjects for KEDI's Experimental Schools and Traditional Control Schools Following Full Academic Year Implementation of New Instructional System

	1st Grade		2nd Grade		3rd Grade		4th Grade		5th Grade		6th Grade		TOTAL		Diff*	Percent
	KEDI	Trad.	KEDI	Trad.	KEDI	Trad.	KEDI	Trad.	KEDI	Trad.	KEDI	Trad.	KEDI	Trad.	(K–T)	Increase
Large City	89.4	83.2	78.8	68.1	78.3	71.3	75.0	66.0	76.9	69.3	78.6	63.5	79.5	70.2	9.3	13%
Small Town	86.5	78.1	83.5	68.5	81.6	68.6	79.5	58.7	84.2	66.3	86.2	67.6	83.6	67.9	15.7	23%
Rural	81.4	76.6	73.3	64.1	76.5	64.2	72.8	59.1	75.3	61.9	78.4	63.9	76.5	64.9	11.6	18%
Total	86.2	79.8	79.5	67.2	79.4	68.5	76.4	61.5	80.0	66.1	81.9	64.9	80.6	67.6	13.0	19%

Source: Korean Educational Development Institute.
*All differences significant (p. <.05).

an Education and Human Resources Sector Assessment (Cieutat, 1983). In 1984, USAID inaugurated a large ten-year project called "Improving the Efficiency of Educational Systems" (IEES) that presently involves eight countries from around the world—Liberia, Botswana, Somalia, Zimbabwe, Haiti, Yemen, Indonesia, and Nepal. Comprehensive educational sector assessments have been completed in all but one of these countries. Technical assistance for the IEES project is provided by a consortium of U.S. institutions that includes Florida State University, the State University of New York at Albany, the Institute for International Research, and Howard University.

Efficiency improvement in the first five-year phase of the project is presently underway and, for each country, the focus of project work has been derived from the sector assessment. Clearly, the countries participating in the IEES project differ in many ways, and their educational problems and priorities are highly diverse. A major curriculum development effort, utilizing the ISD approach, is being undertaken in Botswana, with support activities in pre- and in-service training of teachers and administrators. In Haiti, with the majority of primary schools being operated by private organizations, work is underway to improve the quality of private schooling. The focus of Indonesia is on improving the analysis, planning, and information management functions of the central Ministry of Education and Culture. All of the countries are taking measures to improve their planning and management capacities.

A valuable lesson learned thus far from the IEES experience is the importance of close coordination of the analysis, research, evaluation, planning, and policy formation processes (Kaufman, 1988). When these functions are not linked, with one leading to another, the resulting fragmentation leads to ill-informed decision making and educational systems that are not as efficient as they could be.

REFERENCES

Andrews, D. H., & Goodson, L. A. (1980). A comparative analysis of models of instructional design. *Journal of Instructional Development*, 3(4), 2–16.

Banathy, B. (1969). *Instructional systems*. Palo Alto, CA: Fearon.

Bass, R. K., & Dills, C. R. (Eds.). (1984). *Instructional development: The state of the art, II*. Dubuque, IA: Kendall Hunt.

Bloom, B. S., Englehart, M. D., Furst, E. J., Hill, W. H., & Krathwohl, D. R. (1956). *Taxonomy of educational objectives: The classification of educational goals, handbook I: Cognitive domain*. New York: David McKay.

Branson, R. K. (1981). Applications research in instructional systems development, *Journal of Instructional Development*, 4(4), 14–16, 27–31.

Branson, R. K. (1988). Why schools can't improve: The upper limit hypothesis. *Journal of Instructional Development*, 10, 27–32.

Branson, R. K., & Foster, R. W. (1978). Educational applications research and videodisc technology. *Educational Technology Systems, 8,* 241–262.

Branson, R. K., Rayner, G. T., Cox, J. L., Furman, J. P., King, F. J., & Hannum, W. H. (1976). *Interservice procedures for instructional systems development* (5 vols.) (TRADOC Pam 350–30 and NAVEDTRA 106A). Fort Monroe, VA: U.S. Army Training and Doctrine Command (NTIS No. ADA–019 486 through ADA–019–490).

Briggs, L. J., Campeau, P. L., Gagne, R. M., & May, M. A. (1967). *Instructional media: A procedure for the design of multi-media instruction, a critical review of research and suggestions for future research.* Palo Alto, CA: American Institutes for Research.

Churchman, C. W. (1964). An approach to general systems theory. In Mihajlo Mesarovic (Ed.), *Views on general systems theory.* New York: John Wiley and Co.

Churchman, C. W. (1965). On the design of educational systems. *Audiovisual Instruction, 10,* 361–365.

Cieutat, V. J. (1983). *Planning and managing an education sector assessment.* Washington, D.C.: U.S. Agency for International Development.

Coombs, P. H. (1970). The need for a new strategy for development. *Comparative Education Review, 14,* 75–89.

Cummings, W. K. (1986). *Low-cost primary education: Implementing an innovation in six nations.* Ottawa, Canada: International Development Research Centre.

Dick, W., & Carey, L. (1978). *The systematic design of instruction* (1st ed.). Glenville, IL: Scott, Foresman.

Friend, J., Galda, K., & Searle, B. (1986). From Nicaragua to Thailand: Adapting interactive radio instruction. *Development Communications Report, 52.*

Gagne, R. M. (1977). *The conditions of learning.* New York: Holt, Rinehart, & Winston.

Gagne, R. M. (Ed.). (1987). *Instructional technology: Foundations.* Hillsdale, NJ: Erlbaum.

Harbison, F., & Myers, C. A. (1964). *Education, manpower, and economic growth.* New York: McGraw-Hill.

Harrison, G. V., & Morgan, R. M. (1982). *An evaluation of the Improved Efficiency of Learning Project.* Monrovia, Liberia: U.S. Agency for International Development.

Heyneman, S., Jamison, D., & Montenegro, X. (1983). Textbooks in the Philippines: Evaluation of the pedagogical impact of the nationwide investment. *Education Evaluation and Policy Analysis, 6*(2), 139–150.

Kaufman, R. A. (1988). *Planning educational systems.* Lancaster, PA: Technomic.

Kelly, E. (1984a). *Horse races, time trials, and evaluation designs: Implications for future evaluations of the Improved Efficiency of Learning Project.* Albany: State University of New York at Albany.

Kelly, E. (1984b). *Preliminary report no. II—overall test results.* Albany: State University of New York at Albany.

Lockheed, M. E., & Hanushek, E. (1988). Improving educational efficiency in developing countries: What do we know? *Compare, 18,* 21–38.

Mager, R. (1962). *Preparing instructional objectives.* Palo Alto, CA: Fearon.

Montemerlo, M. D., & Tennyson, M. E. (1976). Instructional systems development: Conceptual analysis and comprehensive biography (NAVTRAE-QUIPCEN–257). Orlando, FL: Naval Training Equipment Center.

Morgan, R. M. (1978). Educational technology—adolescence to adulthood. *Educational Communications and Technology, 26*, 142–152.

Morgan, R. M. (1979). *The Korean Educational Development Institute—its organization and function.* Paris: United Nations Educational, Scientific, and Cultural Organization (UNESCO).

Morgan, R. M., Adams, M., Cooper, D. M., Kraft, R. H. P., & Vinton, D. (1986). *The feasibility of integrating programmed learning with conventional instruction in Liberian primary education.* Tallahassee: Learning Systems Institute.

Morgan, R. M., & Chadwick, C. B. (1971). *Systems analysis for educational change: The Republic of Korea.* Tallahassee: Florida State University.

Morgan, R. M., & Jeon, U. H. (1979). *Field evaluation processes in formal and nonformal education.* Tallahassee: Florida State University.

Nielsen, H. D. (1982a). *Analysis of achievement test scores for PAMONG and regular primary schools of Gianyar Bali trimester, 1, 1981–1982.* Jakarta, Indonesia: Department of Education and Culture.

Nielsen, H. D. (1982b). *Improving the process of peer group learning in PAMONG primary schools.* Jakarta, Indonesia: Department of Education and Culture.

Nielsen, H. D., & Bernard, D. C. (1983). *Final report: Self-instructional learning system.* Solo, Indonesia: Universitas Sebelas Maret.

Oxford, R., Clark J., Hermansen, J., Christensen, P., & Imhoff, M. (1986). *Final report: Evaluation of the Kenya Radio Language Arts Project.* Washington, D.C.: Academy for Educational Development.

Pappagianis, G. J., Klees, S. J., & Bickel, R. (1982). Toward a political economy of educational innovation. *Review of Educational Research, 52*, 245–290.

Reiser, R. A., & Gagne, R. M. (1983). *Selecting media for instruction.* Englewood Cliffs, NJ: Educational Technology Publications.

Searle, B., & Galda, K. (1980). Measurement of the effect of radio mathematics lessons on student achievement. In J. Friend, B. Searle, & P. Suppes (Eds.), *Radio mathematics in Nicaragua.* Stanford, CA: Stanford University.

Shin, S. H., Chang, S. W., & Park, K. S. (1984). *Study of impact of E-M Project of Korean education.* Seoul: Korean Educational Development Institute.

Skinner, B. F. (1968). *The technology of teaching.* New York: Appleton.

Thiagarajan, S. (1976). Help, I am trapped inside an ID model! Alternatives to the systems approach. *NSPI Journal, 15*(9), 16–17.

Tuckman, B. W. (1979). *Evaluating instructional programs.* Boston: Allyn and Bacon.

Weiner, Norbert. (1948). *Cybernetics: Systems development manual. USAF PERT, Vol. 3. PERT COST.* New York: Doubleday.

Windham, D. M. (1983a, January). *Cost issues in the Liberian Improved Efficiency of Learning (IEL) Project (Report No. 1).* Monrovia, Liberia: Ministry of Education.

Windham, D. M. (1983b, March). *Internal economies of the Liberian Improved Efficiency of Learning (IEL) Project (Report No. 2).* Monrovia, Liberia: Ministry of Education.

Windham, D. M. (1983c, June). *The relative cost-effectiveness of the Liberian Improved*

Efficiency of Learning (IEL) Project (Report No. 3). Monrovia, Liberia: Ministry of Education.

Windham, D. M. (1983d, June). *Cost issues in the dissemination of the Liberian Improved Efficiency of Learning Project (Report No. 3)*. Monrovia, Liberia: Ministry of Education.

Windham, D. M. (1983e, September). *Cost estimates of the revised Improved Efficiency of Learning (IEL) Project (Supplemental Report to the IEL Cost Analysis Project)*. Monrovia, Liberia: Ministry of Education.

Windham, D. M. (1988). *Indicators of educational effectiveness and efficiency*. Tallahassee: Florida State University, Improving the Efficiency of Education Systems Project.

Witherell, R. A., Morgan, R. M., Yoon, H. W., Kim, S. U., & Lee, C. J. (1981). *Korean elementary-middle school project* (AID Evaluation Special Study No. 5, Working Paper No. 530). Washington, D.C.: U.S. Agency for International Development.

5

The Donor Role in Instructional Improvement

Joan M. Claffey

This chapter describes the changing context in which some donors and recipient countries are coming to approach the task of instructional improvement. Three areas of emerging consensus are beginning to guide approaches to educational assistance. The first area of agreement is that strikingly new conditions exist in many developing countries regarding expanding educational demand and the ability of resources to keep pace. This situation of rapidly accelerating demand and resource constraint is causing educational quality to decline and evoking the second point of agreement, that investments in education systems must become more efficient. A strategy for how to proceed with strengthening education systems comprises the third area of consensus. This strategy involves formulating more fruitful policies to guide educational systems, allocating both internal and external resources to maximum benefit, and revitalizing the entire schooling process. Each of these areas of agreement is discussed in order to finally describe the context in which instructional improvement is likely to receive greater impetus from donors supporting education and human resources development.

Donor organizations regard their support of education as instrumental to achieving and sustaining social and economic growth. New research and experience continually document the importance of basic skills to meeting a broad range of development objectives. Donors have accepted the beneficial link between education and improvements in food production, income, health, nutrition, and the management of fertility, because the case for these links has been adequately made. Today, the key issue is one of strategy for making education systems more productive. Which organizational structures, processes, and mixes of instructional resources yield optimum student learning, under what conditions, and at what cost? What education policies at the national level can result in more effective schools? In what ways can educational improvements be marketed to broaden support? How can policy effects be monitored and assessed? How can donors best support educational improvement? Before suggesting some directions in which donors and country leaders may be moving on these questions, three points of growing consensus will be presented.

EXPANDING DEMAND, DECLINING QUALITY, AND RESOURCE CONSTRAINT

A chief cause of concern about the future of education in many developing countries is the fact that resources for education are not likely to expand in proportion to need. Shaping this need in stagnating, even declining, instructional quality for those in school and growing numbers of children without schooling at all. Although the twin tasks of improving educational quality while serving larger numbers of students require new resources, especially in low-income countries, great opportunity exists for more effectively using resources already being invested in education.

Even now, after decades of remarkable progress around the world, access to schooling is limited in many countries. Large numbers of children are not in school, especially in Sub-Saharan Africa and south Asia,[1] and female enrollment lags behind that of males.[2] Children in rural areas have considerably less access than those in urban areas to schools and learning materials.

Demand for schooling will continue to grow, not only from those currently without access but also as a result of growing numbers of school-age children. In addition to the estimated 100 million school-age children not in school, another 100 million will be added to the age cohort in the next 10 years. By the year 2000, six of every seven school-age children will be in the world's lower-income countries. Without concerted national effort and external assistance, universal primary education by the year 2000 will remain an elusive target.

To enroll more children than are being added to the population will be a formidable task indeed. Consider the situation of Pakistan, with 70 percent (11 million) of its 6 to 11 year olds out of school. Even if it were possible to increase annual enrollment by 5 percent until the year 2000, half of the primary school-age children would still remain out of school.

Several figures from a recent World Bank (1988) study illustrate the conflict between demand and resources in Sub-Saharan Africa. The region has experienced serious economic decline with per capita income falling 4 percent annually between 1980 and 1984. Population growth in Africa burgeoned an average of 2.9 percent annually between 1970 and 1980, about 1.5 times the world rate, and by 1989 had edged up to 3.2 percent. By the year 2000, Africa's primary and secondary school-age population is projected to be 70 percent more than it was in 1984. To have all children enrolled then would require a 157 percent increase in primary school places alone. Simply to keep pace in the year 2000 with the primary and secondary gross enrollment ratios of 1983 (75 percent and 20 percent, respectively) would require a 75 percent increase in recurrent costs (in 1983 dollars)—to $9.4 billion. This is more than all African countries spent for primary, secondary, and tertiary levels combined in 1983. Many African countries already allocate a large part of their budgets to education, and enlarging this percentage significantly is unfeasible for most.[3]

Low enrollment rates and dim prospects for financing expansion are perhaps not the greatest concerns, however. Particularly troubling is the failure of schools in lowest-income countries to teach effectively those children who are in school. In many instances, students are without basic learning materials and teachers without instructional guides and technical support. Primary school completers and secondary school students from low-income countries, who generally constitute a small and more advantaged percent of their national age cohorts, tend to greatly underperform students in industrialized countries when comparative achievement tests have been conducted in science, mathematics, and reading comprehension.

Due in part to the low quality of schooling, education systems throughout much of the world are burdened by high attrition and grade repetition rates that result in high cycle costs.[4] In many developing countries 15 to 20 percent of the students are repeating a level, and fewer than half of those entering the first grade of primary school finally complete fifth grade. The lowest-income countries spend about 9 years of schooling resources to produce one fifth-grade completer compared with 5.4 years of investment in industrialized countries.[5] This inefficient flow of students through school raises its cost and results in unnecessary pressure on education budgets.

IMPROVING EDUCATION SYSTEM EFFICIENCY

Because of accelerating education demand coupled with low schooling quality and severe resource limitations, national decision makers and donors alike are eager to find ways to increase the impact of their educational investments. Generally, the types and amounts of these investments are amenable to policy change because they concern educational resources and processes that educational managers can alter as needs require. In most low-income countries, supplemental funding for education will remain a necessary part of donor assistance, particularly where more than three-fourths of the school-age population are without primary education. As many donors are admitting, albeit informally, many of their other development assistance programs in such sectors as agriculture, health, and population are stymied where a critical mass of the population is without the basic skills of literacy, numeracy, and reasoning.

The problem is not one simply of additional funding, as necessary as that is, but also better allocation of education aid. One analysis of direct education aid to Africa for the 1981/83 period concluded that the amount of aid was not correlated with educational need in terms of existing enrollment rates (World Bank, 1988, pp. 103-104). It found that only about 7 percent of the aid was used to finance primary education, covering only about 2 percent of the cost of primary schooling. This is the level that must absorb additional numbers of new students and ensure their mastery of basic skills, challenges that are not now being met. Secondary and tertiary schools in many developing countries find their own work seriously constrained by the poor preparation of students at the lower educational levels.[6] In addition, goals in other development sectors are less likely to be met when schools do not adequately prepare the country's youth. At the top of the education pyramid, the amount of direct aid for secondary vocational/technical education and tertiary education was 17 percent and 34 percent, respectively, covering about half of the costs of schooling at those levels. Yet secondary vocational/technical schools enroll only a small fraction of all secondary students (about 1 in 20 of the secondary students in Sub-Saharan Africa), while tertiary institutions enroll a still smaller number (only about 3 percent of the age cohort in low-income countries: and a 1.4 percent gross enrollment ratio in Sub-Saharan Africa).

Besides funding imbalances by enrollment rates, education aid has not been particularly well tied to need in terms of its expenditure categories. The same analysis indicates that for the 1981/83 period, only 11 percent of direct education aid was for operating costs, the category in which constraints to instructional improvement have been particularly great owing to a lack of materials. Another 17 percent of direct education aid went for overseas fellowships for a few students, 44 percent for technical assistance, and the balance for capital and other expenditures.

In addition to better use of external funding, attention is increasingly being given to ways to improve the use of the vast resources that countries themselves are putting into education. In many countries there is inefficient allocation of resources between salary and nonsalary expenditures. For instance, many of the low-income countries spend less than

2 percent of their recurrent primary education budgets on educational materials (the figure is only 1.1 percent for the median African country, but nearly 4 percent for industrialized countries) (World Bank, 1988, p. 35). This means less than $1 per student for instructional materials in many countries (but about $100 per student yearly in developed countries). As a result, most students are without textbooks and must rely on marginally prepared and frequently absent teachers to copy or recite texts. With teachers' salaries and benefits currently comprising about 90 percent of recurrent education budgets at the primary level, and with the dearth of spending for nonsalary instructional resources, greater attention is being drawn to the relative cost-effectiveness of various educational inputs. Certainly, the underfunding of such nonsalary resources as textbooks and other instructional materials, and teacher guides and training, thwarts teaching and learning. In fact, the influence of instructional resources on student achievement is greater in developing countries than in industrialized countries where nonschool factors, such as socioeconomic background, exert relatively greater influence.

National investments among the educational levels also may merit adjustment. Some countries find that the ratio of per-pupil spending between higher and primary education is more than 30:1, despite indications that rates of return for primary education can be much higher (Komenan, 1987). Others find excess social demand for upper secondary and higher education, yet have made little attempt to recover costs.

The case of one country suggests opportunities for better leveraging of instructional resources. At the country's predominant tertiary institution, instructional expenditures were only about 44 percent of the total nondevelopment budget; at another higher-level institution they were only 33 percent. With both student achievement and instructors' nonteaching contributions rather mediocre, the low levels of support for instructional materials seem in serious need of redress. At the primary level, enrollments declined about 24 percent during a recent 2 year period, but the number of teachers and noninstructional staff increased by about 9 percent. Salaries for teachers and nonteaching staff totalled about 96 percent of annual expenditures for public primary and secondary schools, while the amount for educational materials and supplies was only 1.3 percent, or about $0.24 per pupil.

As these examples show, providing education of good quality, in a context of severe budgetary constraint and past imbalances in the external and internal allocation of resources, demands greater efficiency. Educational efficiency is said to exist when the desired mix of outputs (i.e., student educational attainment and learning achievement) is maximized for a given level of material and nonmaterial inputs (i.e., teachers, facilities, equipment, educational materials, instructional processes, and administrative arrangements), or when inputs are minimized for a desired set of outputs. Efficiency concerns both effectiveness (the extent to which the desired outputs are achieved) and cost (the economic value of the inputs used to achieve a desired output) (Windham, 1988, p. 6). The concept of the internal efficiency of education implies a ratio of learning to costs of educational inputs and offers a basis for considering how funds for education can be best apportioned. For example, textbooks, interactive radio, in-service teacher training, and cooperative learning are among the inputs found to be relatively cost-effective, and secondary vocational schooling and some types of pre-service teacher training among those less so (Lockheed & Hanushek, 1987).

Improving the efficiency of education systems serves several purposes. First, it raises the average level of student achievement by mobilizing cost-effective instructional resources and processes that boost learning. Second, it reduces cycle costs that are due to inefficient student flows through the system. Third, it reduces the portion of unit costs coming from unproductive uses of staff and facilities. Fourth, it obviates the need for extensive remediation for students at successive levels of the system. Fifth, it manages education components with a view to optimal resource allocation for present and future societal needs.

STRATEGY FOR IMPROVING EDUCATIONAL QUALITY

As a result of pressures for a broader, more integrated approach to the education sector, several new directions for improving educational quality are taking clearer shape among persons charged with strengthening national education systems and those assisting them. Central to the approach is an agenda of action larger than merely instructional improvement, one that regards the educational policy and management environment as basic to educational quality. Attention is directed to assisting countries to improve the performance of their education systems and to develop sustainable capacity for planning and managing efficient systems. The orientation reflects a desire to better balance the component parts of the education system in terms of social needs, what is produced, resources required, and costs. Several stages define the strategy.

Formulating Appropriate Education Policy

The task of improving instruction is seen in tandem with the task of developing coherent packages of educational policies to better relate the sector to national priorities and available resources. Sought from this process of policy formulation is a set of choices that reflects a country's education sector realities and guides action with respect to

1. improving educational quality (internal efficiency);
2. strengthening educational relevance and links with employment (external efficiency);
3. selectively expanding educational services to under-served groups (access and equity);
4. managing education costs and financing; and
5. improving educational management (sector organization, planning, administration, and supervision).

Improving educational quality concerns the inputs to educational processes (teachers, textbooks, curriculum and instructional delivery, and facilities) and the results in terms of learning achievement. Examples of actions to improve quality include curriculum structuring for more effective teaching and learning of core knowledge and skills, strengthening the competence of practicing teachers through cost-effective means, providing adequate levels of classroom textbooks and furniture, and improving school organization and classroom management.

Actions to strengthen external efficiency typically involve vocational training programs and strategies for linking them more effectively to labor demand by increasing employer involvement. Efforts also may address how well schools help students acquire the basic skills of literacy and numeracy necessary for employment.

Access concerns the proportion of the relevant age cohort reached by the education system, while equity refers to the extent to which educational opportunities are available to all segments of the population without restriction due to factors beyond the individual's control, such as gender, economic status, or rural/urban location. Actions to increase access and equity may simply expand enrollment capacity at various school levels, especially at the primary level when enrollment is low. In addition, actions may target females, rural youth, or other under-served segments, and may include efforts to "market" schooling to them and their families.

Efforts to manage education costs may be aimed at aggregate cost reductions, generally for the teacher cadre or for new facilities. They also may phase out programs judged too costly for the product provided. Reducing teacher costs may be pursued by linking salary more closely with productivity, greater use of junior-level or assistant teachers, and increasing student/teacher ratios. Holding costs down for new school facilities can be realized by lower-cost designs and better planning of the placement of new schools. Financial policies usually target cost recovery or cost sharing opportunities. They may also focus on finding new sources of educational financing. At a macro level, policies to improve resource allocations can be important for adjusting finances in favor of basic schooling when unmet needs at this level are most severe. Other kinds of financial actions may seek to alter the mixes of public and private support for education, based on demand and equity considerations.

Actions to improve sector management often seek to develop effective education management information systems to bolster sector analysis and planning, and to link these with decision making. They also may target the training of provincial education administrators and school headmasters to better manage and maintain local school systems.

The process of analyzing policy options within all of these content areas involves countries first in identifying the major issues to be resolved. At the level of national decision making, the issues concern the adequacy of public resources designated for education relative to other government expenditures, and the apportionment of education financing among educational levels according to national needs and investment returns. Relative to the education sector itself, particular issues might include the emphasis to be given to improving school quality relative to expanding access, improving instruction while containing costs, ensuring performance standards, maintaining facilities and equipment, and diversifying sources of finance. Of central concern to education managers are opportunities for reallocating existing resources—educational personnel, facilities, materials, and processes—to raise student achievement.

Policy decisions address such choices as

- apportionment of resources among the different schooling levels or programs (e.g., among primary, secondary, and tertiary levels, vocational/technical school programs, and scholarships for overseas study);
- the relative amount for student subsidies by education level and type, together with scholarship and loan schemes;
- institutional types by level (e.g., at the secondary level, among boarding schools, day schools, general academic schools, vocational schools, distance learning, etc.);
- the relative amounts for various schooling inputs (e.g., teachers, instructional and student learning materials, facilities and equipment, supervision);
- the relative contribution of private schools and of the individual or family, by schooling level;
- types of instructional formats in terms of their cost-effectiveness at various educational levels (e.g., schooling and its duration; distance learning; traditional instruction; media-based instruction as a supplement to, or as a substitute for, a teacher); and
- options for financing schooling.

After a country identifies its most germane issues amenable to policy choice, the next task is to probe each issue in terms of alternative courses of action that are based on research-supported relationships between education inputs and outputs. Consideration must also be given to constituents' interests, the extent to which these might be influenced along desired lines, and what effect these interests might have on various courses of action.

A few examples illustrate this dilemma with interest groups. If personnel are being carried on the education payroll but neither teaching nor contributing significantly to the educational process, decision makers must consider not only whether they can be redeployed, but also how they and other under-utilized staff can be eased from the payroll if need be. If university students are accustomed to receiving full tuition and boarding subsidies, how will government prepare them and the public for the need to rechannel some of these resources to other educational system priorities? If teachers are to work longer hours or be responsible for more students, in return for the government's ability to afford more instructional materials, how can their support be fostered?

Policy analysts need to assess each alternative course of action with respect to its (a) concreteness of outcomes; (b) feasibility as to timeline, cost, and institutional (administrative/managerial) capacity for implementation; and (c) overall probability for being implemented, achieving the intended outcomes, and avoiding unintended ones. Finally, the policy options—documented as to outcomes, trade-offs, and costs—need to be presented clearly to decision makers for selection.

The political aspects of policy reform seem to have been its most neglected dimension. Important in this regard is how policy formulation takes place and is "marketed." Relatively little attention has been given to political feasibility, those conditions either conducive or problematic for developing and implementing coherent education policy. Among these, broadening the constituency for education policy development, building national consensus, and creating incentives for those expecting to be disadvantaged by a policy change all merit heed since they can strongly influence successful policy implementation.

Mapping Policy Implementation

Because many worthy education policies fail for want of a workable implementation strategy, the next major effort is to map a detailed, feasibly strategy to implement the reformulated national education policies. This involves specifying concrete outcomes to be achieved for groups, and by program level and type, at successive points in time. Indicators of quality and efficiency could include, for example, supply of textbooks and workbooks per student, supply of teacher guides per school and level, grade repetition and attrition rates, curriculum-related knowledge and skills of teachers, student achievement, unit and cycle costs by level, teacher productivity, and school usage figures. Indicators would also concern progress toward greater equity, such as female enrollment relative to that of males, and rural enrollments relative to those in urban areas. The policy implementation strategy would also indicate which performance criteria would be met at specific points of time, how implementation would occur, what resources are required (financial, personnel, material, organizational), how the resources would be made available, the administrative arrangements (what institutions or groups are responsible for what and when), and how and when progress would be evaluated.

To illustrate, one desired outcome for a particular country might be to increase the number and effective use of curriculum instruction guides for teachers, from the current lack of any to a set for each primary school, covering the subjects taught at each grade level. Benchmarks for each year would set intermediate targets for the guides' preparation, production, and distribution to schools, given resources reasonably available. Targets would also specify availability and usage numbers over time, methods for training teachers to use the guides, and levels of student achievement.

Assessing Impact

Countries will want to assess the effectiveness of their education policy adjustments and their progress in improving education system efficiency. This work would benefit from greater knowledge about how education policies and their implementation affect educational productivity. At a minimum, however, countries that have set operational benchmarks can monitor policy implementation and regularly assess system performance and improvement.

Education management information systems help track changes by functioning to collect data on education efficiency benchmarks, analyze the data in reference to national education policies and strategies, and link up with education decision-making processes at national and local levels. Data can be iteratively expanded as needed and as resources permit to cover key inputs in the educational process (characteristics of students, teachers, administrators; curriculum and educational materials for students and teachers; facilities, and equipment), education exchanges (teacher behavior, student behavior, administrator behavior), and outputs (student attainment, student achievement, equity effects). To the extent possible, data would also concern education outcomes (future educational attainment and achievement, employment, and earnings).

The ultimate value of an education management information system comes not merely from a rich supply of descriptive data but also from the policy questions put to it. Data system managers should be proactive and undertake the analysis of key issues and policy options for decision makers. As the quality of an information system strengthens, its user constituency should broaden, particularly at regional and local levels.

The discussion to this point has sketched the macro context of education policy, demand, resource availability, and scarcity that is shaping thinking about the best use of resources for education and human resources development. In sum, a consensus is emerging among international donors and host country officials that existing and new resources for education can be used most efficiently within a structure of national education policy that is comprehensive, consistent, and affordable, together with a detailed strategy for its implementation and validation. In the following section, the ways in which the future role of donors may adapt to these sector requirements are examined.

THE FUTURE CONTEXT FOR INSTRUCTIONAL IMPROVEMENT

In view of the convergence of conditions already described, there are several ways in which the roles of donors are likely, indeed need, to change. This section describes some of these shifts and points to obstacles that may arise in implementing the changes.

1. *From micro project to sector approach.* Much previous project assistance has been piecemeal and noncumulative in terms of helping countries devise and maintain comprehensive education development strategies tailored to their own situations. New efforts are likely to increase support to countries to develop more efficient national education programs. This will entail assistance for sector assessment, policy development, national consensus building, and policy implementation.

To date, education sector policies have not been improving dramatically nor in an integrated way. National decision makers are not readily identifying the points of leverage that could make their education systems more productive. The ability to do this depends, in part, on the availability of information about the system. It also depends on the capacity both to identify and analyze policy options, costs, and likely outcomes, and to devise appropriate implementation and monitoring strategies.

Countries are seeking more guidance on which education policies prove effective in raising school quality and education system efficiency, which circumstances may influence successful implementation, and what means can be used to evaluate progress. As supporters of these efforts, donors need fuller knowledge about the content, structure, and progress of education sector development. Part of this search will entail support of diverse national approaches and ongoing synthesis of lessons learned from previous experience. It will depend, too, on more rigorous education sector study by each country in order to apportion national resources and donor assistance among the greatest priorities.

Developing a sector approach may meet with resistance. Collaborative sector analysis and decision making can threaten special interests. Consider an instance where there are separate ministries of education and higher education competing for control of teacher training, or where a country's university is accustomed to receiving a steady 25 percent of the national education budget without having to justify its allotments relative to the primary and secondary levels. Officials who have spent considerable energy claiming resources for their respective ministries may balk at greater sector cooperation, sensing it would mean their loss of influence or funding. Decisions that my cost certain interest groups may provoke resistance. This was seen during recent upheavals by university students in several countries when faced with the loss or reduction of their full tuition and boarding subsidies.

Another form of resistance to the sector approach may come from national officials who believe too much time and donor resources are spent studying problems instead of being invested in more concrete development activities. This concern is most valid when, as often happens, duplicative types of sector analysis are demanded by several donors. However, the solution to this inefficiency is to coordinate sector study, not to forego it. The onus is to ensure that the scope of the study is vital for policy direction. Experience shows that the ability of policies to improve the efficiency of education systems is based, in large part, on broad participation in the policy development process. Building a base of support usually requires interministerial and other professional participation in sector analysis, and consensus as to the diagnosis of inefficiencies in the system and to the kinds of actions that need to be taken. Action that calls for trimming resources in one area of the sector is more likely to be supported if the cost savings are redeployed within the education sector rather than taken from it. Nevertheless, the practical difficulties of involving senior officials and analysts in the sector review process are real because of their numerous other responsibilities. In some countries top officials have found that their contributions could be maximized by engaging selected staff in sector analysis, and reserving their own time for pivotal, interministerial meetings to guide and assess work in progress.

2. *Policy-based loans and grants.* An important new trend in projects and lending is donor support of educational policy development and implementation. This trend can mean assistance to countries to diagnose and relieve sector problems as they analyze them to be, rather than aid foreordained by donors for predetermined uses—for example, school construction, teacher training, or new university programs. In the fiscal year ending in 1988, about half of the World Bank's education sector

lending included support for some facet of policy development. In 1984 the U.S. Agency for International Development launched a 10 year effort to assist selected countries to improve the efficiency of their education systems, chiefly through training and assistance in sector assessment, policy analysis, planning, and sector management. Policy-based loans and grants have tended to focus on measures to increase educational quality and efficiency, improve equity for females, reduce costs, diversify sources of educational financing, and build sector management capacity. While policy reforms have focused on general and tertiary education, they are likely to concentrate also on vocational and technical education, where unit and cycle costs have been high and quality generally low.

There are three thorny issues that country leaders and donors will have to address if these efforts are to succeed. The first concerns the political aspects of policy reform and how to go about building national consensus for educational policy change. Popular support for policy reform needs to be broadened, especially where decisions may make new demands on certain groups. Leaders have to forestall any disturbances that would preclude policy implementation. Because shaping the political context for reform is so important, the occasional practice of donors to prematurely set policy conditions as requirements for funding may need to be restrained. National decision makers and donors might agree to a process first of educational sector analysis to build agreement about problems and actions to correct them. This would then lead to reforms in the various subsectors to be implemented in stages rather than fully enacted at once. For example, in higher education, strategies could be developed to: improve instruction by training faculty to use teaching modules for sets of skill and knowledge objectives, curtail costs by eliminating less critical and under-enrolled programs, and gradually reduce student subsidies and institute a loan scheme.

A second issue in policy-based lending concerns balancing funding for policy development with that for physical inputs. If donors wait until educational policy is well formulated in all facets before providing more tangible forms of support (e.g., textbooks, curriculum guides for teachers, and classrooms), they may deny incentives to undertake the policy reforms. Basic instructional resources are so urgently needed in most countries to raise educational quality that moving ahead with their supply, concurrent with policy review, has considerable merit if an adequate curriculum is in place. Donors face a challenge to come up with innovative loans and projects to help countries develop more effective educational policies while, at the same time, providing immediate resources to improve instruction.

A third issue in lending for educational policy development concerns how to measure progress. From a donor's perspective, is a country to show its willingness to make certain kinds of policy changes, to mandate and carry out the changes, or to produce actual improvements at the school level? From a country leader's viewpoint, is it satisfactory merely to satisfy donors' desires for visible policy changes at the national level or also to muster popular support and build indigenous management capacity to carry out the policies? Devising mutually satisfactory ways to define and measure progress toward educational efficiency is important beyond tracking compliance. The more difficult task is to assess the impact of educational policies—the extent to which they have a positive impact on indicators of educational quality and efficiency. A related problem concerns causal links at two levels—how to assess the effects of national decisions about educational allocations and financing on the system's efficiency, and how to assess the effects of more localized policies on school quality.

3. *From solutions in search of a problem to greater consensus on priorities and strategy.* Donor proclivities to promote certain kinds of instructional improvements, such as curriculum revision, pre-service teacher training, or radio-assisted instruction, in isolation from a coherent, nationally developed strategy to improve the performance of the system, usually fail to have the desired effect. A cost-effective instructional tool or method is potent only to the extent that it is employed appropriately. For example, a curriculum development project that results in well-designed model texts for primary school and instructional guides for teachers, but is not carried out concurrently with a scheme to ensure timely production and distribution of the materials and training in their use, is apt to yield little. Similarly, an instructional radio project introduced before a country has the school textbooks it considers of higher priority or without having built consensus among teachers who are expected to use the radio, will be unlikely to produce the learning effects it could produce if the larger educational system were taken into account.

Countries, too, may fail to follow their own educational strategies even after they are well formulated. In one country, a project to revitalize instructional quality at the junior secondary level recently was diverted toward shorter-term interests of the host government. Expensive foreign experts, intended to help local educators strengthen instructional delivery in the schools and at the new teacher training college, instead taught understaffed courses not requiring their particular level of expertise.[7] In this case, the donor tolerated the diversion to avoid political strain with the government, and a project designed to meet a high priority national need was allowed to dissipate its resources on a more immediate but less critical staffing problem.

Besides the scope and sequence of assistance to the education sector, the type of donor assistance is coming under close scrutiny. Money spent on capital construction, supplies and materials, training, technical assistance, and institutional development all can have very different implications for the long-term obligations of the host government. For instance, massive capital construction projects can saddle countries with recurrent expenses they cannot handle. Then, too, providing materials and conventional training can have limited results if governments are not first helped to better manage their recurrent education budgets and address policy choices that can improve the overall operation of the education system. Problems can also occur if technical assistance to countries for sector review and policy analysis is short term and ad hoc. Such assistance can fail to build the trust, collegiality, and skills necessary to grapple successfully with budget and policy issues. Yet, when longer-term collaborative technical assistance is available from highly qualified collaborators, it may be at the cost of adequate funding going directly to host country institutions, which results in those institutions not developing independent capacities for managing their own education system.

Although there is growing agreement that donors' efforts in education need to focus more on countries' own priorities and employ a more consistent strategy among donors in addressing those priorities, there are substantial hurdles to achieving this. One set of problems concerns the fit between national priorities and programming preferences of the various donors. National priorities may be poorly defined and articulated. If the priorities are thoughtfully derived, they still may not be in line with a particular donor's funding interests or comparative expertise. In some cases, donors may wish to fund only those parts of national programs for which they can claim recognition. Another problem of fit between donors' preferences and national priorities can occur when a donor designs a project to test an instructional application in a pilot setting. If a contractor for the donor is charged with obtaining sites for the trials, pressures may be put on countries to proceed with the instructional practice before appropriate sector review takes place and decisions are made about related policy and strategy for the subsector.

4. *Greater attention to sustainability.* To enable ongoing educational improvement, national decision makers and donors must pay greater attention to building capacity for requisite analysis, planning, evaluation, and management to sustain efficient education systems. Sustainability refers to the capacity for continuing to provide valued outcomes at acceptable cost. Sustainable education systems are those able to maintain a level of efficient production (considering student attainment, achievement, and cost) necessary to meet increasing educational needs of an expanding population. Sustaining a national education system involves optimally allocating and managing resources to address changing educational demand in an environment of resource (financial, material, human expertise) scarcity.

What will it take to establish permanent capacity for managing education systems? Country leaders themselves must insist that donors provide the kinds of assistance to enable their country to become self-sufficient in policy analysis, sector planning, and evaluation. Providing incentives to retain trained personnel and making full use of their skills are subsequent tasks. Donors will need to sustain their own project and lending efforts to ensure not only that enough individuals are proficient in skills to manage the education system, but also that organizational structures and processes are in place for ongoing sector development and staff training. Also required of donors is the provision of high-caliber technical expertise on education systems development from within their organizations and from professionals at large.

National decision makers and donors are apt to focus more on how to build support for difficult decisions affecting the allocation of educational resources. Almost certainly, they will put more effort into establishing education management information systems to inform policy decisions and to monitor policy effects.

Constraints to achieving sustainable capacity for managing efficient education systems come from a variety of sources. Perhaps most troublesome is the tendency of some bilateral donors to severely alter their funding and programming agenda as political mandates change from year to year. This may mean that an agreement between governments to engage in a 10 year education development project will last only as long as the donor government maintains its funding level for the concerned country, continues to value education as an investment sector, and has the professional staff to guide the effort. A parallel type of constraint exists in developing countries. Changing political priorities affect how much of the national budget is allocated to education and at which levels of the sector. An inability to recruit and maintain high-caliber educational personnel, especially in analyst and managerial positions, also can slow the progress of educational improvement.

The rapid turnover of personnel involved in educational development in countries and in donor agencies can also impede sustainability. In one small country, scores of top government personnel were moved from their positions the day before a donor's team arrived to design a large management training program for government officials. Most of the government officials responsible for developing the training proposal were suddenly out of roles to support the scheme. Even in donor organizations, a change in personnel managing education efforts can mean a loss of support for ongoing work in a country.

Still another type of constraint is the difficulty for both donor or lending agencies and recipient governments to mobilize a continuing core of top-quality technical experts to help revitalize education systems. Part of the problem is that the kinds of skills needed for the task—for example, sector assessment, policy analysis, cost analysis, education systems planning, and management—simply have not been fostered adequately in graduate schools of education. Another aspect is that not enough individuals who do have the requisite technical skills also have the interpersonal and managerial competence to provide leadership in cross-national settings and have a desire to serve under the difficult conditions that sometimes characterize developing countries.

5. *More operational research and knowledge building.* Education development efforts are hampered also because basic knowledge about the ways education systems work, how they might be improved, and the cost-effective mixes of resources and processes needed to increase learning is scarce. Also hampered is our understanding of the influence of various "policy packages" on educational development and of the conditions that support or impede their implementation. Nor has much attention been focused as yet on ways to support a country's building of national consensus for educational reform and revitalization.

Donors can be expected to support operational research to assess the cost-effectiveness of national education policies. Such research would suggest what courses of action and what types of investment can affect certain learning outcomes. It also could point to the kinds of resource allocation decisions that affect productivity within the educational system.

Donors also are likely to fund more study of the cost-effectiveness of different combinations of educational inputs. Examples of such research include: the cost and learning achievement associated with different types of in-service teacher training, the cost and effectiveness of curriculum guides for teachers relative to pre-service training or to a higher ratio of textbooks for students, and the cost-effectiveness of different types of vocational and technical training.

Still another body of research that donors are likely to encourage is akin to that being conducted on the characteristics of effective schools. This research examines not only more quantifiable inputs such as amounts and kinds of training, instructional materials, and teachers and facilities, but also probes the impact of how learning environments are organized, the attitudes of educational managers, and the function of incentives. Besides further study on effective schools, there is particular interest in cost-effective modes of learning out of school and in the employment setting. At the tertiary level, more knowledge is needed on cost-effective ways to develop the skills needed by the society, and on the optimal blend of teaching and research given the level of development of higher education in the country.

Another important, yet difficult research area concerns the education policy environment: Which conditions are conducive and which are problematic for formulating and implementing more strategic education policy? Issues of political feasibility also need to be probed with respect to educational planning.

Valuable, too, will be ongoing synthesis of the types of policy levers that have been tried and their cost-effectiveness in improving quality at the different educational levels. Also of interest are experiences with the use of education management information systems in tracking indicators of educational system efficiency, student achievement, and school quality.

6. *From donor independence to greater collaboration.* A major problem is that external assistance in the education sector has been fragmented and not well focused on a country's greatest needs by host governments or among the donors. This has led to redundant or unnecessary effort in some areas and unmet need in others. There is growing recognition that competing or poorly coordinated efforts among donors are themselves causing a fair amount of inefficiency. Correcting this will not be easy for a variety of reasons.

First, international donors and lenders have quite different philosophies about the purpose and supposed benefits of assistance. Multilateral lending institutions, such as the World Bank, the Inter-American Development Bank, the Asian Development Bank, and the African Development Bank, are first and foremost economic institutions. Their missions are to lend funds that will increase production and thereby return the investment. Such institutions tend to seek policies in the borrower countries that they consider conducive to economic growth. Within this context, borrower countries may be given considerable latitude in selecting among or within productive sectoral investments and among sources of technical assistance that may be needed. Until recently, funding in education by large lending institutions has tended more toward construction, equipment, and furniture than technical assistance and educational materials, and much less for recurrent expenses.

Bilateral donors tend to grant or loan monies that further national political objectives such as private sector development, expanding trade relationships, or securing land or sea rights. To the extent that donors provide "grants" rather than "loans," the recipient country may have less of a say about the content of the grant, either in terms of the sectors being assisted or the focus within a sector. Also, in the case of bilateral project assistance, the recipient country generally must obtain project-related goods and services from the donor country. Yet, donor countries vary greatly among themselves in terms of the conditions they attach to their aid and the degree of oversight they provide. Nevertheless, divergent donor approaches can impede effective collaboration in a country.

A second reason why donor coordination will not be easy is because many countries fail to specify clearly their educational priorities, policies, and strategies and to base these on comprehensive study of the sector. Similarly, countries may lack effective mechanisms for ensuring that donors attend to the educational development priorities of the country rather than to an agenda more of the donor's choosing. To the extent that countries have thoroughly analyzed sector needs and trade-offs among policy options, they are in a better position to persuade donors to support their national education strategy.

Even if a country has a clearly articulated educational strategy, officials may not regard cooperation among donors to be in their best interest if they think they can gain more by dealing with donors separately. This constitutes a third obstacle to coordination.

A fourth obstacle to coordination lies within donor organizations that may have problems coordinating their own activities. In one country, two education consultant teams sent by a donor organization found themselves competing for the attention of government officials and promoting somewhat duplicative strategies for developing education information management systems. In another country, two donor institutions essentially ignored the fact that the instructional strategies they were propounding—provision of standard textbooks in one case, and development and supply of student curriculum modules without textbooks in the other—conflicted in terms of the resources and teacher training needed to support them. Even where there is cooperation among donors in a country, the proposed package of assistance may meet resistance. In one country, cooperative agreements among three donors to support the country's primary education improvement strategy collapsed when two of the donors' home offices decided to stop or reduce funding for education in the country.

CONCLUSIONS

Broad agreement that education is in worsening crisis in most developing countries is leading national officials and donors to consider a comprehensive, integrated strategy to improve educational quality. This strategy is grounded in broad-based sector analysis and policy formulation to direct countries' own limited resources, and those of donors, to the best advantage for the education system as a whole. To support the strategy, some donors and lending institutions are signaling key changes in their modes of assistance. Whether these new shifts by donors can overcome the difficult obstacles described will strongly affect how well and how quickly countries can revitalize the quality of their education systems.

NOTES

1. Even official records, which tend to greatly over-report enrollments and largely discount chronic absenteeism, show that fewer than 70 percent of the 6 to 11 year olds in Africa and south Asia are in school (less than 50 percent in many of the countries), and fewer than 40 percent of the 12 to 17 year olds in those regions are enrolled at any level (UNESCO, 1983). Worldwide, nearly 70 percent of the 100 million school-age children not in school are in south Asia and Sub-Saharan Africa.

2. In the lower-income countries in 1984, 59 percent of the 6 to 11 year old girls were in primary school (compared with 77 percent of the boys), and only 15 percent of the females of secondary school age were enrolled at that level (compared with 27 percent of the males).

3. Sub-Saharan countries allocated a median of 15.3 percent of their national budget to education in 1983, more than developing countries in general (World Bank, 1988).

4. Cycle cost refers to the average number of student years of schooling provided by an education subsector (e.g., primary) relative to the number of completers of that subsector, multiplied by the average unit cost per year. Cycle cost is the investment required to produce a completer of an educational level at current rates of completion. Unit cost consists of the cost of education (recurrent budget) inputs for a particular education level divided by the total number of students in that level.

5. World Bank data for 1984.

6. One West African country enrolls approximately 4,900 students in at least 47 separate degree-granting programs at the tertiary level. This in itself raises questions about the ability to deliver quality programs in so many areas of specialization. In addition, over 70 percent of the students admitted to the largest institution are accepted conditionally and must spend an initial period in remedial study to build the language and mathematics skills that were not developed at earlier levels of schooling.

7. A technical expert from an industrialized country working in a low-income country may cost $175,000 per year (e.g., salary- $60,000; insurance, pension, and other benefits—$14,000; supplement for working in a difficult post—$12,000; housing—$30,000; dependents'; schooling and allowances—$10,000; travel and transportation—$20,000; indirect costs for the contracting institution—$29,000).

REFERENCES

Komenan, A. G. (1987). World education indicators: An annex to improving the efficiency of education in developing countries (Discussion Paper EDT 88). Washington, D.C.: The World Bank.

Lockheed, M. E. & Hanushek, E. (1987). *Improving the efficiency of education in developing countries: Review of the evidence* (Discussion Paper, EDT 77). Washington, D.C.: The World Bank.

United Nations Educational, Scientific, and Cultural Organization (UNESCO). (1983). *Trends and projections of enrollment by level and age, 1960-2000*. Paris,

France: UNESCO, Division of Statistics on Education, Office of Statistics. As cited in Coombs, P. H. (1985). *The world crisis in education.* New York: Oxford University Press.

Windham, D. M. (1988). *Indicators of educational effectiveness and efficiency.* Tallahassee: Florida State University, Improving the Efficiency of Education Systems Project.

World Bank (1988). *Education in Sub-Saharan Africa: Policies for adjustment, revitalization, and expansion.* Washington, D.C.: The World Bank.

Part Two

ISSUES IN IMPLEMENTING QUALITY IMPROVEMENT PROGRAMS

6

An Integrated Approach to Primary Teacher Support and Training

Sivasailam Thiagarajan

This chapter is about the support and training for teacher performances that contribute to the improvement of education in Third World classrooms. It begins by challenging some basic assumptions about the role of teachers in educational quality enhancement. It recommends and illustrates an integrated approach in which teacher training is perceived as a component of a larger system for facilitating student learning in schools. The chapter also briefly explores appropriate strategies and tactics for teacher training programs. The discussion of teacher support (and teacher training) in this chapter is in the context of primary education. With some obvious modifications, several comments may be extrapolated to other levels of education.

ASSUMPTIONS ABOUT PRIMARY TEACHING AND TEACHER TRAINING

In several developing nations, the quality of primary education is perceived to be alarmingly low by educators and policy makers. There is widespread agreement about the urgent need to improve the quality of education and about the fastest way to bring about this improvement: Recruit and train more teachers. This quick-fix solution is based on a number of assumptions, many of which are questionable.

Assumption 1. Teachers are the most important component of primary education. Teachers do have a significant role to play in providing quality education. They are necessary, but not sufficient. A focus on the outcome of primary education—improved learning by children—enables us to identify other equally essential components of the system. Instruction without appropriate textbooks, equipment, and facilities cannot be effective or efficient even in the hands of highly trained teachers. Without instructional support and professional supervision, it is unlikely that teachers can provide the desired quality of primary education.

Assumption 2. The more basic education the primary teacher has, the higher will be the quality of instruction. Sufficient knowledge of different curricular areas is essential for effective teaching. However, excessive knowledge of the content areas does not contribute to the quality of instruction. It is not necessarily true that a college graduate can do a better job of primary teaching than a secondary school graduate. The ability to solve quadratic equations (as taught in secondary schools) or the ability to solve differential equations (as taught in college classes) does not directly contribute to the ability to teach children to solve equations of the type $2 + \_\_ = 5$. Greater student learning is produced by primary teachers trained in efficient methods of teaching basic computational skills than by those educated in advanced concepts of set theory. Similarly, basic language skills in the first few grades do not require high-level linguistic capabilities on the part of the teacher. Sophisticated and superfluous subject-matter expertise is often counterproductive since it may reduce the teacher's ability to understand the naivete of a beginning learner and to appreciate the need for patience and empathy.

Assumption 3. Educating teachers is more important than training them. Education provides broader, generalizable knowledge while training supplies specific skills. A popular assumption holds that education on basic concepts of developmental psychology, educational philosophy, and learning theories will enable the primary teacher to design, develop, and implement appropriate instruction for his or her classroom. An opposing assumption holds that targeted training related to the implementation of a specific curriculum will result in immediate improvement in classroom instruction. Obviously, there is truth in both assumptions. However, judging from the urgency of the task, scarcity of resources, and rapid turnover of primary teachers, the practical training approach promises greater efficiency.

Assumption 4. We know what to teach teachers. Curricula for training (or educating) teachers seem to be based on three questionable axioms. The first is that *what* to teach is more important than *how* to teach. This results in remedial secondary or anticipated university education in teacher training programs. Thus, primary teacher trainees learn more language, more mathematics, more science, more social studies, and more of other topics that (as we discussed above) may not directly contribute to improved effectiveness in the classroom. The second axiom is that traditional pedagogical topics from the past decades are always relevant to primary education. Thus, primary teacher trainees learn about Herbart, Pestalozzi, and other great educators of yesteryear. The third axiom— often the converse of the second—is that a nationalized curriculum is more effective than a foreign one. This results in discarding universal teaching strategies just because they were not invented locally.

In many cases, what is taught to primary teacher trainees becomes an end in itself, requiring memorization and mastery. No attempt is made to check the external validity of the training program and the correlation between the knowledge taught to teachers and the instructional outcomes in the classroom.

Assumption 5. Primary teaching provides a career path. The education of primary teachers is based on the assumption that trainees will become permanent professionals. However, data from different developing countries during the past decade record rapid turnover in primary teaching. Only the earners of second incomes could afford to take up primary teaching as a permanent job. Others treat the job as a temporary one until they qualify for a better-paying job or for entrance to the university. This reality of teaching as a temporary (or as a secondary) job has important implications for the recruitment and training of teachers. An intensive, no-nonsense, lean training is needed to accommodate less-qualified teachers and to utilize the nonpermanent cadre.

For optimum efficiency, training and support for primary teachers in developing nations should be based on realistic assumptions about teacher roles and functions. While conditions differ from one country to another, here are some appropriate conservative assumptions:

1. Teachers are a necessary component of the primary education system; however, this component will function efficiently only if certain other components are present at the threshold level.
2. The additional cost of advanced education for primary teachers does not result in any worthwhile return.
3. Primary teacher training curricula should be relevant to the needs of real-world classrooms.
4. Practical training of teachers on instructional and classroom-management skills is more important than their theoretical education on pedagogical principles.
5. A significant number of primary teachers are unlikely to stay in their jobs for long periods of time.

PERFORMANCE ANALYSIS OF PRIMARY TEACHING

Confronted with the lack of quality of primary education, planners and decision makers turn to providing more of the training that failed to produce the required performance in the first place. Political expediency and wishful thinking encourage them to handle all primary teacher deficiencies with the shotgun approach of more pre-service and in-service training for more people—regardless of whether the deficiency is caused by a lack of skill, motivation, incentives, supervision, or instructional materials. It is dangerous to assume that all primary teacher problems can be remedied through increased training. The way to avoid this danger is to rationally analyze the causes of teacher deficiencies and to systematically remove them. A multidisciplinary approach called *human performance technology* (Smith, 1986) provides appropriate tools for this purpose.

The steps in the application of human performance technology include the following:

1. specifying the goals of a performance system;
2. identifying the elements of ideal performance;
3. identifying the levels of actual performance;
4. determining the discrepancies between the ideal and the actual performance;
5. hypothesizing the causes of these discrepancies;
6. selecting suitable interventions to eliminate or reduce these causes;
7. implementing appropriate interventions; and
8. monitoring and modifying the interventions until the actual performance reaches the desirable level.

The following is an application of the first five steps in the performance technology process to primary teaching:

Goal of primary teaching. Children's learning is the ultimate goal of primary teaching. Although obvious, many educational planners tend to forget this ultimate goal in their pursuit of such secondary goals as recruiting teachers, training them, and keeping them satisfied. (For a detailed discussion of the inefficient focus on secondary goals to the neglect of the primary one, see the following chapter.)

Ideal performance. The ideal performance required of a primary teacher includes many tasks. The teacher is required to play the roles of an instructional designer, instructional presenter, evaluator, classroom manager, and an assistant school administrator. Sample tasks under each of these roles is shown in Figure 6.1.

Actual performance. The actual performance of primary teachers falls significantly short of this ideal. Even well-trained and well-supported teachers in affluent nations have not acquired this level of performance, suggesting that our ideal is unrealistic. Most teachers usually concentrate on the tasks of instructional presentation ("teaching") and of behavior management ("maintaining discipline") and ignore the other tasks of instructional design and evaluation.

Figure 6.1
Primary Teachers: Ideal Performance

Instructional Preparation

Curriculum analysis
Learner analysis
Task analysis
Lesson planning
Specifying objectives
Specifying content
Selecting learning activities
Sequencing instruction
Preparing instructional materials
Trying out and modifying instructional
     materials

Instructional Presentation

Motivating learners
Providing orientation to the lesson
Reviewing prerequisite skills and
     knowledge
Presenting new knowledge
Demonstrating new skills
Eliciting responses
Providing practice
Providing feedback
Integrating lesson elements
Reviewing the lesson
Facilitating transfer

Evaluation

Specifying evaluation purposes
Selecting appropriate evaluation
     strategies
Test construction
Test validation
Test administration
Diagnosing learner problems
Learner placement
Prescribing instructional activities for
     individual learners

Prescribing remedial and enrichment
     activities
Tracking progress of individual learners
Reporting learner progress to parents and
     others
Making learner promotion decisions

Classroom Management

Managing Learners

Grouping learners
Seating learners
Behavior management
Counseling individual learners

Managing Equipment and Materials

Selecting suitable equipment and
     materials
Acquiring equipment and materials
Organizing materials for use
Using equipment and materials
Monitoring use of equipment and
     materials
Ensuring security of equipment and
     materials
Repairing equipment

Managing Activities

Scheduling instructional activities
Scheduling noninstructional activities

**Participation in School
Administration**

Interacting with parents
Soliciting community support
Working with community groups
Assisting school administrators

Determining discrepancies. Gaps between the ideal and the actual performance are present in almost all aspects of teacher performance. These gaps are particularly salient in the areas of instructional preparation and evaluation and least visible in different aspects of classroom management.

Causes of the performance discrepancy. The discrepancies between the ideal and the actual performance of primary teachers are due to several

different causes. Performance technology provides a convenient classification system for identifying probable causes:

- Organizational deficits
- Job design deficits
- Facilities deficits
- Motivational deficits
- Skill/knowledge deficits

Organizational deficits include inappropriate institutional structures
(that encourage clashes and conflicts within and among different levels
of management), and a counterproductive culture (that discourages productivity). In the primary schools of developing nations, the workload
among different teachers differs considerably resulting in complaints
about inequity. For example, the first-grade teacher (usually the least
qualified and the most demoralized) is entrusted with hundreds of children who require the most individual attention. High rates of attrition
ensure that the final grade in the primary school has relatively few
children. In addition, the cultures of most primary schools place a very
high value on covering the syllabus and on teaching rather than on
achieving instructional objectives and learning. This discourages teachers from spending time on instructional design and evaluation.

Job design deficits include inappropriate personnel selection standards, unrealistic expectations, lack of feedback, and lack of support
personnel. Most primary teachers are expected to undertake a set of
responsibilities beyond the reach of most competent human beings. As
a result, teachers redesign their jobs by eliminating the unpleasant and
invisible tasks and by focusing on the public tasks of teaching and maintaining discipline. They regress to the level of least effort—of having
students read from textbooks and copy from blackboards. Instructional
supervision and constructive feedback is almost completely absent from
the primary education systems of most developing nations. There is
very little differentiation among the members of the teaching staff; no
paraprofessional aides or other support personnel help reduce the teacher's load even in the most crowded classrooms.

Facilities deficits include a lack of appropriate facilities, equipment,
and materials. Most primary schools in developing nations are hindered
by crowded classrooms that lack proper ventilation and light. These
schools are often closed during the rainy season. Many classrooms do
not have blackboards or furniture, teachers do not have reference books
or charts, and children do not have textbooks or pencils. Even when
textbooks are available, they are often alien and obsolete.

Motivational deficits include lack of intrinsic interest, sense of accomplishment, and extrinsic incentives. Teaching young children can often be a frustrating and boring task with its demand for dull drill-practice activities. Incentive systems for primary teachers (see chapter 8) are not designed to encourage teacher attendance, performance, or retention. The opportunity cost of primary teaching is seldom worth the meager financial and psychic rewards associated with it.

Skill/knowledge deficits are caused by ignorance and incompetence on the part of the performer. Primary teachers in developing nations lack skills and knowledge in many of the tasks identified in Figure 6.1.

There is not enough time or money to remove or reduce all the deficits that hinder the performance of primary teachers. Nor is such an ambitious effort a requirement of performance technology, whose major prescriptions include these two: (1) attack those deficits that promise major benefits at minor costs, and (2) ensure that all factors that contribute to the system performance are maintained above the threshold level.

AN INTEGRATED APPROACH TO TEACHER SUPPORT AND TRAINING

After analyzing discrepancies and identifying possible causes, the next step in the performance technology process is to select and implement suitable interventions to remove or reduce these causes. A variety of interventions are available to the performance technologist and a sample set is listed and defined in Figure 6.2.

Efficiency in eliciting maximum teacher productivity requires an integrated approach that combines teacher training and other forms of teacher support. Such an integration is not a new concept in primary education; examples include the interactive radio instruction (Jamison & McAnany, 1978) and, much earlier, the Montessori Method (Montessori, 1917). The most flexible strategies among these integrated approaches are grouped under the generic name of *low-cost learning systems* (Nichols, 1982). Cummings (1986) and Pasigna (1988) have recently published comparative reviews of the features and the impact of various systems, including the IMPACT (Instructional Management by Parents, Community, and Teachers) system in the Philippines (Pasigna, 1985), the PAMONG (Pendidikan Anak oleh Masyarakat, Orang tua Murid, dan Guru) system in Indonesia (Dilts & Mudjiman, 1984), the UPE/IMPACT (Unified Primary Education/Instructional Management by Parents, Community, and Teachers) system in Bangladesh (Claveria, 1982), and the Posterized Programmed Teaching Technology Project in Belize (Thiagarajan, 1988).

A successful version of the low-cost learning systems is currently being implemented in Liberia as the Improved Efficiency of Learning system.

Figure 6.2
Sample Performance Technology Interventions

1. **Reducing Organizational Design Deficits**

   Culture change. Identifying and altering beliefs, values, artifacts, and habitual procedures of a group.

   Teambuilding. Collaboratively establishing and accepting common goals, accepting and respecting individual differences, communicating in an open and supportive manner, sharing leadership responsibilities, and participating in the improvement of interactive processes.

2. **Reducing Job Design Deficits**

   Job redesign. Altering the workflow and redistributing the workload among different workers.

   Staffing. Selecting and recruiting more appropriate workers and assigning more appropriate task responsibilities.

   Feedback system. Providing constructive, timely, and useful feedback to improve the performance of individuals and groups.

3. **Reducing Facilities Deficits**

   Facilities design. Providing well-lit, ventilated, and furnished space.

   Materials Support. Providing the workers with appropriate tools, supplies, equipment, and materials.

   Ergonomics. Redesigning the physical facilities, furniture, equipment, materials, and tools to make them more user-friendly and efficient.

4. **Reducing Motivational Deficits**

   Job enrichment. Making the tasks more interesting, meaningful, and integrated.

   Incentive systems. Changing the nature of monetary and nonmonetary rewards and changing the ways in which different performances are rewarded.

5. **Reducing Skill/Knowledge Deficits**

   Job aids. Providing appropriate guidance (through checklists, worksheets, decision tables, etc.) while the worker is in the process of performing.

   Training. Providing instruction on immediately applicable skills and knowledge.

   Education. Providing generalizable skills and knowledge for long-term application.

This system is described below to illustrate different aspects of an integrated system. The description is based on the overview presented in the *Final Contractor's Report* of the IEL Project (Thiagarajan & Pasigna, 1985).

THE IEL SYSTEM

In the IEL system, the instructional strategies are not left to the teacher as in the conventional classroom but programmed by a team of instructional designers. In the first three grades, the IEL system uses Programmed Teaching (PT); in the latter three grades, Programmed Learning (PL).

Programmed Teaching (PT)

In the PT classrooms, children are taught in a two-step sequence: direct instruction and review. Each of these steps lasts 20 minutes. Allowing for a 5-minute break between steps, the full class period lasts for 45 minutes. This sequence is repeated four times each school day, once for each of four subject areas (Language, Mathematics, Reading, and Science or Social Studies).

In a typical PT classroom, children are divided into two groups. While one group is in direct instruction, the other is in review. In direct instruction, children are taught by the teacher who uses PT modules. Both the content (what is to be taught) and the method (how it is to be taught) are prescribed in these modules. The teacher is guided in presenting the content, eliciting student responses, reinforcing acceptable responses, and correcting errors. The content in the PT module may be presented in a graphic or text mode. The teacher holds up the module so all children can see it clearly. The content may also be written on the blackboard or orally presented by the teacher from a script. The PT module contains a large number of questions that require the children to process the content. The children respond as a group. The teacher uses a signal to ensure that responses are made exactly at the same time, thus preventing slower children from imitating earlier responses. From time to time, the teacher varies the procedure and requires individual responses to keep the children alert.

The teacher uses the rapid question-response format for the 20 minutes of direct instruction. After this, the group moves to a different part of the classroom for review. At the same time, the group that was in review moves to direct instruction. The teacher spends about 5 minutes to orient the review group on their task and to distribute copies of the *Review Booklet*. The review group divides into smaller groups of three to five children. The review activities cover the same content that was taught in the preceding direct instruction session. These activities include asking and answering questions; reading aloud; show-and-tell; team game; copying or tracing; writing from dictation; and writing answers to questions from the *Review Booklet*.

At the end of the next 20 minutes, the two groups change activities again. The two-step sequence is repeated four times each day. An additional 45-minute period at the end of the school day is reserved for local scheduling.

Programmed Learning (PL)

This strategy is used in grades 4 through 6 in the IEL schools. Whereas programmed teaching (PT) structures *teaching* behaviors, programmed learning (PL) structures *learning* behaviors.

The majority of PL activities take place in learning teams of three to seven children who study together, helping each other. The teacher monitors, corrects, and reinforces positive learning behaviors. Students use self-contained PL modules, completing each module in 2 days or less. Each team shares three copies of the same module, which is different from those studied by any other team. When one team finishes a module, another team may check it out.

In the learning teams, students take turns being the group leader. PL modules contain specific instructions for the leader. Some typical instructions are to read together; read alone; take turns reading sentences; take turns reading paragraphs; make up questions; answer as a group; take turns answering questions; answer in notebook; make up examples; and tell each other.

Following these instructions, the team proceeds through the lessons in the module. Children take turns reading new information and answering carefully sequenced questions, either collaboratively or individually. In the latter case, they compare and discuss the answers. The leader then checks with the feedback section at the back of the module. Children discuss any discrepancy between their answers and the module answers and correct their mistakes, checking with the teacher only if absolutely necessary.

After completing a module, children take a criterion test that measures their mastery of the instructional objectives. After completing the test, children exchange their notebooks and, using an answer key, check each other's answers. The teacher rechecks the test performance and prescribes suitable follow-up or remedial activity for the team or its individual members.

PL activities are followed for only 4 days out of the 5-day school week. All Fridays are left open for local scheduling of such activities as arts and crafts, science experiments, agriculture, and remediation.

How the Integrated Approach Improves Primary Teacher Performance

The IEL system is an example of an integrated application of performance technology. Different component interventions in the IEL system are briefly discussed below, using the framework from Figure 6.3.

Reducing Organizational Design Deficits

Culture change. In the IEL system, no deliberate attempt is made to change the culture of primary teachers. However, after a couple of years in the system, it is obvious that the values, vocabulary, and views of these teachers have become drastically different from those of traditional teachers. Teacher values have shifted from covering the curriculum to helping the learners achieve instructional objectives; from keeping the children quiet to encouraging active participation; and from single-shot examinations to continuous evaluation. Teachers talk knowledgeably of mastery learning, criterion testing, and remedial recycling. They have become fluent users of rapid-fire questions and immediate correction procedures.

Team building. IEL teachers are trained through an intensive 3-week workshop along with their principals. During and after the workshop, the principal and the teachers of each school implement the system as a team. In the implementation of the IEL system, a special arrangement is used to balance the workload among the teachers: Usually, programmed teaching (PT) requires an intensive effort because the instruction is mediated by the teacher, because the early grades are the most crowded, and because they are the most difficult to teach. In contrast, programmed learning (PL) requires less effort because children learn on their own and because the classrooms are less crowded. Rather than assigning a teacher to a specific grade, all teachers in an IEL primary school rotate among different PT and PL classrooms during the week. This team-teaching arrangement redistributes the workload more equitably and encourages teachers to collaborate with each other.

Reducing Job Design Deficits

Job redesign. A major innovation in the IEL system is the separation of instructional *preparation* from instructional *presentation*. The teacher does not prepare the lesson; instead, all curriculum analysis and instructional design activities are carried out by an interdisciplinary group of experts and incorporated in the PT and PL materials. This ensures that the content is up to date and accurate and the scope and sequence of instruction is appropriate and relevant to the children, to the local environment, and to the national curriculum. Instructional design specialists specify the objectives to be achieved, construct criterion tests to be administered, and select the learning activities to be used. The team applies its superior knowledge of learning theory and developmental psychology to design effective and efficient materials. The teacher's task now becomes one of implementing the instructional package. This division of labor between the instructional designers and classroom teachers is analogous to the relationship between a composer and musicians (Ellson, 1976).

The teacher in a PL classroom has no instructional preparation tasks since they are also completed by the external instructional design team. In addition, the PL teacher does not have many of the instructional presentation tasks since they are shifted to the learners in peer groups.

Figure 6.3
Curriculum for IEL Training

General

    Overview of programmed teaching and
    programmed learning

    The team teaching concept

    Workshop content and format

Programmed Teaching (PT)

    Annual school calendar
      Preliminary activities
      Regular sessions
      Tests and examinations

    Daily schedule
      Language
      Mathematics
      Reading
      Science
      Social Studies
      Remedial period

    PT instructional materials
      PT modules
      Reading booklets
      Review booklets
      Test booklets

    Establishing PT learning groups
      Class size and number of groups
      Heterogeneous ability grouping

    Conducting direct instruction
      Overview of job aids
      Preparation
      Initial information presentation
      Specifying the instructional task
        Group tasks
        Individual tasks
        Oral tasks
        Written tasks

Signaling
  Hand signal
  Pointing signal
  Silence signal
Processing students' response
  Using correct response from the
  module
  Deciding if a response is acceptable
Reinforcement
  Immediate reinforcement
  Varying type of reinforcement
Correcting student errors
  Modeling procedure
  Analysis procedure
  Brightening procedure

Conducting review activities
  Preparation
  Grouping students
  Giving directions to groups
  Student activities
    Oral activities
      Answering questions
      Reading
      Show and tell
      Team game
    Written activities
      Tracing
      Copying
      Drawing
      Writing from dictation
      Writing answers
  Monitoring student activities

Homework
  Assigning homework
  Correcting homework

Testing
  Module tests
    Individual
    Group
  Semester tests
  Annual examination

Figure 6.3 (continued)

Remedial instruction
Reviewing difficult lessons
Tutoring absentees
Preparing transfer students

Recording student progress
Maintaining the PT class log
Keeping track of review activities
Recording student grades
Recording remedial sessions

Maintaining PT materials
Teacher responsibilities
Student responsibilities
Storage of materials
Security of materials
Storage during annual vacation
How to obtain replacement
materials

Programmed Learning (PL)

Annual school calendar
Preliminary activities
Regular sessions
Tests and examinations

Weekly and daily schedules
Language
Mathematics
Reading
Science
Social Studies
Other activities
Science experiments
Arts and crafts
Agriculture
Remedial instruction

PL instructional modules
PL modules
Student guides
Module test booklets
Module test answer keys
Block and semester test booklets
Arts and crafts manuals

Establishing learning teams
Class size and number of teams
Size of each team
Heterogeneous ability grouping

Managing PL activities
PL module selection
Orienting the learning teams
Monitoring team activities
Read together
Read alone
Take turns reading
Group answer
Tell each other
Take turns answering
Answer in notebook
Make up questions
Copy on blackboard
Selecting new leader
Intervening in the team activities

Homework
Assigning homework
Correcting homework

Testing
Module tests
Individual tests
Scoring by team
Reviewing test performance
Block tests
Semester tests
Annual examination

Remedial instruction
Remediating group deficiencies
Remediating individual deficiencies
Tutoring absentees
Preparing transfer students

Recording student progress
Maintaining learning team log
Keeping track of homework
assignments
Recording individual student grades
Recording remedial sessions

Maintaining PL materials
Teacher responsibilities
Student responsibilities
Storage of materials
Security of materials
Storage during annual vacation
How to obtain replacement materials

Thus the major role of the PL teacher is limited to instructional management.

Staffing improvement. In some variations of low-cost learning systems, the teacher's task is further reduced: In the IMPACT system in the Philippines, PT instructional presentation responsibilities are entrusted to students of grades 5 and 6. In this cross-age tutoring arrangement, older students teach younger ones in grades 1 and 2, to the benefit of both. The classroom teacher monitors and manages this arrangement.

In the IEL system, another staffing change is that of team teaching (described earlier) in which all teachers handle different PT and PL classes to equalize their workloads. In addition, some of the supervisory tasks of the principal are shared with a special cadre of instructional supervisors. Modeled after the school inspectorate in many postcolonial educational systems, these instructional supervisors are trained and supported to play a key role in providing feedback to teachers.

Feedback system. Instructional supervisors in the IEL system visit the schools in their region on a regular schedule. They observe every teacher in PT and PL classrooms, focusing on specific behaviors related to IEL materials and methods. This observation is structured by a set of checklists and behaviorally anchored rating scales (Nichols, 1979) that specify what the teacher should do before, during, and after instruction. The supervisors also use an observation system to record timed samples of classroom interactions among the children in PT review groups and PL learning teams and between the teacher and the children. Immediately after the observation, the supervisors interview the teachers about their progress, problems, and plans.

A feedback session with each individual teacher follows next. This session is characterized by collaborative problem solving (rather than by mutual recriminations) and is based on specific objective data (rather than on vague subjective generalizations such as "You should respect individual differences"). The supervisor comments on the teacher's strengths as well as weaknesses, and provides practical suggestions on how the latter can be reduced. The supervisor refers to the modules, teacher manuals, and training materials and provides demonstrations of the correct behaviors—often in an actual classroom with children. The collaborative nature of this activity is further emphasized by the supervisor receiving (and acting upon) feedback from the teachers on how the IEL system can be improved.

Reducing Facilities Deficits

Facilities design. The IEL system is implemented in several rural schools in Liberia that lack appropriate physical facilities, furniture, and equipment. To help these schools to reach the threshold level, an analysis of minimum physical facilities requirements has been completed. Based on this analysis, the IEL system supplies blackboards for the teacher, lapboards for the children, and storage bins for the classrooms. These equipment are manufactured locally and inexpensively. The blackboard is created by applying two coats of black enamel to a 6 x 4 sheet of roofing material; the lapboards (which provide flat surfaces for writing) are cut out of a sheet of hardboard; the storage bin is a large wooden crate with a lid. Vertical dividers in this bin permit organized storage of modules in different subject areas. When placed on the side, the bin looks and functions like a bookshelf. It contains naphthalene balls to prevent termites from damaging the modules. In the evenings, the bin is locked to ensure the security of the instructional materials.

Instructional materials. The IEL system is materials-centered. Its success depends heavily on the systematic design, development, and distribution of instructional materials. At the beginning of the first year of implementation, every IEL school receives a large shipment of several instructional materials: PT and PL modules, review booklets, module tests, block tests, semester tests, scoring keys, teacher's manuals, PL student's manual, and so on. At the beginning of each subsequent year, the schools receive replacement materials.

The instructional materials in each classroom are shared among the children. Several strategies ensure the most cost-effective use of the materials: In programmed teaching, a single set of modules is used by the teacher to provide instruction to all children. The number of copies of review booklets are typically one-sixth the number of children in the class since the children work in groups. In the higher grades, by having different learning groups work on different PL modules at any given time, only three copies of each module are needed.

Ergonomics. PT and PL materials are carefully designed to make them user-friendly and durable. The page layout in the modules incorporates several data-based prescriptions for instructional text (Hartley, 1985) while keeping the reproduction costs under control. PT modules are spiral bound with the pages printed on one side to the end and then continued on the reverse direction to permit the teacher to conveniently display the pages. Each PT module is divided into three different booklets to minimize the number of page flips during a typical lesson. The style and size of type and visuals are carefully selected and student-tested to ensure their legibility in a crowded classroom.

Reducing Motivational Deficits

Job enrichment. During the initial project, there were dire predictions from teacher trainers that IEL teachers would complain about the tight structuring of their classroom behaviors. However, field data indicate that the typical primary teacher not only tolerates this tight structuring, but welcomes it. Teacher absenteeism in IEL schools is lower than in conventional control schools (Kelly, 1984). Teacher reports reflect positive reaction to being told exactly what to do and when to do it and being supplied with the tools necessary to do it. Most importantly, teachers comment favorably on being able to observe the children mastering basic skills and concepts in different subject areas. This visibility of results appears to increase teacher feelings of personal efficacy and to contribute to their morale and motivation.

Incentive systems. Due to political constraints of the type discussed in the next chapter, the IEL system is not able to modify the primary teacher incentive system to enhance its effectiveness. Salary payments to IEL teachers are based on original qualifications and not on performances or results. It is obvious that IEL teachers work harder than their conventional counterparts. In a typical PT lesson, for example, teachers elicit and process an average of seven student responses per minute and continue this fast pace for 20 minutes at a stretch, for a total of eight sessions a day. This is in contrast to their earlier passive behavior of having the students read and copy materials from the blackboard throughout the school day. There are frequent complaints from IEL teachers about receiving the same salary for harder work and more effective results. However, these complaints do not appear to have seriously dampened their enthusiasm.

Reducing Skill/Knowledge Deficits

Job aids. In the IEL system, the main intervention used for providing teacher skills and knowledge is a special form of guidance known as job aids (Harless, 1987). The job aid, usually in the form of a checklist, worksheet, or decision table, is used to guide the performance of a worker without the need for learning the steps of the task. Job aids are used in the implementation of both programmed teaching and programmed learning materials.

The most important type of job aid in the PT materials is the *teaching procedure box*, which is found on every page of the PT module, adjacent to the items to be presented to the children. This procedure box may include preparation, directions, scripts, signal, and correction. Each of these elements is briefly described below.

Preparation. A few PT lessons require the teacher to complete some preparatory activities. In a grade 1 language lesson on colors, for example, the teacher is required to bring common objects (e.g., green leaf, white paper, black charcoal, and red fabric) to the class. Directions for this preparatory activity are given at the beginning of the lesson.

Directions. All teaching procedures boxes begin with explicit directions for teacher action (e.g., POINT TO THE ADDITION PROBLEM). The same action is repeated with each item in the lesson until a new teaching procedure box is presented. All action directions are printed in capital letters.

Scripts. Anything that the teacher is to say (including short lectures, questions, and commands) are printed after a "SAY:" tag. In the case of questions and commands, the script provides a general pattern with substitutable words or phrases in parentheses. For example, when the teacher sees the script,

SAY:This word is (sky).
   What color is the (sky)?

he or she substitutes different words in different items for the word "sky."

Signal. During a PT lesson, children respond simultaneously at a given signal. Depending on the nature of the task, the teacher may use any one of three different signals (hand, pointing, or silence). The teaching procedure box specifies the signal for the lesson items.

Correction. When the children give the correct answer, the teacher praises them and proceeds to the next item. When they make an error, the teacher immediately uses a modeling, analysis, or brightening procedure. The teaching procedure box identifies the appropriate correction procedure.

Feedback. In addition to these elements in the teaching procedure box, a feedback job aid is also incorporated in the PT modules. Because the teacher is required to attend carefully to children's behaviors, he or she may not have the time to process their responses. To simplify the task, all lesson items have the correct answers printed below.

Review directions. At the end of each PT lesson, specific directions for the review session are provided. This job aid identifies the nature of the review task and the appropriate pages in the review booklet. The teacher uses this information to orient the group of children on the review activity.

Other job aids. The job aids described above are all incorporated in the PT modules to provide the required guidance at the most appropriate location for use in the act of presenting instruction. Several additional job aids for pre- and post-instructional activities are found in a *Handbook for IEL Instructional Management* (Nichols, 1979). These checklists, tables, and worksheets deal with the following topics:

- Establishing PT learning groups
- Conducting direct instruction
- Conducting review in PT classrooms
- Assigning homework in PT classrooms

- Providing remedial instruction in PT classrooms
- Administering tests to PT groups
- Recording student progress in PT classrooms
- Maintaining PT materials

Programmed learning modules also make use of job aids. However, these job aids provide guidance to the leader and the members of the learning team rather than to the teacher, since the instructional responsibility is entrusted to the children. Additional job aids for the teacher are found in the *Handbook for IEL Instructional Management*. These job aids deal with the following areas:

- Establishing learning teams
- Monitoring and managing learning teams
- Assigning homework in PL classrooms
- Providing remedial instruction in PL classrooms
- Administering tests to PL groups
- Recording student progress in PL classrooms
- Preparing transfer students for PL classrooms
- Maintaining PL materials

The IEL handbook also contains job aids for principals on supervising and managing IEL schools and on procedures for installing the IEL system for the first time.

Training. The IEL system provides three types of teacher training:

Initial workshop. This 3-week workshop provides the basic competencies required to implement programmed teaching and programmed learning materials in the IEL classroom. The curriculum for the workshop is given in Figure 6.3. In general, teachers learn how to present the PT content, give the appropriate signals, elicit and process student responses, and use suitable correction procedures. They also learn to manage the PL classroom, administer tests, and provide suitable remedial instruction. The workshop features hands-on learning activities. The leaders give demonstrations of various PT and PL procedures and require the trainees to immediately apply them in a simulated microteaching situation. Each trainee teaches the other participants (who play the role of primary school children), and receives feedback from peers and the workshop leader. At the end of the workshop, the trainees are able to function effectively in the IEL classrooms with the guidance provided by the various job aids.

On-the-job training. During the first couple of months, IEL teachers receive appropriate on-site training from instructional supervisors. This training is completely individualized, based on observations and analyses of the teacher's performance in the classroom. The supervisor diagnoses the teacher's performance, demonstrates the required skills, and provides immediate opportunities for practice and feedback.

Mid-year training. A short 1-week training workshop is conducted at the end of the first semester to review and refine teacher competencies. The content of the workshop is based on the common problems identified by the supervisors, principals, and teachers. This workshop maintains a practical format and facilitates teachers learning from each other.

All aspects of IEL teacher training have the following common features:

- *The training is relevant.* Only skills and knowledge that are of immediate applicability are taught to the teachers.
- *The training is lean.* Every training objective is checked for its relevance to improving children's learning. No superfluous knowledge on the subject area or on child psychology is included.
- *The training is integrated.* It is designed around the specific instructional materials, classroom conditions, teacher roles, supervisory system, and job aids.
- *The training is reflective.* It practices what it preaches. For example, teacher trainees use PT modules to learn about programmed teaching and PL modules to learn about programmed learning.

Education. The IEL workshops include demonstrations and discussions of *how to* teach specific content from different subject areas. However, they do not deal with the subject-matter content of what is to be taught. Teachers are encouraged to preview the lessons before presenting them to children. In this process, they master different subject areas through incidental learning. This phenomenon of teachers learning along with the children has also been reported in other low-cost learning projects in the Philippines, Indonesia, and elsewhere.

SECTIONAL SUMMARY

The IEL system is an integrated application of different performance technology interventions to improve primary teacher performance—and children's learning. The following are the major performance technology interventions incorporated in the system:

Job redesign to redistribute the responsibilities for instructional design, presentation, and management to outside teams of instructional designers and inside team of students so that the teacher's job becomes more manageable.

Feedback system that provides constructive suggestions to the teacher on his or her performance.

Instructional materials to provide the teachers and students with tools to achieve the objectives.

Job aids that are incorporated both within and outside these materials to enhance the teaching and learning performance.

Training to ensure effective implementation of these interventions.

The IEL system uses a few other interventions in a partial fashion:

Facilities for use in the classroom.

Teambuilding activities (such as team teaching) to ensure more collaboration among teachers.

Ergonomics to improve the usefulness of instructional materials.

The IEL system achieves incidental integration of a few other interventions:

Culture change in teachers' values, views, and vocabulary.

Job enrichment through the immediate and visible evidence of student learning.

Incidental education in different subject-matter areas.

Because of political constraints, the IEL system is not able to include rational improvements to the *incentive system* by relating the pay to performance or results.

Transitional Strategies for Teacher Training

The IEL system is not perfect, but it is a significant example of an integrated primary education system. The development of such a comprehensive system may not be possible in other developing nations that lack the necessary time, money, technical expertise, and political will. A partially integrated system, although not as efficient, is much more feasible. For example, the Reduced Instructional Time (RIT) Project in Thailand provides targeted teacher training (in direct and distance education modes) for the implementation of specific instructional materials (Potart, 1982; Pasigna, 1988). In Somalia, the Curriculum Development Center has systematically developed and distributed the New Reform Curriculum Textbooks and is now currently developing an integrated set of teacher training modules to facilitate their implementation (Improving the Efficiency of Education Systems (IEES) Project, 1988).

Developing nations can begin to significantly improve primary education by integrating teacher training with the systematic design and distribution of textbooks.

Teacher Training Strategies and Tactics

The major contention of this chapter is that without supporting interventions teacher training is inefficient and counterproductive. With appropriate support, however, such training can be a significant component in the improvement of primary education.

Both in-service and pre-service teacher training can benefit from innovative instructional development. The following section briefly discusses some teacher training strategies and tactics.

Competency-Based Teacher Training

Competency-based teacher training provides an important organizing principle for designing, developing, and delivering efficient teacher training. This approach is based on providing trainees with skills and knowledge that have a positive effect on teacher performance—and on student learning. In a competency-based program, instructional objectives are clearly specified in terms of teacher performances. The training program—and the method of evaluating its impact on teacher performance—are directly based on these objectives.

Competency-based programs are developed through the application of the systematic instructional systems design (ISD) process presented in Chapter 4 by Robert Morgan. ISD activities for a teacher-training program should include analyses of the following (Thiagarajan, Semmel, & Semmel, 1974):

- Activities of the primary teacher during a typical day
- Activities of the primary teacher during a typical year
- Features of the instructional materials used in local primary schools
- Behaviors required for effectively implementing these instructional materials
- Classroom management strategies (for the management of time, materials, and student behaviors)
- Evaluation procedures that support individualized instruction

Once these analyses are completed, developmental activities proceed to the simultaneous construction of tests and design of instructional materials. The tests are criterion-referenced; that is, they are designed to directly measure the achievement of prespecified objectives. They are also performance based, requiring the trainees to actually teach in real or simulated classrooms. Measurement of teacher behaviors in performance tests require rating scales and other observation instruments. While paper-and-pencil tests may also be used to measure the trainees' recall of basic principles, they cannot replace performance tests for the measurement of teacher skills.

The design of training is based on the principal that for maximum transfer, teachers should receive their training in as close to an on-the-job situation as possible. Teaching skills should be taught using a behavior-modeling paradigm. A master teacher should first demonstrate the teaching procedure. Trainees should be required to practice these procedures by teaching each other in a simulated microteaching situation. This should be followed by practice teaching in actual classrooms. Immediate and specific feedback should be provided through systematic observation and rating scales. Basic teaching concepts (such as types of questions or behavior problems) should be presented to the trainees through protocol materials (Thiagarajan, 1980), which are authentic recordings of actual classroom interactions. These recordings may be on videotapes (which are beginning to be fairly easily available in developing nations). Alternatively, print or audiotape protocols may be used to present various concepts. While text and lecture may form the basis for theoretical instruction, they cannot replace authentic examples of classroom interactions. Attitudes, values, and other affective outcomes for the competency-based program are best attained through experiential learning approaches such as roleplaying.

Competency-based programs can significantly improve the internal and external efficiencies of primary teacher training. They can reduce the time and the cost of both pre-service and in-service training while improving the effectiveness of the system in achieving its ultimate goal: improved student learning. Once again, however, it must be emphasized that even the most effective training program may not be efficient unless the desired teacher performance is supported by other interventions such as incentives, instructional materials, job aids, job redesign, and supervision.

REFERENCES

Claveria, O. B. (1982). *Report on the implementation of the IMPACT experiment—universal primary education (IDS)*. Dhaka, Bangladesh: Institute for International Research.

Cummings, W. K. (1986). *Low-cost primary education: Implementing an innovation in six nations*. Ottawa, Canada: International Development Research Centre.

Dilts, R., & Mudjiman, H. (1984). *UPT PAMONG: The technical implementation unit for primary school instructional management by parents, community, and teachers*. Unpublished manuscript. Jakarta: Ministry of Education.

Ellson, D. G. (1976). Tutoring. In N. Gage (Ed.), *The psychology of teaching methods*. Chicago: National Society for the Study of Education.

Harless, J. H. (1986). Guiding performance with job aids. In M. E. Smith (Ed.),

Introduction to performance technology. Washington, D.C.: National Society for Performance and Instruction.

Hartley, J. (1985). *Designing instructional text* (2nd ed.). New York: Nichols.

Improving the Efficiency of Education Systems (IEES) Project. (1988). *Somalia country plan*. Tallahassee: Florida State University, IEES Educational Efficiency Clearinghouse.

Jamison, D. T., & McAnany, E. G. (1978). *Radio for education and development*. Beverly Hills, CA: Sage Publications.

Kelly, E. F. (1984). *Evaluation of the Improved Efficiency of Learning Project in Liberia, Africa: Overview and peculiar problems*. Albany, NY: The Evaluation Consortium, School of Education, State University of New York at Albany.

Montessori, M. (1917). *The Montessori elementary material*. New York: Schoken Books.

Nichols, D. G. (1979). *Handbook for IEL instructional management*. Gbarnga, Liberia: Improved Efficiency of Learning Project.

Nichols, D. G. (1982). Low-cost learning systems: The general concept and some specific examples. *NSPI Journal, 4* (September), 4–8.

Pasigna, A. L. (1985). Success story: Liberia's Improved Efficiency of Learning Project. *NSPI Journal, 24*(9), 7-8.

Pasigna, A. L. (In Press). *A post-hoc analysis of "low-cost" learning systems*.

Potart, N. (1962). *Report on the reduced instructional time project*. Bangkok, Thailand: Ministry of Education, RIT Project.

Smith, M. E. (Ed.). (1986). *Introduction to performance technology*. Washington, D.C.: National Society for Performance and Instruction.

Thiagarajan, S. (1980). *Protocol packages*. Englewood Cliffs, NJ: Educational Technology Publications.

Thiagarajan, S. (1988). *Belize's Posterized Programmed Teaching Technology Project: An interim evaluation report*. Bloomington, IN: Institute for International Research, Inc.

Thiagarajan, S., & Pasigna, A. L. (1985). *Final contractor's report: Improved Efficiency of Learning (IEL) Project* (Final Report to the U.S. Agency for International Development, Contract No. AID/AFR-C–1494). McLean, VA: Institute for International Research.

Thiagarajan, S., Semmel, D. S., & Semmel, M. I. (1974). *Instructional development for training teachers*. Reston, VA: The Council for Exceptional Children.

7

An Integrated Approach to Primary Teacher Incentives

Frances Kemmerer

INTRODUCTION

The purpose of teacher incentive systems—as of all incentive systems—is to modify the behavior of an individual or a group of individuals in the interest of goal attainment. In the case of teacher incentives the long-term goal or outcome is improved student learning and the short-term objective or output is improved teacher performance. Achievement of the longer-term outcome is indicated by national examination results, school grades, progression rates, attrition rates, and measures of various other student attitudes and behaviors (Windham, 1988). Achievement of output goal is indicated by teacher behaviors related to instructional preparation, presentation, evaluation, and classroom management (see Chapter 6).

There are two approaches to designing or reforming a teacher incentives system in order to maximize the impact of available resources on these outcomes and outputs. The traditional or fixed input approach is characterized by taking as given a narrowly defined pool of candidates for teaching (e.g. secondary school graduates with one year of teacher training) and focusing on their needs and wants. Yet, as suggested in the previous chapter, enhancing teacher effectiveness as defined by mastery of a broad range of skills from lesson preparation to evaluation is not a necessary intermediate goal. When resources are sharply constrained, this approach generally leads to confusion of ends and means (student learning and upgrading teachers) and to reduced opportunities for improved system performance. As the opportunity set decreases, interest in low-cost or nonmonetary incentives increases proportionally. However, where direct and indirect monetary incentives are small by either absolute or relative standards, the nonmonetary incentives are likely to produce few or negligible benefits at the margin.

An alternative approach is to view teacher incentives as part of a larger resource allocation problem. The integrated approach requires beginning with the goal or output desired and then selecting means or inputs on the basis of their potential contribution to the goal. The questions of which students get what resources and why, which are central to the integrated approach, prohibit the transposition of ends and means and result in the definition of the greatest possible opportunity set. Although the policy outcomes of the two approaches may be the same, the latter approach forces explicit choice while the former does not. In terms of improving teacher performance, the policy maker is forced back to the decision of which students are to receive what resources and at what cost. The choices of who should be hired to teach, the availability and length of pre-service or in-service training, the medium of instruction, strong or weak supervision, and so on, represent ancillary decisions. For instance, in resource-poor systems an optimal choice might be less educated and therefore less "expensive" teachers combined with radio instruction or programmed teaching. If, however, the pool of potential teachers is already defined (e.g. secondary student graduates with 1 year of postsecondary teacher training), then the option set is reduced. Resources that could have been used to improve the effectiveness of curriculum or supervision have already been committed to salary.

This chapter treats teacher incentives as part of a broader resource allocation question. This approach is justified on two counts. First, few countries can afford to provide incentives for teaching that are unrelated to improved teacher performance and student learning. And secondly, many of the extrinsic motivators of teachers (guides, textbooks, supervisory support) are major inputs in the production of school learning.

The chapter focuses on primary teacher incentives since primary schooling is the only formal education most of the population in developing countries will receive and since the number of teachers and their geographic distribution make the issues related to incentives more difficult. First a choice model for teacher incentives is presented. Second, the criteria for an efficient incentive system are defined. Third, typical problems of central and local-level incentives systems in developing countries are examined in light of the model, and criteria and solutions offered. The chapter concludes with a discussion of the political constraints to reform of incentive systems in developing countries.

Figure 7.1
A Choice Model for Teacher Incentives

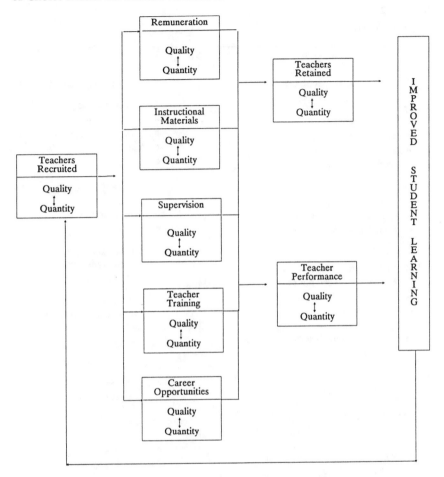

A MODEL FOR TEACHER INCENTIVES

A simple choice model for a teacher incentive system, which is an integral part of a plan for the allocation of resources for schooling, is shown in Figure 7.1. A partial listing of the incentives contained in each of the Figure 7.1 categories is provided in Figure 7.2. The model assumes that teacher performance directly affects the quantity and quality of student learning (Berliner, 1979, 1980; Joyce & Weil, 1986), and second, that teacher performance is a function of the quality and quantity of the individuals recruited and retained, instructional support, supervision, training, and other forms of direct and indirect support (see Chapter 6).

Figure 7.2
Incentive Categories

Remuneration

Salary
- Beginning salary
- Salary scale
- Regularity of payment
- Merit pay

Allowances
- Materials allowance
- Cost-of-living allowance
- Hardship allowance
- Travel allowance

In-Kind Salary Supplements
- Free or subsidized housing
- Free or subsidized food
- Plots of land
- Low interest loans
- Scholarships for children
- Free books

Bonuses
- Bonus for regular attendance
- Bonus for student achievement
- Grants for classroom projects

Benefits
- Paid leave
- Sick leave
- Maternity leave
- Health insurance
- Medical assistance
- Pension
- Life insurance
- Additional employment
- Additional teaching jobs
  (e.g. adult education)
- Examination grading
- Textbook writing
- Development projects

Working Conditions
- School facilities
- Classroom facilities
- Numbers of students
- Age Range of students
- Collegiality

Instructional Support

Instructional Materials
- Teacher guides
  on time
  in all subject areas
  in appropriate language
- Student textbooks
  on time
  in all subject areas
  in appropriate language
- Classroom charts
- Science equipment
- Copy books
- Pencils
- Chalkboard
- Safe storage for materials

Supervision
- Observation
- Feedback
- Coaching

Teacher Training
- Classroom management
- Materials usage
- Lesson preparation
- Test administration

Career Opportunities
- Master teacher
- Principal
- Supervisor
- Post-service training

Of this list of factors affecting teacher performance and consequently student learning, the one most questionable is teacher retention. It is included here on the belief that the findings of studies conducted in the United States and other developed countries that show a doubtful or nonsystematic relationship between teacher experience and student learning (Murnane, 1975; Summers & Wolf, 1975; Rosenholtz & Smylie, 1984) cannot be readily generalized to developing nations, where the entry qualifications of teachers are typically much lower. The lower entry qualifications suggest that teachers acquire mastery of the curriculum content on the job, which in turn might indicate that in later years they would be more competent than in earlier years, regardless of student characteristics.

The model defines teacher incentives to include all the direct and indirect monetary and nonmonetary benefits offered to teachers as extrinsic motivators. Direct monetary benefits are defined as the package of salary and fringe benefits (allowances, bonus, sick leave, maternity leave, pension) offered to teachers. Indirect monetary benefits comprise all other resources provided to teachers that are financed by government and communities. These include teacher professional support benefits in the form of guides, textbooks, supervision, pre-service and in-service training, appropriate classroom facilities, and personal support incentives such as free or subsidized housing, food, or transportation. Finally, nonmonetary incentives are incentives for which it is difficult to calculate the provider's cost in dollar terms. Status in the community, exemption from military service, choice of location for the next assignment, and recognition of effort and excellence are examples of nonmonetary incentives.

Remuneration is a basic system requirement and is related to both retention and recruitment. While many studies of teachers indicate that teachers join the educational service and remain in it because they like working with children and consider teaching an important, if not critical, contribution to society, few could afford to engage in it on a voluntary basis. Interestingly, poor compensation is more often cited as the primary reason for not becoming a teacher but as a secondary reason for leaving teaching (Lortie, 1975; Rosenholtz & Smylie, 1984).

In the lesser-developed nations and in the early stages of educational systems development in more developed nations, low salaries have been successfully offset by provision of housing or food. District officers who have been able to engage communities in this form of support have improved both teacher attendance and retention in their schools.

If meeting the basic salary requirements of teachers (which includes both adequate salary and benefits and payment of salary on time) is the sine qua non of a functional educational system, the provision of appropriate working conditions and instructional support are the basis for system performance. Low social status, shortages of storage space, lack of collegial relationships, fear of physical safety, large class size, and considerable non-teaching responsibilities are complaints heard equally in developed and developing countries. In developed countries, 36 percent of former teachers report unfavorable working conditions as the primary reason for leaving teaching. In developing countries, poor working conditions, including instructional support, are listed second only to low salary as the reason for leaving teaching (The Metropolitan Life Insurance Company, 1986; Improving the Efficiency of Education Systems (IEES) Project, 1988a).

Instructional support, which includes training, instructional materials, and supervision, acts as an incentive since it is a requirement for a sense of personal efficacy—the belief that the teacher can help students learn. A teacher who does not know what to do in the classroom and has little opportunity to learn will eventually attend less, or if he or she attends, use instructional time for other activities (Ashton & Webb, 1986).

The emphasis on the theoretical rather than the practical dimensions of teaching in pre-service training is cited as one of the factors responsible for teachers' feelings of incompetence (Lortie, 1975; Dreeben 1970; Rosenholtz & Smylie, 1984). It is probable that the emphasis on theory rather than practice is responsible for the fact that there appears to be no significant relationship between the number of education courses taken and a teacher's instructional effectiveness (Denton & Lacina, 1983). For instance, basic skills such as learning to manage students and present a textbook lesson are only infrequently taught in pre-service programs (Chapman & Hutcheson, 1980; Rosenholtz & Smylie, 1984; see also Chapter 6 of this volume). In developing countries, lack of a practical curricular orientation is compounded by the absence of systematic practice teaching. As a result, beginning teachers, who are younger and have less education than their developed-country counterparts, are much less likely to be comfortable with the multifaceted performance requirements of classroom teaching.

Much of the typical trial-and-error learning of new teachers can be overcome by appropriate in-service training. In-service training also serves to break down the isolation experienced by most teachers and renew a sense of professionalism and purpose (Verspoor & Leno, 1986). For these reasons, if a choice had to be made between the provision of 1 or more years of pre-service and in-service training, teachers might benefit more from the latter rather than the former. The poor results of many in-service programs suggest, however, that the scope and content of such training should be narrowly focused and specific to the materials teachers actually use.

Instructional materials, like appropriate teacher orientation, play a crucial role in teachers' assessments of their own instructional competence. Where teachers are provided with a blueprint for organizing students, presenting the lesson, providing feedback and practice, they are much more likely to acquire a sense of competence than if the inverse were true (see Chapter 6). Textbooks, particularly in developing countries where other reading materials are scarce, have been shown not only to affect teacher performance but to have a separate and independent effect on student learning (Heyneman, Farrell, & Sepulveda-Stuardo, 1978; Verspoor, 1986; Sepulveda-Stuardo & Farrell, 1983).

Teachers, particularly new ones, require supportive supervision. Such supervision can reduce the need for in-service by frank discussion of the teacher's skill deficits and strengths. This type of supervision requires the interpersonal and professional skills of a master teacher and regular visits by the supervisor. Supervisory systems in developing countries, however, are often characterized by untrained personnel, who may have less experience than the teacher, insufficient travel funds, and an emphasis on evaluation rather than training. Given the resource constraints of most countries, a more cost-effective approach to supervision might be assignment of this responsibility to the principal.

The provision of career opportunities within the educational subsector reinforces the instructional support system and provides a stimulus for continued teacher involvement. The teacher, particularly if head of household, who can look forward to the possibility of becoming a principal, a master teacher, or district officer is much more likely to remain in primary education than one who has no opportunity for promotion (Rosenholtz & Smylie, 1984; Chapman & Hutcheson, 1982).

Post-service training, which is listed under the category of Career Opportunities in Figure 7.2 is assumed to mean training as a primary school master teacher, principal, or supervisor rather than liberal arts education or training in secondary teaching; this is for the simple reason that the former reinforce the goal of improved teacher performance while the latter not only are not reinforcers but are contrary to the goal.

The categories of personal and professional incentives taken together represent a support network for teachers. None of the concerns represented in the categories can be ignored with impunity, and changes cannot be successfully made in any given category without reference to other categories. For instance, efficiency is not likely to be enhanced if the qualifications of those recruited are raised while salary, the content of pre-service and in-service training, and career opportunities remain the same. Similarly, the level of language in teacher guides and textbooks should be closely related to the average teachers' ability or they will not serve as useful tools.

The reciprocal arrows between categories indicate, however, the possibility of input substitution. Substitution among inputs simply means that, within limits, more of one input can be combined with less of another input to produce the same results. For instance, better tools for the teacher (guides, textbooks, reference materials, and supplies) can be substituted for teachers with higher qualifications, or post-service training for greater remuneration. An even more fundamental set of trade-offs is imbedded in the descriptors "quality" and "quantity" within each category. The arrows are drawn to indicate that, within limits, quality can be substituted for quantity, resulting in an overall gain rather than loss of efficiency. An example of this would be the substitution of higher quality teacher guides for a textbook for every child. Students, particularly at an early age, benefit more from a competent teacher than from printed matter (Thomas, 1977), and students at any age can successfully share books (Windham, 1983).

The criteria for selecting an efficient *combination* of incentives are discussed in the next section.

CRITERIA FOR EFFICIENT INCENTIVE SYSTEMS

Efficiency is defined as the least-cost means of achieving a specific goal or the most productive use of available resources in terms of goal attainment. As Windham has noted "It is important to recognize from these definitions that the concept of effectiveness (how well or to what extent the desired outputs are achieved) is subsumed in the concept of efficiency (effectiveness relative to cost)" (Windham, 1988, p. 6).

Efficiency in the production of optimal teacher performance requires internal consistency, adequacy, and equity. An incentive system simply will not work if the means are not compatible with each other or with the goals, if the incentives or motivators are perceived as inadequate, or the distribution of benefits considered unfair. Each of these standards is discussed in turn.

Internal Consistency

Internal consistency refers to the relationship between the means and the goal and among the means. By definition efficiency demands clear statement of both goals and means, as well as compatibility between the goal and means.

At a minimum, goal statements should provide detailed output and outcome standards against which the incentive system can be evaluated. While the value added to student achievement by participation in a particular teacher's class is difficult to measure given the error of teacher-made tests and the problematic relationship of national examinations to the actual curriculum, evaluation techniques such as criterion-referenced tests imbedded in teacher guides can be used to provide reasonable measures of relative student mastery (Kelly, 1984; Chapman & Windham, 1986).

Measures of teacher performance are in contrast fairly easy to develop and apply. As Thiagarajan delineated in the previous chapter, they flow from a task analysis of the teacher's job, beginning with very obvious behavioral requirements such as regular attendance to more complex behaviors governing the presentation of different types of lessons, the provision of feedback to students, and student evaluation and remediation (see Chapter 6).

Once the goals have been defined in concrete terms, the relationship between and among goals and means, or outputs and inputs, needs to be examined. Internal consistency is generally violated through reductionism or transposition of means and ends. The original goal—enhanced student achievement through improved teacher performance—is reduced to two or more goals that previously had been defined as means. For example, the original goal of improving teacher performance is often reduced to increasing recruitment and retention, which are properly considered means. In the first place, the new goals may be rivals, in which case one can only be reached at the expense of the other. In other words, the high cost of recruitment incentives might require a smaller investment in the incentives that affect retention. In the second place, even if the new goals are not mutually exclusive, their attainment is not synonymous with reaching the original goal. For instance, sufficient salary incentives might result in reaching targeted recruitment and retention goals without affecting teacher performance or student learning.

Consistency among means requires a close fit between the characteristics of the inputs into the production of teacher performance. The attributes of teachers, remuneration, teacher training, supervision, instructional materials, and career opportunities must be related to each other in a systematic fashion. On the one hand, provision of teacher guides purchased abroad would represent a poor fit to primary graduate teachers, since the books are most likely geared to a higher level of reading than the average teacher has attained and require the intermediate step of translation if not in a local language. Training focused on the textbooks used in the classroom, on the other hand, represents a good fit because it is closely related to the teacher's task in the classroom.

Adequacy

Adequacy is the condition of being sufficient for a given purpose. The concept of adequacy by definition then corrects a common misconception about efficiency, that is, that greater efficiency always results in cost savings. In fact, gains in efficiency can result in either lower costs or in higher costs. Enhanced efficiency obviously would generate higher costs in situations where the original investments were inadequate to the task.

Adequacy also connotes relativism. What is perceived as adequate by one individual or group of individuals may not suffice for another. For example, few would expect secondary graduates and primary graduates to respond similarly to the same set of incentives. One measure of adequacy is, therefore, the opportunity cost related to choosing one occupation rather than another. The characteristics of an individual in a given labor market determine, to a large extent, the employment opportunities available to them. Where non-teaching opportunities are available and are related to both better monetary or nonmonetary rewards, individuals will opt for those alternatives, regardless of whether such choice demands a long search period or not. This is particularly true if it is difficult to exit the teaching service when and if better opportunities present themselves.

A second and narrower measure of adequacy results from comparison of both the direct and indirect benefits offered to teachers and the cost of living. Where salary falls far below the cost of living, the teacher, if head of household, will leave teaching or seek second and third jobs, in which case attendance at school and performance in the classroom will suffer.

Both these measures (opportunity cost and cost of living) rely chiefly on the comparison of the monetary benefits of teaching to other standards. It is argued here, however, that there is a threshold value for each type of incentive. When the value falls below that threshold, competent teacher performance, as measured on a scale from regular attendance to gains in student achievement scores, is improbable at best. While this is most easily seen in terms of salary incentive, it is equally true of instructional support incentives. Teachers without guides and texts operating in poor facilities have little motivation to perform competently, and in the case of poorly educated teachers, will be unable to perform even at a minimally acceptable level. It is axiomatic that the poorer the craftsperson the better the tools required.

Equity

Incentives systems only work if they are perceived as fair. Equity requires both that unequals are treated differently (vertical equity) and that equals are treated similarly (horizontal equity).

Levels of education, experience, and scope of work are almost universally perceived as fair ways of distinguishing among individuals. Thus differential rewards for headmasters or head teachers, for secondary as opposed to primary graduate teachers, or for experienced as opposed to beginning teachers, are rarely questioned and, in fact, define the structure of many incentive systems. Vertical equity is also violated by noncompensated differences in teaching loads. Where some teachers teach more hours a week, significantly larger classes, or more difficult classes (in terms either of student ability or discipline) than others, dissatisfaction, which generally adversely impacts performance, is likely to ensue.

Even incentive systems characterized by vertical equity, however, often remain ineffective because they neglect dealing with the more troublesome issues related to distinguishing among so-called "equals." If all teachers with the same training and experience receive the same compensation but some perform better than others, morale and effort tend to deteriorate. The non-performers, in some cases non-attenders, send a very strong message to their colleagues that rewards do not change with level of services rendered.

A number of solutions to this problem have been offered. The first is to compensate teachers on the basis of the success of their students on examinations. There were many experiments in "performance contracting" of this type in the late 1960s in the United States. Technical problems related to measuring the value added by a particular teacher, as well as widespread allegations of teaching to a particular test rather than for the acquisition of a broad range of cognitive and affective skills, led to the virtual abandonment of this approach (Murnane & Cohen, 1986).

More acceptable solutions have been the public recognition of individuals' contributions to the school and community. Recognition may take the form of either monetary or nonmonetary awards. Educational research provides surprising little guidance about the relative benefits of various types of award systems that might be expected from the institution.

Merit pay systems, which are cyclically proposed in the United States, appear to be more popular with policy makers than with teachers themselves. Because of the differences between a teacher's work and the piece-rate work in factories, where these systems were developed, the cost of developing appropriate evaluation systems tends to be exceptionally high both in terms of time and money. The complexity of the teacher's task also makes it difficult to prove beyond doubt that the teacher evaluations were impartial and objective. Administrators tend to worry that merit pay evaluations promote divisiveness among the faculty, and teachers that merit pay drains the resources needed for more basic across-the-board salary increases. The merit pay systems that have persisted are inherently contradictory. They are characterized by rewards for non-teaching service and a reward for almost every teacher (Murnane & Cohen, 1986, Hatry & Greiner, 1985).

Even less research has been conducted on the effects of nonmonetary award systems. National teacher and school of the year awards tend, however, not to be divisive and have the advantage of publicizing the benefits produced by good teachers and schools.

Gender and geographical location of assignment represent both vertical and horizontal equity issues. Active recruitment of women teachers is desirable for two reasons. First, women teachers have a positive impact both on the enrollment and continuation of girls in school. And second, in many lesser-developed countries cultural norms effectively lower women's opportunity cost for teaching. On the one hand, few alternative employment opportunities are available, and on the other, school teaching by reason of its hours is one of the few occupations compatible with traditional child-rearing practices. It was, after all, not by chance that the educational systems in the developed countries came to have a predominance of women teachers at the primary level. (Obviously, women, when hired, cannot be paid less than men for the same task without violating horizontal equity and having a strong negative impact on motivation.)

The criteria of consistency, adequacy, and equity are interdependent. An incentive system characterized by marked inconsistencies between and among the means and goals will almost invariably also be characterized by inadequate investments in one or more of the incentive categories. Interestingly enough, some of these inadequacies could be remedied if greater attention was paid to equity. Where current teacher salaries are considered inadequate, greater effort could be made to recruit women who might consider the current salaries acceptable both because they are secondary breadwinners and because the hours of teaching do not conflict with their own preference for child-rearing. In fact, much of the increase in gender equity in the hiring of teachers results from personal economic decisions rather than policy directives (see, for example, IEES, 1988b, pp. 18-26).

PROBLEMS IN INCENTIVE SYSTEMS

Difficulties in recruiting new teachers and high teacher attrition rates are signs that the incentive system in place is not working. Identification of the problems and their solution requires examination of all the rules and regulations governing teachers and talking to teachers. There is no substitute for understanding teachers' perceptions of the current incentive systems and their analysis of what works, what does not work, and why. The original intent of policy makers who designed the system is less relevant than teachers' point of view. For as Windham has pointed out,

planners, no matter how much discretionary power they have, never determine the actual outcome of policy. They can only set in action forces which they anticipate, with or without rational justification, will have certain effects. The effects themselves are the result of the millions of micro decisions made by individuals who are responding to the planners' policies in terms of (a) the actual pattern of rewards (positive or negative) which their decision matrix presents and (b) their perception of this pattern. (Windham, 1978, p. 4)

The typical teacher incentive system in developing countries is described below from the teachers' perspective and is based on the IEES Education and Human Resource Sector Assessments.

THE TYPICAL INCENTIVE SYSTEM

The typical candidate for teaching in a developing country has few other career options. He or she is attracted to the profession by the promise of pre-service training often conducted in English or another international language and promise of post-service training at the university.

The pre-service training itself is generally 1 or 2 years in length and takes place either in the capital or a regional center. The general nature of the training and the medium of instruction often results in more marketable skills, causing the graduate to reconsider the opportunity costs of teaching relative to new options.

Should he (and it is usually he rather than she) decide to continue in education, he or she is likely to be posted to a rural area where health services, second jobs, and entertainment opportunities are scarce. These deficits will not be offset by a hardship allowance.

After placement in a school, the new teacher expects a long delay in the start of salary as bureaucratic paper work does not keep pace with the new assignments. The delay may be anywhere from 4 months to over a year. More often than not, once payment begins the teacher leaves his or her school each month to travel to the capital or a regional center to pick up his or her salary. The round trip will take anywhere from a few days to over a week and is a non-reimbursable expenditure.

On the job, the typical school teacher has few instructional materials to aid in preparation for class, and what materials are available provide little guidance to selection of the core lessons or lesson presentation. Students come to class without copybooks and pencils and the teacher has none to give them. He or she receives little supervisory support since the supervisors, even if trained, have inadequate travel allowances and the headmaster provides no guidance in instruction. The teacher's salary, youth, and inexperience, combined with the physical condition of the school and classroom and the lack of textbooks and materials, sends a strong message to the parents of his or her students that schooling is not a priority and teachers are not very important. As a result, lack of appropriate direct and indirect monetary support is compounded by lack of community regard and involvement.

As he or she becomes experienced, the teacher does not receive any increment in salary, other than the across-the-board increases mandated for the civil service. If the teacher is able, he or she leaves primary teaching after a few years' service to attend the university training in secondary teaching. If he or she is less able, the teacher will remain in teaching (or more rarely become a headmaster or supervisor). When the teacher retires, he or she will not receive a pension.

This description of the typical incentive system for primary teaching, if rewritten in the form of an advertisement for teaching, would result in applications from only the most selfless or desperate (see Darling-Hammond, 1984). It is important to note, however, that the primary cause of the inadequacies detailed above is not monetary. It stems more from inefficiency in the allocation of resources than from scarcity of resources.

Comparison of the typical incentive system with the model suggests that the typical system is characterized by profound inconsistencies between the goal of the incentive system (enhanced student achievement through improved teacher performance) and the means (recruitment of teachers, training, instructional materials, and supervision), and further, marked incompatibility among the means.

The system emphasizes recruitment incentives at the expense of all other incentives. The individuals recruited have characteristics such that 95 to 99 percent of the educational budget is invested in their salaries (see, for example, IEES, 1988a). To correct this imbalance, it is necessary to review the original rationale for selecting teachers who are secondary (or higher level) graduates and heads of households. More than likely, one of the justifications was that improving the quality of the teachers would result in better teacher performance, and therefore, in enhanced student achievement. In a situation where all else was truly equal (investments in other incentives were adequate), this approach to quality improvement might have a good probability of success. In a system operating under severe resource constraints, however, the improbability of a change in teacher educational attainment affecting either his or her performance or student achievement is dictated by the lack of an enabling instructional support system. The skill levels of secondary graduates and even college graduates generally do not stretch to instructional development and student evaluation.

Available options include lowering the entry qualifications and recruiting more women and individuals who are economically tied to a local area, or training principals in instructional supervision. Either of these options would produce cost savings in salary, which could then be used to increase investment in materials printing and distribution.

(Materials development, which is an extremely costly exercise, is also one for which it is not difficult to elicit donor assistance.)

To the extent that cost savings realized by recruiting from different pools are not sufficient to create a functioning instructional support system, the personnel needs of the ministry itself (central, regional, and district offices), including the supervisory system (which is rendered obsolete in many countries by the lack of travel funds) should be examined. At a minimum, no-show personnel in whatever position should be fired, and excess personnel transferred to teaching. It is not uncommon to find that the resources actually allocated to schools are a relatively small percentage of the Ministry of Education's budget. Large amounts of money are spent on maintenance activities that have no productive role in student achievement (see, for example, IEES, 1988a, Government of Somalia, 1985).

Additional cost savings could be obtained by providing teacher training as an integral part of the secondary curriculum, and therefore obviating the need for lengthy pre-service training and support for expensive faculties and facilities. The budgetary savings realized through reductions in the workforce and less ambitious pre-service schemes would then be available for the redevelopment of instructional materials, where appropriate, and their printing and distribution, and materials-oriented in-service. These changes would result in greater productivity in the production of education and a more effective teacher incentive system.

If a more balanced investment scheme (and thus more adequate incentives) is the necessary condition for goal attainment, the sufficient condition is consistency among the means and between the means and the goal. If these two conditions are met, nonmonetary incentives, such as providing a choice in assignment after a number of years of rural service, reserving places in the university for teachers' children who met the entrance requirements, and recognition of effort, are likely to have benefits at the margin.

The question of why these fairly obvious reforms have not been implemented is discussed in the next section.

THE POLITICAL CONSTRAINTS TO EDUCATIONAL REFORM

Systematic reform of the educational system, including teacher incentives, requires unequivocal consensus on the goal of the system. Goal statements about education typically err on the side of rhetoric and idealism and generally serve as a very poor basis for system design and evaluation (Windham, 1988). Nonetheless, the goal statements tend to focus on students and their cognitive, affective, and physical development. However, just as there is a difference between the syllabus and what is actually taught in schools (called the hidden curriculum), there is an obvious difference between the stated goals of the system and actual patterns of investment. The major unexpressed agenda of the educational system is employment. Evidence for this is found in the size of central, regional, and district staff, the poor match of incumbent qualifications with job descriptions (where such exist), the lack of personnel evaluation, the low incidence of hiring freezes or dismissals for cause, the maintenance of nonfunctioning system components, and the apparent preference for institution building (plants and equipment) rather than capacity building (increasing the system's ability to respond to the needs of schools and teachers).

Full employment is a legitimate goal of government. In developed countries, employment is considered a joint product of the productive sector. When the productive sector is expanding, the goal is attained, and when the sector is contracting, unemployment rises. Governments, through public works, welfare programs, or direct subsidization of industry, become the employer of last resort. In developing countries, where the productive sector is small and welfare systems nascent, government, regardless of ideology, is often the employer of first instance— if not in prestige, certainly in volume. And within government, the Ministry of Education is the largest employer, with schools requiring staffs and administrators spread throughout the nation.

Very little has been written about the constraints faced by ministry officials in making decisions. In most countries, however, a reduction in force is not a decision taken within ministries. Ministers and permanent secretaries rarely have the authority to use personnel cuts as a means of financing system reforms. When and if personnel are retrenched, funds from the salary line in the ministry's budget are simply reduced. Similarly, educational policy makers do not necessarily have a great deal of say about who is recruited and why. Patronage aside, the recruitment of secondary graduates, rather primary graduates, for primary school teaching is probably more likely to result from the political liability attached to having a large surplus of secondary graduates than from an educational rationale.

The rivalry between the employment goals and the system's goals of improved teacher performance and student learning is aggravated by very real resource constraints. Government is left with what seems to be an unacceptable choice between maximizing employment and maximizing student achievement. Although additional resources could reduce the exclusivity of the goals, the result might well be greater inefficiency rather than less.

Studies and the results of studies such as the *Civil Service Study* in Somalia (Government of Somalia, 1984a) suggest that the reform of the educational system (and other sectors) must begin at a higher policy level than the ministry. The cabinet or the legislature alone can alter the incentives and disincentives faced by decision makers in the ministry. To the extent that disincentives for basic reform are replaced by incentives, ministry decision makers will be free to act on the information they have on system strengths and weaknesses, balance investments in educational resources, and alter the incentives and disincentives of their own employees. This is neither a simple task nor an impossible one. It is, however, a necessary one if the goals of improved teacher performance and student learning are to be reached.

REFERENCES

Ashton, P. T., & Webb, R. B. (1986). *Making a difference: Teachers' sense of efficacy and student achievement*. New York: Longman.

Berliner, D. C. (1979). Tempus educare. In P. L. Peterson & H. J. Walberg (Eds.), *Research on teaching* (pp. 120-136). Berkeley, CA: McCutchan.

Berliner, D. C. (1980). Studying instruction in the elementary classroom. In R. Dreeben & J. A. Thomas (Eds.), *The analysis of educational productivity, vol. I: Issues in microanalysis* (pp. 191-122). Cambridge, MA: Ballinger.

Chapman, D. W., & Hutcheson, S. M. (1982). Attrition from teaching careers: A discriminant analysis. *American Educational Research Journal, 19*, 93-105.

Darling-Hammond, L. (1984). *Beyond the Commission Reports: The coming crisis in teaching*. Santa Monica, CA: The Rand Corporation.

Denton, J. J., & Lacina, L. J. (1983). *Quantity of professional education coursework linked with process measures of student teaching*. Paper presented at the annual meeting of the American Educational Research Association, Montreal, Canada.

Dreeben, R. (1970). *The nature of teaching*. Glenview, IL: Scott, Forseman.

Government of Botswana. (1984). *Botswana education and human resources sector assessment* (Report). Gaborone: Ministry of Planning and Economic Affairs.

Government of Liberia. (1988). *Liberia education and human resources sector assessment* (Report). Monrovia: Ministry of Education.

Government of Somalia. (1984a). *Somalia civil service study* (Report). Mogadishu: Ministry of Labor and Sports.

Government of Somalia. (1984b). *Somalia education and human resources sector assessment* (Report). Mogadishu: Ministry of National Planning.

Government of Somalia. (1985). *Enhancement of school quality in Somalia* (Report). Mogadishu: Ministry of Education.

Hatry, H. P., & Greiner, J. M. (1985). *Issues and case studies in teacher incentive plans*. Washington, D.C.: The Urban Institute Press.

Heyneman, S. P., Farrell, J. P., & Sepulveda-Stuardo, M. (1978). *Textbooks and achievement: What we know* (World Bank Staff Working Paper No. 298). Washington, D.C.: The World Bank.

Improving the Efficiency of Education Systems (IEES) Project (1988a). *Preliminary results of the teacher incentive study in the Yemen Arab Republic*. Tallahassee: Florida State University, IEES Educational Efficiency Clearinghouse.

Improving the Efficiency of Education Systems (IEES) Project (1988b). *Somalia country plan.*

Joyce, B., & Weil, M. (1986). *Models of teaching* (3rd ed.). Englewood Cliffs, NJ: Prentice-Hall.

Lortie, D. C. (1975). *Schoolteacher: A sociological study.* Chicago: University of Chicago Press.

The Metropolitan Life survey of the American teacher, 1986: Restructuring the teaching profession. (1986). New York: Metropolitan Life Insurance Company.

Murnane, R. J. (1975). *The impact of school resources on the learning of inner city children.* Cambridge, MA: Ballinger.

Murnane, R. J., & Cohen, D. K. (1986). Merit pay and the evaluation problem: Why most merit pay plans fail and a few survive. *Harvard Educational Review, 56*(1), 1-17.

Rosenholtz, S. J., & Smylie, M. A. (1984). Teacher compensation and career ladders. *The Elementary School Journal, 85*(2), 149-166.

Sepulveda-Stuardo, M. A., & Farrell, J. P. (1983). *The use of textbooks by teachers and students in learning and teaching* (World Bank Staff Working Paper No. 530). Washington, D.C.: The World Bank.

Summers, A. A., & Wolf, B. L. (1975). *Equality of educational opportunity quantified: A production function approach.* Philadelphia: Department of Research, Federal Reserve Building.

Thomas, J. A., & Kemmerer, F. (1983). *Money, time, and learning* (Final Research Report to the National Institute of Education, Contract No. 400-77-0094). Chicago, IL: University of Chicago.

Verspoor, A. M. (1986). Textbooks as instruments for the improvement of the quality of education. (World Bank Discussion Paper, EDT 50).

Verspoor, A. M., & Leno, J. L. (1986). Improving teaching: A key to successful educational change (World Bank Discussion Paper, EDT 50). Washington, D.C.: The World Bank.

Windham, D. M. (1978). Incentive analysis and higher education planning: Alternatives in theory, research, and policy (IIEP Research Report, No. 29). Paris: International Institute for Educational Planning, UNESCO.

Windham, D. M. (1983a, January). *Cost issues in the Liberian Improved Efficiency of Learning (IEL) Project* (Report No. 1). Monrovia, Liberia: Ministry of Education.

Windham, D. M. (1983b, March). *Internal economies in the Liberian Improved Efficiency of Learning (IEL) Project* (Report No. 2). Monrovia, Liberia: Ministry of Education.

Windham, D. M. (1983c, June). *The relative cost-effectiveness of the Liberian Improved Efficiency of Learning (IEL) Project* (Report No. 3). Monrovia, Liberia: Ministry of Education.

Windham, D. M. (1983d, June). *Cost issues in the dissemination of the Liberian Improved Efficiency of Learning (IEL) Project* (Report No. 4). Monrovia, Liberia: Ministry of Education.

Windham, D. M. (1988). *Indicators of educational effectiveness and efficiency.* Tallahassee: Florida State University, Improving the Efficiency of Education Systems Project.

8

Affective Context of Schools as a Potential Indicator of Teacher Receptivity to Instructional Change and Teacher Worklife Quality

Conrad Wesley Snyder, Jr.

In the movie "The Gods Must Be Crazy," a Coca-Cola bottle is discarded unceremoniously from an airplane over the Kalahari Desert. This "new" object from "heaven" changes the lives of a (Botswana) Bushmen family. Although at first the indestructible bottle presents multiple possibilities that appear valuable, eventually its impact is considered too dramatic and problematic for the family. Because the Gods must have made a mistake in offering this intrusive tool, an attempt is made to give it back, to throw the bottle "off the end of the earth." The lessons are well known—change is never as simple or as easily assimilated as it first appears, and there are always trade-offs to the advantages of change.

Modern Botswana is deluged with more than Coke bottles from "developers" of the world. Since the time of David Livingstone, who with Botswana assistant teachers presumed to set up the first Westernized school for Botswana at Kolobeng (about 30 km from the present capital city) in 1847, formal schooling has been sought at considerable personal sacrifice by the populace, hoping no doubt to accrue the perceived and promoted advantages of this form of education. Over the years, many changes have been introduced into the educational system, even altering the program emphasis from the doctrinal inclinations of the London Missionary Society (whom Livingstone represented) to the wider, secular instructional program of today—perhaps also changing the overall system goal from personal spiritual salvation to national economic salvation. Since educational systems are hard-pressed to deliver "salvation" of any kind or quantity, many schemes, some undoubtedly good and some quite clearly bad, have been concocted to lead to "improved quality" of instruction. Despite a voluminous literature of systematic research on innovation and diffusion since the early 1940s, our understanding of the process of adoption and implementation of an intervention, in general and in education in particular, is still rather limited. We do know that few interventions are really adopted by the target group, fewer are implemented as expected, and almost none are incorporated as permanent features of the program.

In the face of this pessimistic scenario, educational development projects still usually target system-wide change in the instructional program. It turns out that education is complex and changing it makes it more so. Most projects, even good ones, flounder on their inability to deal with the complex interactions associated with the changes introduced in the host system. That is, it may be that we have many ways to help a national educational system, but we don't know how to get them in place to have some impact.

This chapter arises out of this kind of situation. Botswana, since national independence in 1966, has expanded its educational system dramatically, growing over 3-fold at the primary level and over 20-fold at the secondary, and has now set its sights on universal access to education through 9 years of instruction (through junior secondary schooling in a 7–2–3 system). The trade-off for expansion is usually deterioration of quality, so Botswana proposes to offset the potentially lower capacity of the wider student population with improvements in the instructional program. To assist in the promotion of ideas and development of the program, two large educational projects, both sponsored by the United States Agency for International Development, are operational in Botswana. The question arises, if at the national level there is a will to change and improve the instructional program, is this will likely to be translated into real changes in the classroom? Both projects offer maintenance support for the expansion, but their raison d'etre is a higher-quality program, which will necessitate changes at the classroom instructional level.

In order to have a sustainable impact, the instructional design must be tailored to the context of implementation. Although "mathematics is mathematics" wherever it is taught, not only must content be adapted to local context to effectively convey abstractions, so too must instructional interventions attend to implicit social and cultural conditions so that instruction has a chance of being effective. We no longer "impose" a curriculum, but rather work with local professionals to adapt or develop an indigenous instructional program. The timeline is much longer, and monitoring progress becomes an important element in the overall design.

This chapter attends to the preconditions that may impact later formative evaluations of particular instructional interventions. The problem is that unless teachers at a target school are receptive to change in their worklife (in particular, the perceived impact on the quality of worklife), the intervention may be "corrupted" or ignored. Formative evaluation information will be more useful if it takes into account these affective preconditions to change. Furthermore, if we can predict (with understanding) the receptivity of a school to a change in its instructional program, we may be able to alter the intervention to accommodate the local affective environment, as well as its cultural and social predilections. This additional information helps us to fine-tune the otherwise general intervention in the school system. And, as indicated, we can make more informed judgments about interventions and their immediate and long-term effectiveness. Good contextual understanding will better help us know what should be "thrown off the end."

AFFECT AND ASSIMILATION RESISTANCE

Interventions in schools can be enacted only if the teachers understand the intervention and are willing participants in the change process. We sometimes forget that educational institutions are employers as well. Teachers are employed to teach and the school is their workplace. Their view of their worklife is therefore a potentially important variable in the change process. Instructional interventions necessarily alter the activities of the classroom and, therefore, seriously impinge upon the worklife of the teacher.

Teachers develop certain means-end cognitive structures to deal with the enactment of teaching. These schema provide psychological balance for the individual's actions and also serve to test new events and information. According to Eckblad (1981a, p. 12), the overall scheme structure of an individual "serves as the perceptual and conceptual context into which the person's experience is assimilated, as a system of intentions and plans for action, and as a system of goals toward which purposive activity is directed."

Interaction with the environment is guided by the individual's scheme structure—specifically through the processes of assimilation and accommodation. In the worklife of a teacher, the events and activities of the classroom are assessed in terms of the individual's intentions and plans. If they are congruent, then the individual experiences psychological equilibrium. If, however, the attempts at assimilation are not matched with or adapted to the environmental inputs, then the schemes must adapt or accommodate these new experiences. The degree to which assimilation fails and accommodation is necessary is referred to as assimilation resistance.

If we can picture, then, a teacher with marginal training and experience working in the Botswana classroom, we can understand that each day the teacher is potentially changing as a result of the instructional activities experienced. There may be considerable assimilation resistance and accommodation taking place in the teacher as well as in the students. Any intervention or change in instructional procedure is cast over these dynamic patterns already present. It therefore seems reasonable to better understand the perceptions of teachers about their worklife so that we can predict their reaction to proposed changes.

The cognitive activities that we employ to cope with the world are related to the judgments we make about our feelings. Affect reflects the assimilation resistance experienced. At very low levels of resistance, the affective report is Boredom. As resistance increases moderately, we report Mastery and Pleasure. At the edge of assimilation, where accommodation is likely but not easily attained, we report Interest and Challenge. But at the high levels of resistance, we are likely to report Stress and Difficulty. The result is a spectrum of affect related directly to cognitive activities and experiences.

In terms of instructional interventions, we can speculate how teachers may be receptive to change on the basis of their affective status. If, at present, they experience Stress, they are unlikely to welcome further change; if Interest, then they may already be challenged and the intervention should be framed to assist in the process of accommodation; if Mastery, then modest changes may improve motivation; and if Bored, then larger changes may be tolerated if attention can be fostered. The spectrum of affect may provide a window to the receptivity to innovation and change.

QUALITY OF WORKLIFE

Quality is a personal evaluation. Although this evaluation may be influenced by physical conditions and circumstances, quality entails feelings, attitudes, and values, and is more than the sum of objective indicators. In the assessment of worklife, quality refers to the evaluation of activities and experiences in carrying out the specific job and its relationship to the general world of work.

An unstated, but implicit goal of educational institutions is to provide an enriched environment that enhances the academic experiences of students and the quality of worklife for the teachers. Changes in the educational system affect the quality of the teaching experience for the teacher. The teacher continues to grow intellectually and, depending upon the changes introduced, that growth may be capitalized by increased motivation or wasted in an empty regimen of activities.

The spectrum of affect should be related to quality assessments. If a teacher is either Bored or Stressed, then the quality of worklife will probably be lower than when the teacher is Interested. This potential relationship means that the monitoring of affect may provide useful information about the quality of teacher worklife and the likely receptivity to change aspects of that worklife. Only with this contextual understanding is the intervention likely to be structured appropriately for adoption and implementation.

EDUCATIONAL QUALITY AND WORKLIFE QUALITY

The relationship between educational quality, usually defined in terms of student academic achievements, and the quality of worklife for teachers is not direct, but it is important for the delineation of the intervention process. Interventions are intended to improve instructional quality and related achievements. This can only happen if the intervention is actually implemented.

Classically, we thought that an intervention must be implemented in some precise form, as per an independent variable in an experimental design. However, education is dynamic and we now understand that although interventions are intended to change contexts they must also change to accommodate the contexts they are changing. We need to better understand the context in the change process so that we can more accurately and appropriately monitor and evolve an effective intervention.

Therefore, although we can anticipate on logical grounds that there is no reason why a change in worklife quality will necessarily affect directly the achievement of students, it is clear that unless an intervention of some kind is possible, there is little likelihood of spontaneous instructional improvement. The analysis of context alerts us to the problems of implementation of an intervention and the form it might take to be more readily accepted.

SCHOOL CONTEXT

Much of the early research on change focused on the adoption of innovation by individuals. However, it is the nature of educational interventions that they are introduced at a school or system-wide level. The particular array of individuals and their sociological patterns may have substantial influence over the personal inclinations of individuals for intervention adoption. Of course, for interventions in the instructional program, when the teacher closes the door there is no audience besides the students to influence implementation. Although organizational behavior is important in influencing the receptivity of an educational system to a system-wide intervention, in this particular case the constructed school assimilation resistance scale links the school to the individual psychology of the potential participant and may be more informative than a more sociological organizational variable.

In this chapter, the selected model of affect is based on individual scheme theory (Eckblad, 1980, 1981a, 1981b).[1] The affective central tendencies of component scores for teachers at particular schools were used to characterize the affective context of the schools. In order to add some assessment of interaction, two additional variables were included: communication and information flow, and control and autonomy. It is expected that the general rating of worklife quality at a school will be nonlinearly related to affect/assimilation resistance (that is, higher quality at medium levels of assimilation resistance), directly related to communication (but possibly negative because increased information flow and interaction for any Botswana school are usually indicative of problems and its consequent reporting), and directly related to the teacher-perceived level of personal control and autonomy in the job.

Two studies are reported that analyze the individual affect structure to establish construct validity for the notion of a *spectrum of affect* reflecting assimilation resistance. Then, the larger first study is analyzed in terms of constructed school variables to examine the relationships of average assimilation resistance, communication, and control component scores with the average quality of worklife for the teachers at each school. The results present some insights and problems for the understanding and facilitation of receptivity to innovation.

ANALYSES OF INDIVIDUAL AFFECT STRUCTURE

Study 1

Background. Questionnaires, comprising 14 affect variables, 6 communication variables, 7 control variables, and 2 ratings of worklife quality, were administered to 147 teachers at 25 junior secondary schools across the country (out of 54 possible schools). Data collection was carried out by 13 Botswana Masters' students enrolled at the Florida State University. The questionnaire was administered as part of a general interview with teachers about the educational program of Botswana.[2]

Rating scales for each of the variables ranged from 0 to 10, anchored as None = 0; Slight Amount = 1 or 2; Fair Amount = 3 or 4; Moderate Amount = 5 or 6; Considerable Amount = 7 or 8; and Great Amount = 9 or 10, and presented as a "ladder" of magnitude for each of the attributes. Worklife quality was rated at the beginning as an "initial feeling" and then again at the end after rating all the other attributes as a "considered assessment." After elimination of incomplete

Table 8.1

Means and Standard Deviations for the Study 1 Sample on the Quality, Affect, Communication, and Control Variables (N = 147)

VARIABLE	MEAN *	STD DEV
Quality of Worklife 1	5.97	2.18
Quality of Worklife 2	6.14	2.08
Satisfaction	5.34	2.51
Happiness	6.24	2.33
Complexity	5.36	2.45
Interest	6.24	2.08
Gratification	6.61	2.32
Structure	5.98	2.19
Challenge	7.07	2.19
Stress	5.31	2.68
Diversity	5.53	2.27
Clarity	7.00	2.22
Arousingness	6.06	2.21
Uncertainty	4.14	2.37
Difficulty	4.50	2.73
Unity	6.71	2.22
Control over Job Content	6.65	2.20
Control over Job Process	6.88	2.14
Control over Others	4.74	3.22
Control over Goals	6.06	2.40
Responsibility	7.61	1.97
Power	4.90	2.44
Autonomy	6.76	1.84
Communication	6.08	2.44
Information Received	5.44	2.51
Information Stored	6.83	2.50
Information Processed	6.91	2.05
Information Generated	5.82	2.55
Information Given	4.73	2.79
Efficacy	7.78	1.66

Note: Scales range from 0 (None) to 10 (Great Amount of).

data, 130 teachers' responses for 24 schools were available for analyses.

Results. The means and standard deviations for the first sample data are presented in Table 8.1. Table 8.2 provides the principal component weights and variance accounted for in the structural analyses of the affect, communication, and control variables. Figure 8.1 illustrates the "curvex" pattern of affect variables in a two-dimemsional principal component space. These results indicate that the "spectrum of affect" model does provide a reasonable description of the pattern of relation-

Table 8.2
Study 1 Sample: Principal Component Analyses of the Affect,
Communication, and Control Variables (N = 147)

VARIABLE	COMPONENT			
	AR I	AR II	CTRL I	COM I
Satisfaction	.661	.012		
Happiness	.687	-.077		
Complexity	.194	.620		
Interest	.820	.198		
Gratification	.765	.049		
Structure	.624	.040		
Challenge	.325	.402		
Stress	-.055	.551		
Diversity	.320	.480		
Clarity	.574	-.080		
Arousingness	.704	-.133		
Uncertainty	-.132	.700		
Difficulty	-.304	.679		
Unity	.560	-.207		
Control over Job Content			.758	
Control over Job Process			.741	
Control over Others			.637	
Control over Goals			.744	
Responsibility			.603	
Power			.441	
Autonomy			.521	
Communication				.583
Information Received				.702
Information Stored				.818
Information Processed				.777
Information Generated				.770
Information Given				.706
Total Variance Accounted For:	44%		42%	53%

Note: AR = Assimilation Resistance; COM = Communication; and CTRL = Control.

ships among affect variables, and that the variables selected to represent communication and control can be combined into single scales respectively.

In the affect results, the array of variables did not "fan" as much as expected (see Figure 8.1). The clustering of variables along the dimensional axes means that these axes can be interpreted (although the interpretation is in terms of variance rather than "latent variables"). Axis I reflects the hedonic tone or pleasantness associated with teaching and accounts for the largest share of variance. Axis II reflects the complexity or difficulty associated with teaching. Component scores for each in-

Figure 8.1
Configuration of Affect Variables (from Study 1) in Two-Dimensional Principal Component Space

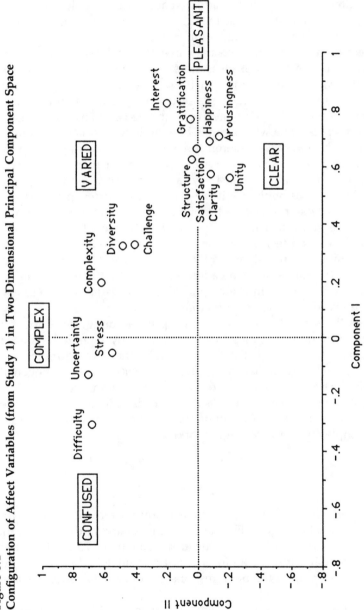

Note: The sectors of the space are marked by boxed descriptors in terms of Eckblad's "spectrum of affect" to provide a frame of reference for the interpretation of the observed structure.

dividual were calculated for each dimension (that is, 2 scores for each teacher). School affect variables were created by averaging the same dimensional component scores across teachers in the school. Therefore a school can be located in the affect space. The variables, Diversity, Challenge, and Interest, provide the spread between the axes to interpret school results in terms of assimilation resistance.

In affect terms, it can be said that, overall, teaching worklife is differentiated more in terms of pleasantness than in terms of complexity of the job. Teachers discriminate their worklife on the basis of hedonic tone more than the structural tasks of teaching. Since assimilation resistance is a function of the objective cognitive complexity of a task or situation, there is not a wide a range of assimilation resistance as might be expected in a task as inherently complex as teaching. Classroom observations in Botswana bear out the fact that teachers rely on expository approaches almost exclusively, and therefore, don't sample the methodological possibilities available in instructional design for teaching conceptual understanding (see Prophet, 1987). There are two implications for receptivity to change: First, any instructional design change introduced in this affect context at any school is likely to dramatically increase complexity and significantly impact on assimilation resistance; and second, the range of assimilation resistance that does exist may be an extremely important indicator (more so than usual) of where even modest interventions may be attempted.

Perhaps these results are not surprising for a young, developing instructional program, and they may underline why seemingly good interventions are often resisted. Although the opportunities and possibilities for instructional change are great (with higher homogeneity present in the system, there are more ways to try to improve instructional quality), the affective climate warns that considerable care must be taken in the introduction of interventions that are likely to increase the perceived complexity of the teaching worklife.

Study 2

Background. The same questionnaire was administered in the following year by one of the original Florida State University students in partial fulfillment of a practicum research course. This time, 73 teachers were interviewed at 10 different junior secondary schools. After elimination of incomplete data, 70 teachers' responses were available for the analyses.

Results. The results are remarkably similar to the first sample results. Table 8.3 presents the means and standard deviations, and Table 8.4 the principal component weights for the structural analyses of affect,

Table 8.3
Means and Standard Deviations for the Study 2 Sample on the Quality,
Affect, Communication, and Control Variables (N = 73)

VARIABLE	MEAN *	STD DEV
Quality of Worklife 1	5.82	2.10
Quality of Worklife 2	5.67	1.87
Satisfaction	4.82	2.21
Happiness	4.92	2.68
Complexity	5.36	2.42
Interest	6.03	2.19
Gratification	5.77	2.38
Structure	5.63	2.06
Challenge	6.37	2.65
Stress	6.05	2.76
Diversity	5.22	2.24
Clarity	6.60	2.37
Arousingness	5.37	2.42
Uncertainty	4.26	2.58
Difficulty	4.44	2.76
Unity	5.63	2.28
Control over Job Content	6.11	2.66
Control over Job Process	6.08	2.53
Control over Others	4.70	2.77
Control over Goals	5.47	2.67
Responsibility	7.48	2.01
Power	5.25	2.28
Autonomy	6.18	1.89
Communication	6.08	2.56
Information Received	4.88	2.30
Information Stored	6.14	2.36
Information Processed	5.92	2.05
Information Generated	5.52	2.55
Information Given	4.83	2.63
Efficacy	7.86	1.78

*Note: Scales range from 0 (None) to 10 (Great Amount of).

communication, and control variables. The pattern of results conforms
to the original interpretation.

CORRELATES OF SCHOOL WORKLIFE QUALITY

As alluded to earlier, from the individual teacher data of Study 1, five
variables were constructed to describe schools: Quality 1, Quality 2,
Assimilation Resistance, Communication, and Control. The last three
scales were related to the quality variables in separate regression equa-

Table 8.4

Study 2 Sample: Principal Component Analyses of the Affect, Communication, and Control Variables (N = 73)

VARIABLE	COMPONENT			
	AR I	AR II	CTRL I	COM I
Satisfaction	.808	-.131		
Happiness	.747	-.101		
Complexity	-.012	.556		
Interest	.622	.244		
Gratification	.756	.028		
Structure	.405	-.098		
Challenge	.420	.643		
Stress	-.477	.588		
Diversity	.174	.723		
Clarity	.321	-.262		
Arousingness	.638	.306		
Uncertainty	-.233	.629		
Difficulty	-.041	.692		
Unity	.174	.019		
Control over Job Content			.808	
Control over Job Process			.776	
Control over Others			.781	
Control over Goals			.761	
Responsibility			.511	
Power			.501	
Autonomy			.401	
Communication				.539
Information Received				.780
Information Stored				.782
Information Processed				.672
Information Generated				.816
Information Given				.765
Total Variance Accounted For:	43%		44%	54%

Note: AR = Assimilation Resistance; COM = Communication; and CTRL = Control.

tions. Based on the projected relationships, the following equation was tested for each quality index:

$$\text{Quality} = \text{Constant} + \text{AR} - \text{AR*AR} - \text{Com} + \text{Ctrl},$$

where AR represents assimilation resistance, AR*AR is the nonlinear portion of this scale as related to quality, Com indicates the level of interaction and information flow for the school, and Ctrl reflects the general level of personal control reported for the school. Table 8.5 summarizes the results.

Two of the constructed school scales related as predicted to the quality

Table 8.5
Regression Equations for Quality of Worklife

Scale	Coefficient	Standardized Coefficient	t (Probability)
Quality 1 = Constant + AR - AR*AR - COM + CTRL			
Constant	3.984	0	.00
Assimilation Resistance (AR)	1.231	2.409	.01
AR*AR	-0.130	-2.421	.01
Communication (COM)	-1.448	-0.792	.00
Control (CTRL)	1.231	0.514	.05
Multiple R = 0.73; N = 24; p < .01			
Quality 2 = Constant + AR - AR*AR - COM + CTRL			
Constant	4.530	0	.00
Assimilation Resistance (AR)	1.051	2.539	.01
AR*AR	-0.118	-2.722	.01
Communication (COM)	-0.598	-0.403	.12
Control (CTRL)	0.787	0.439	.11
Multiple R = 0.69; N = 24; p < .05			

Note: AR = Assimilation Resistance; COM = Communication; and CTRL = Control.

of worklife; the constructed information variable took on a negative sign. Given the difficulties of collecting this field information and the time pressures under which teachers participated, the data were remarkably reliable, demonstrated by the variance accounted for. Assimilation resistance was curvilinearly related to quality, communication was negatively related, and control positively related. The results for the "initial" rating of quality and the "considered" rating of quality reflect the slight general increase in reported quality (note the differences in the constants, which correspond to the mean differences noted in Table 8.1) after teachers considered affect, communication, and control items.

Nevertheless, the combination of variables yielded similar multiple Rs, cross-validating the relationships.

IMPLICATIONS

Minimal Change and Continuing Field Support

The results indicate that assimilation resistance is an important component in the overall quality of teacher worklife. Many consequences for receptivity to change have already been discussed. Schools with low resistance can perhaps tolerate greater changes; schools with high resistance need special assistance to handle the problems currently faced and are unlikely to be receptive to innovations. Unless the affective environment is given its due consideration, good ideas and interventions may falter from teacher neglect and avoidance.

In terms of strategy for innovation diffusion, the affect picture would suggest introduction by minimal change, reminiscent of "Minimum Change Therapy" (see Tyler, 1983). The rationale is that a small (simple) change in a dynamic system will make a large difference later. And, at the time of introduction, the complexity of the innovation will be less difficult to assimilate, also allowing time to accommodate scheme structures to the new context as the system evolves.

The above scenario is unlikely to be advocated by educational development projects. Donors want fast, dramatic results over large domains of the system. If the intervention is to be complex, then, as indicated, the assimilation resistance will be high, particularly for those who are already overwhelmed by their teaching worklife. One hope for effective implementation and diffusion may be to target the intervention on those teachers currently underwhelmed by their situation (as administratively concentrated at particular schools) and offer constant assistance and support as the intervention unfolds.

The role and importance of in-service support is clear in the affect model (although perhaps different from the usual training orientation): to monitor assimilation resistance and assist in accommodation to the new instructional program or approach. To the extent that wider teacher groups (in terms of affect) are involved, greater in-service support will be required. Unfortunately, attention is usually given to the development of the innovation rather than to effective support of its implementation, even if only a small change in the instructional program is intended. Complex changes require extensive and continuing support. As affect changes toward higher levels of assimilation resistance, cognitive capacity is exceeded as well. An effective in-service scheme would tailor the innovation to the individual differences of schools and teachers to "protect" the quality of teacher worklife while striving for a better instructional outcome.

Information Architecture

The negative weight associated with communication and information flow in the quality equation must be interpreted carefully. Communication and Control are significantly correlated (0.54), so their weights are affected by their respective relationships with the quality ratings, which Control dominates. Communication may have a touch of nonlinearity in its relationships with the quality ratings that are emphasized in these equations or be operating as a suppressor variable due to its association with other features of the context that are unrelated to quality. If we include a multiplicative term for Communication in the regression equations for Quality 1 and 2, the multiple Rs increase to 0.77 (p < .01) and 0.83 (p < .01), respectively, indicating an important negative and nonlinear component to the relationship between Communication and Quality of Worklife.

The bivariate relationships of Communication and the quality ratings are positive, and Communication is positively correlated with perceived Efficacy (0.32). Clearly, information is perceived to be important to doing a better job and achieving a higher-quality worklife. However, when Assimilation Resistance and Control are taken into account, the positive role of Communication may be covered—that is, when resistance is lowered, there is understanding, and when personal control is increased, there is consultation.

Schools, of course, are constantly bombarded with information about policy and instructional issues. An innovation increases the information load, and may in fact counter other information related to old activities. The lesson here for innovators may be that a rapid introduction of a new program with masses of preliminary and unsuspected information may be ignored as part of ongoing background noise and crisis management, unless attention is given to "understanding" and "personal control" on the part of the teacher. This implies that information must be marketed to serve a new program well. Otherwise, it is likely that further "information" may lead to premature dismissal or avoidance of the innovation.

This is another argument for strong field support. Any innovation must be accompanied by extensive descriptive and expository information. There are any number of communication potholes in a school system that will bury a new initiative. Field support is essential to link the innovators with the implementors and ensure that teachers are involved and effectively accommodating to the change.

Teacher Individuality

One of the problems in instructional intervention is that it potentially shifts the control over instruction from the teacher to those intervening. In the hierarchical organizational structure of a Ministry of Education, for example, changes are "handed-down" from central agencies in charge of program development. The teachers are frequently viewed as passive recipients of this wisdom. The affect model shifts perspective so that teacher affects and cognitions become central to diffusion considerations.

In these results, greater personal control (over goals, content, processes, and others), communication, and responsibility are associated with higher quality of teacher worklife. The teacher may prefer a central role in the change process, to be part of the development, not merely as a recipient but as an active participant. The diffusion strategy is therefore coupled with the development strategy. They are operationalized within a field-oriented research and development approach to changes in instructional design (e.g., Snyder & Nagel, 1988) and they are dependent upon a comprehensive formative evaluation subsystem (e.g., Chapman & Windham, 1986). The approach is a little like painting in oil:

In oil painting every new spot of pigment laid on the canvas creates some kind of pattern that provides a continuing source of new ideas to the painter. The painting process is a process of cyclical interaction between the painter and the canvas, while the gradually changing pattern suggests new goals. (Simon, 1981, p. 187)

Naturally, there are boundaries to this approach delineated by the definitional features and strategies of the intervention, but this is the essence of development—to create effectively. And, as suggested by the present research, this means involving the teachers (and schools) in the creation of the innovation so that they have some stake and control in the development. Responsibility and control may be an important part of an enriched work experience for the teacher, which in turn may influence effective diffusion of the initiative intended to improve academic outcomes.

Map of School Affect

The survey of affect enables us to conceptually code the map of schools in terms of assimilation resistance. Selection of schools for interventions can then be made with an understanding of the general affect climate of teachers at the schools and the awareness of possible intrusions on the quality of worklife for those teachers. Similar codes can be included for communication and control summaries of schools as well. Although this chapter related the research to receptivity to change, other important topics can also be addressed. In current research in Botswana, the Junior Secondary Education Improvement Project is looking at relationships between affect climate for the worklife and the classroom (with the students) with structural and behavioral aspects of classroom activities. Over 1,400 classrooms have now been surveyed and observed across the country. There is no doubt that affect is an important variable in the education situation, but we know so little about it. The prospects look interesting—that is, they lie at the edge of our assimilation resistance and promise further understanding.

NOTES

1. More detailed and technical assessment of Eckblad's work can be found in Snyder (1988) and Kroonenberg and Snyder (in press).
2. Appreciation is expressed to the Florida State University (FSU) Botswana students for their role in the collection of these data. Supervision was carried out by the author, C. Howard Williams of FSU, and Felicity Leburu of the Botswana Ministry of Education. Particular thanks is offered to Modise Maphanyane, who participated in the first study and later collected the second sample on his own.

REFERENCES

Chapman, D. W., & Windham, D. M. (1986). *The evaluation of efficiency in educational development activities*. Tallahassee: Florida State University, Improving the Efficiency of Educational Systems Project.

Eckblad, G. (1980). The curvex: Simple order structure revealed in ratings of complexity, interestingness, and pleasantness. *Scandinavian Journal of Psychology, 21*, 1–16.

Eckblad, G. (1981a). Assimilation resistance and affective responses in problem solving. *Scandinavian Journal of Psychology, 22*, 1–16.

Eckblad, G. (1981b). *Scheme theory: A conceptual framework for cognitive-motivational processes*. London: Academic Press.

Kroonenberg, P. M., & Snyder, C. W., Jr. (In Press). Individual differences in assimilation resistance and affective responses in problem solving. *Multivariate Behavioral Research*.

Prophet, R. B. (1987, September). Rhetoric and reality in science curriculum development in Botswana. Paper presented at the British Education Research Association Meeting, Manchester, UK.

Simon, H. A. (1981). *The sciences of the artificial*. Cambridge, MA: The MIT Press.

Snyder, C. W., Jr. (1988). Multimode factor analysis. In J. R. Nesselroade &

R. B. Cattell (Eds.), *Handbook of multivariate experimental psychology* (pp. 289-316) (2nd ed.). New York: Plenum.

Snyder, C. W., Jr., & Nagel, J. (1988). *Indicators of quality in Botswana primary education*. Tallahassee, FL: Learning Systems Institute.

Tyler, L. E. (1983). *Thinking creatively*. San Francisco, CA: Jossey-Bass.

9

Evaluating Instructional Improvement Programs

Carol A. Carrier

INTRODUCTION

This chapter will focus on the process of conducting evaluations of instructional programs within developing countries. Much as been written about how to conceptualize, conduct, and report evaluation studies of new programs, but the context for these studies typically has been developed countries where conditions differ markedly from those in the Third World. Published and unpublished reports of Third World country evaluations are less plentiful and rarely include in-depth discussions of the practical problems associated with conducting the evaluation. Further, more general papers on the topics of conducting program evaluation in developing countries do not necessarily address the specific needs of instructional program evaluation (Ross, 1984; Chapman & Boothroyd, 1988). This chapter, then, will first review the process of instructional program evaluation and set forth a set of five factors that impact the conduct of such evaluations in developing countries. Next, a framework of instructional program components is proposed, each of which must be systematically addressed in order for the evaluation to yield comprehensive information to decision makers. A discussion of the challenges inherent in each of these components is presented.

Evaluation Within an Instructional Systems Design Context

Instructional systems design (ISD) models prescribe ongoing evaluation to provide feedback to program designers at all phases of design and development (Dick & Carey, 1985; Gagne, Briggs, & Wager, 1988). In the needs assessment phase, constituents are encouraged to define the parameters of the perceived problem to aid designers who must determine whether instruction, versus the application of better incentives or improved management, offer the most appropriate solution. Consensus-generating tools, such as Delphi methods or the normative group technique (NGT) may be used by program designers to assist in the validation of a set of preliminary problem statements. Once a content/ task analysis has been performed on the topic of interest, subject-matter experts review it for accuracy and completeness. When a prototype of the instructional program has been developed, a series of one-to-one or small-group tryouts involving representatives of the intended target population are conducted to detect both simple and more substantive errors in the format and content of the program. This sequence of tryouts leads to revisions that may be as minor as clarifying directions to students or as major as eliminating aspects of the program. The next stage, the field test, monitors the new or revised program as it is implemented for the first time in the intended setting. Data collected in the field test informs decisions about how best to administer the program, use instructional materials, train teachers, and assess student learning. The formal evaluation of new instructional programs often ends with a field test. Program implementors who perceive they have sufficient information about a new program may be unwilling or unable to invest further resources in evaluation.

When decision makers have the opportunity to select which program to adopt from among several alternatives, evaluation designs can be implemented to provide comparative data. Summative evaluation describes the processes of determining the overall worth of a product or program, implying comparisons between or among programs across a variety of criteria including cost, efficiency, achievement, and appeal. Based on the outcomes of such analyses, decision makers can choose to accept, modify, or reject a program.

But this range of options is rarely practical for decision makers in developing countries. Host governments and/or other groups, most notably donors, make heavy up-front investments in experimental programs prior to any data collection: teachers are trained, materials produced, and contracts with vendors negotiated. Because such large-scale commitments precede the analysis of the actual outputs of the program, a decision to accept or reject a program based on data from an evaluation often is not a realistic one. At best, decision makers may seek data as a means of detecting modifications that are needed to strengthen components of the new program or as fuel to improve public relations. Ambiguity surrounding the *use* of evaluation data is but one of many factors that complicate evaluation work in developing countries.

FACTORS THAT CONSTRAIN EVALUATORS IN DEVELOPING COUNTRIES

While ISD models can provide guidance to evaluators working in developing countries, at least five factors make strict adherence to principles from these models difficult. First, the mere presence of the program is confounded with the value of individual program components. A case in point is the role of instructional materials. Because schools characteristically can supply instructional materials to so few classrooms, the sheer presence of adequate material in experimental program classrooms, irrespective of how meaningfully such materials present content or how effectively they are sequenced into an overall instructional program plan, improves the classroom environment. For example a new reading program may be the first systematically designed approach to the teaching of reading ever offered within a nation's schools. In the conventional classroom, no consistent approach to teaching reading may exist, within even a single school. Comparative analyses may demonstrate higher achievement for the experimental reading program classrooms, but the superiority is difficult to interpret. The quantity of the input (e.g., students now have workbooks) may be a more powerful factor than the quality of the instructional design used in the reading program. As Fuller (1986) concludes, simple material inputs such as textbooks have strong effects on school achievement in developing countries.

The imbalance of power among the multiple stakeholders of a program is a second factor. In developing countries, ministry personnel hold greater power than either teachers or parents. Ministries control resources and wield political clout. Uneducated parents of low economic status are not equipped to critique the programs their children attend nor are they inclined to communicate their concerns to persons in key positions. The isolationism of rural communities further removes many parents from influencing decisions made in the cities. Teachers fare no better. In much of Africa, for example, teachers have less than a high school education, are not organized to lobby for their views, and are unaccustomed to involvement in matters of educational policy formation. These conditions dictate that only a small subset of eligible stakeholders are likely to influence the selection of criteria, indicators, and standards for the evaluation.

Related to the problem of the imbalance of power among stakeholder groups is a third factor, the need to accommodate the interests of stakeholders with different priorities and agendas, working within the same subsector. These stakeholders may be jointly sponsoring a particular program or sponsoring different instructional programs within the same subsector. Well-meaning donor agencies may work at cross purposes within the same subsector. A glaring example of this problem was seen in Liberia with two projects, the Improved Efficiency of Education (IEL) program sponsored by the U.S. Agency for International Development (USAID), and the World Bank Textbook Project. The goal of both donors was to improve primary education, but each chose a different method. The USAID advocated the use of highly structured, programmed instruction-like materials that required the teacher to use a group drill and practice format. The World Bank project, also targeted at the primary level, supported the use of the textbook as the primary focus of instruction. When it became clear to many that the two programs were on a collision course, efforts were made to remedy the situation. In 1985, a study was conducted to determine the feasibility of integrating the two approaches into a single primary curriculum (Government of Liberia, 1986). Based on results of this study a third approach, now labeled the Liberia Primary Education Program, was initiated.

For the evaluator, multiple program donors can mean that extra resources are expended to arrive at a plan that is acceptable. Agencies with different priorities may request different types of data. Governments, needing the resources and eager to enjoy the good will of all donors, are motivated to ensure that each one has its data needs met. Skillful negotiation may be essential to ensuring that parties with competing agendas are accommodated in the evaluation design.

A fourth factor that complicates evaluation plans within developing countries is that centralized ministries of education are willing to promote the national implementation of new programs without empirical evidence of the value of those programs. In Liberia, for example, the Primary Education Project is scheduled to be implemented in all public primary schools within the next 5 years, but no systematic assessment of student achievement has been undertaken in schools that have by now used the current version of the program for 1 to 2 years. Assessment of student achievement was carried out on an earlier version of the program, then known as the Improved Efficiency of Learning. When evaluators report negligible student achievement differences between new and traditional programs or point out flaws in aspects of the new program, their findings might be discredited or not widely disseminated. The primary function that an evaluation can serve under these conditions is to alert program administrators to problems to be attended to as additional schools join the project.

A fifth factor that makes evaluative work difficult is that the actual data collection is often delegated to individuals who have little training or experience. On donor-funded projects, the evaluation design described in the project proposal may be implemented on a day-to-day basis by individuals unfamiliar with the rigors of data collection, recording, and analysis. In schools, teachers or principals may be asked to record attendance, administer student achievement tests, or keep records of student progress on instructional tasks. If the teachers or principals believe their performance will be judged in terms of student achievement, they may alter the data to reflect more positively on their own performance. When school fees are linked to student enrollment, schools and countries may under-report enrollments in order to keep a portion of the fees at the school level (Government of Liberia, 1988).

Using external personnel does not eliminate data collection problems. When instructional supervisors or other personnel external to the school are used to collect data, the danger of missing data due to inaccessibility of the school during poor weather, lack of vehicles or gasoline, or simple negligence, exists. Because telephones and other methods of communication, such as mail service, are unreliable in developing countries, it is difficult to monitor how effectively data collectors are doing their job.

The quality of data collection will be affected by the number of people involved and their training. Ross (1984) addresses the trade-offs inherent in the decision to use a small or large number of data collection personnel. Training a small number of "enumerators" to collect all of the data offers the benefit of more highly qualified recorders, but in turn, slows the data collection process. Further, when using a small number of observers, any biases that each holds will carry more weight in the overall data set. Using larger numbers of enumerators will speed up the data collection process but perhaps make it less reliable because the individuals are less well trained.

Training of data collection personnel for instructional program evaluation can become more problematic when the data needed include observations of teachers, students, or classroom interactions. The use of interactional schemes such as Flanders, Werner, Elder, Newman, & Lai's (1974), Kouin's (1970), or Goldhammer's (1969) requires a highly trained observer who is able to discriminate subtle changes in teacher or student actions and communications. Training methods for these observers involve various forms of practice, often including videotapes used to simulate classroom activity. Trainees receive feedback from an expert instructor on their performance so that they can refine their skills. While this methodology can be used in developing countries, the expert instructors to deliver the training may need to be imported. Also, the pool of qualified individuals who can be trained for this type of observational task may be small. These constraints can discourage evaluators from including observational data in their plan.

FRAMEWORK OF CRITICAL INSTRUCTIONAL COMPONENTS IN EVALUATION DESIGNS

The factors discussed above suggest that instructional evaluators in Third World countries have extraordinary demands placed upon them.

They must be responsive to a diverse group of constituents representing multiple countries and agencies. They must provide information to assist in national-scale implementation even as such implementation occurs simultaneous to the evaluation itself. They must find ways to prepare local nationals with little experience to assist in data collection. In addition to these special constraints, evaluators must attend to the conventional components of the instructional process, including context, learners, treatments, subject matter, outcomes, and teachers, as shown in Figure 9.1. A brief description of each of these components is provided here and elaborated in the sections that follow:

- Political, economic, cultural, and social context—the context for the new program is an environment shaped by a variety of political, social, cultural and economic conditions

- Treatments, including methods and media—the program's delivery systems, including its methods, approaches, and media, are a major focus of most evaluations

- Outcomes—traditional outcomes for instructional programs include achievement, efficiency, and appeal. Within developing countries, other types of outcomes are significant as well, such as the impact on the local community.

- Learners and their characteristics—the students within the instructional program embody a range of ability and personality characteristics that affect their response to instructional variables

- Teacher and principals—these individuals bear the burden of implementing new programs within their schools and classrooms. Sensitivity to their general characteristics and their special needs in implementing an innovation must be considered.

- Subject matter—the content of the educational program that students are to master

Political, Economic, Cultural, and Social Context

The centralized nature of the Ministry of Education in most Third World countries amplifies the role that political factors play. Ministries become heavily invested in new programs. If ministry personnel help to both define the indicators of program success and participate in the data collection, there is greater likelihood that the statistical analysis of data will support their interests (Sjoberg, 1975). A minister and his or her staff who have been outspoken advocates for a new and visible instructional program that draws heavily upon resources may face serious repercussions if that program does not succeed.

The political climate is likely to determine whether evaluation results impact change. Cousins and Leithwood (1986), in a review of 65 studies focusing on evaluation utilization, found 10 studies that included some

Figure 9.1
Framework of Critical Instructional Components on Evaluation Design

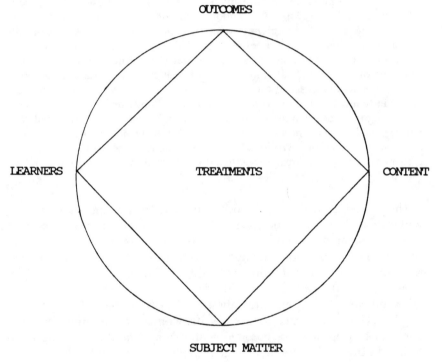

Political, Economic, Cultural, and Social Context

indicator of political climate. All of them showed relationships between these political indicators and evaluation use. For example, there was diminished use of results if they were perceived as threatening, if key people left the organization, or if staff felt "their hands were tied." Interagency rivalry, internal debates, and budget squabbles also reduced the use of findings.

Social or cultural conditions also influence the position that schools occupy in the society of a developing country. Below, Fuller (1987) summarizes the types of influence that operate:

Beyond their applied importance, developing countries present theoretically interesting conditions. First, the school institution often operates within communities where any commitment to written literacy or numeracy is a historically recent event. Therefore, a school of even modest quality may significantly influence academic achievement. Second, social class structures in developing countries often are less differentiated than in highly industrialized societies. Advantages rooted in social class and related parenting practices may be more or less influential within the Third World. In fact, family practices related to the child's cognitive development may be less strongly associated with social class within developing countries. Third, given the low level of material resources available in many Third World schools, the influence of social practices within classrooms may play a greater role than do material inputs, as appears to be the case in the U.S. (p. 256)

The process by which change occurs in a society, and more specifically, within schools within a society, must be understood in order to interpret the meaning of evaluation data. A variety of models of curricular change describe its progression in stages, variously labeled initiation, implementation, and incorporation by Giacquinta (1973); mobilization, implementation, and institutionalization by Berman (1981); or assessment, adoption, initiation, implementation, and institutionalization by Hord and Hall (1986). The early stages are characterized by defining the problem and conceptualizing possible solutions and finally selecting a solution. In the implementation stage the solution is put into place. When the solution is no longer considered new, incorporation has occurred (Giacquinta, 1973). Once incorporation has taken place, continuation of the new curriculum will depend on a variety of school and community context factors, including principal support, attitudes of the community, staff turnover, and student enrollment patterns. Incorporation and continuation, the later stages in curriculum change, are infrequently examined in Third World countries. Instead, evaluations take place at the initiation stage where materials are plentiful, teachers are newly trained, and ministry personnel are enthusiastic. Donor funding may be frontloaded so that there is less support available once a project is incorporated within the system.

Economic instability must also be reckoned with as a hindrance in evaluating programs. To illustrate, teachers in Liberia had salary payment delays of 2 to 3 months at a stretch and then were often forced to travel to the capital city to collect their paychecks once they were issued. Such disruptions not only affect the quality of work that goes on but teachers' attitudes toward their work in general and their level of participation in new programs as well.

Treatments, Including Methods and Media

The focus of most educational program evaluations is the instructional treatment. This term, while often ill-defined, usually refers to that global set of instructional objectives, materials, methods, and media that constitute the "new program." In some instances the treatment is a set of instructional materials, in other cases, an entirely new teaching approach including new materials, teaching behaviors, or organizational configurations for the classroom.

Special concerns that evaluators face when planning an evaluation of instructional treatments in a developing country are the difficulty of ensuring standard administration of the treatment, the challenging of societal or community norms, the ethics of treatment assignment, and the confounding of program effects. Conditions make it difficult to ensure that the treatments are standardized across sites chosen for the study. A major reason is the lack of adequate communications. Local communities and schools have few telephones and fewer still that work reliably. Mail service is unreliable, especially in the rainy season. The remoteness of some locations makes them inaccessible to travel during some parts of the year. Instructional supervisors who are charged with traveling from site to site monitoring the implementation may be unable to visit their assigned sites because of poor weather conditions or lack of transportation. District officers in Liberia, for example, had no fuel for their vehicles, so consequently many had not visited schools in months. The upshot of conditions such as these is that an "experimental" site in one part of one country may implement methods and materials quite differently from another site within the same country! As uniformity in implementation decreases it becomes increasingly difficult to verify which attributes of the experimental program account for any strengths or weaknesses that may be found overall. New instructional treatments may challenge school or community norms and thus pose a threat to the status quo. Schools, and individual teachers within schools, develop ways of conducting their business that over time become quite entrenched. An illustration of the potency of these differences was noted by Snyder and Nagel (1986) in their chronicling of the failures of some of the World Bank education projects. They pointed out that approaches that deviate from "traditional" education, such as the substitution of other materials for textbooks, were viewed suspiciously by community people for whom textbooks are important symbols of learning.

New programs may also disrupt expectations about patterns of work and school attendance. In Liberia, for example, there is high absenteeism among both teachers and students. Because most teachers work at a second job such as farming or marketing, they often leave school early or simply fail to show up at all. Parents may need their children to help out on farms or to care for younger siblings, causing them to miss school. If a new instructional program involves more accountability on the part of teachers or students and their parents it will take time to determine how the participants respond to the new expectations. Longitudinal data collection will be more reasonable than short-term collection if one goal is to see how teachers will adjust to these new expectations.

If the evaluation requires comparison between an experimental and traditional program, the evaluator must grapple with the ethics of subjecting some students to an inferior set of conditions for a period of time extensive enough to make reliable treatment comparisons. New programs carry with them teacher and student materials, training programs for teachers and administrators, and other amenities for the classroom that the "control" or traditional classroom does not have. Though legitimate as a design, many students and parents of students will feel deprived when they learn that other children attend school in a more enriched environment.

The complex array of components involved in many instructional treatments reduces the probability that evaluators will be able to describe the individual contributions of each one. A new program may include, for example, individualized material for students, a new testing system, a student progress management system, teacher and administrator training, and parent information sessions. To assess the individual impact of any of these elements requires a complex multivariate design that would parse out individual contributions to program success or failure.

Outcomes

Traditionally, program evaluators in developing countries have been more effective in assessing the quality of inputs than outputs, perhaps because inputs are less controversial. The number of textbooks and desks can be counted. Teachers can report the amount of training they have received. The socioeconomic level of students can be assessed.

Assessing output from instructional programs is more difficult for several reasons. The first is that stakeholders may not agree on the criteria for success. Donor project staff, responsible for the design of the program, naturally are interested in how well the program achieves its objectives. Do students master math skills? Are teachers able to manage classrooms more effectively? Does a new technology encourage more time on task? Their criteria are likely to reflect traditional outcomes such as achievement, efficiency, and appeal.

Host country representatives may assess success differently. In politized environments, job security is tenuous. One's position may depend on perceptions of program success or failure. The ultimate criterion may be the image of success, not the reality. Given this orientation, programs that appear to be popular, visible, and in demand are more beneficial to Ministry of Education staff than those that produce academic progress but with little fanfare.

Teachers and parents may share similar implicit priorities. Conceived notions of what schooling should look like are the gauges by which new programs are measured. If a teacher's image of the ideal classroom is a set of passive faces responding only when called upon, programs that detract from this scenario are not to be trusted. Different definitions of success, it appears, plague the implementation of evaluation designs.

Should all groups come to agree that student performance is a criterion of importance, they may disagree about appropriate indicators and standards of performance. It is easy to imagine that to some achievement means gain scores on a post-test of program content while to others it means that students attend school more regularly and are thus *exposed* to more instruction. Worthen and Sanders (1987) suggest that the following questions help evaluators decide which of the multiple stakeholders' questions should be addressed:

1. Who would use the information?
2. Would an answer to the question reduce present uncertainty or provide information not now readily available?
3. Would the answer to the question yield important information?
4. Is this question merely of passing interest to someone, or does it focus on critical dimensions of continued interest?
5. Would the scope or comprehensiveness of the evaluation be seriously limited if this question were dropped?
6. Would the answer to the question have an impact on the course of events?
7. Is it feasible to answer this question given available financial and human resources? (pp. 221–222)

Modified, these questions can be raised relative to student achievement in deciding which data to collect and which approaches to use. For example, a modification of Question 1 might read: Who would use this type of information about student achievement? Who wants to know it? Who would it upset if this type of achievement data was not available?

Another reason that outcomes may be difficult to assess is more practical in nature. It is inconvenient and expensive to gather the appropriate data. In assessing achievement, for example, baseline data on students must be collected. Such data are rarely available from school records so evaluators must initiate the process. Tests must be identified or developed and made available for administration at the outset of the evaluation. If tests are to be created, conventional test development procedures should be followed to ensure the appropriateness, reliability, and validity of the instruments. Test administration also can be difficult. Students, often novice test takers, need support to understand what it asked of them. Teachers and other school personnel may be unable to provide this support, which requires, then, that other trained personnel be available to work with students. Crowded classrooms encourage cheating, and high absenteeism rates may mean that many students will not be present on assigned testing days.

When these constraints are accommodated, evaluators are not yet out of the woods. Host country participants may sabotage the data collection process in order to promote a more positive image of student performance. The probability of data tampering increases as the perceived incentives/disincentives for student achievement increase or decrease.

Other chapters in the book address efficiency as a criterion (see Fuller, Chapter 2; Windham, Chapter 3) so it will only be touched upon here. Simplistically the issue is whether the program delivers the product at a cost that is acceptable. As has been argued in many other places, there has been little attempt to do cost comparisons of new instructional programs with existing ones because the "conventional" programs do not represent a conceptual or consensual alternative. There is simply no race when one competitor is severely handicapped!

Indices of efficiency should be addressed only once the implementation has been allowed to "take" within the classroom. Teachers and students need time to adjust to new expectations and behaviors. Mayo (see Chapter 14) reports that many instructional radio programs failed over time because once the novelty had worn off teachers because disillusioned with the difficulties of working around this new medium. First-year data may have looked quite different from second- or fifth-year data.

A longitudinal look at the implementation of new curricula is an important evaluation consideration. Monitoring the incorporation and continuance cycles is no way to enrich knowledge of program outcomes. Several other outcomes to be considered include the quality of teacher, supervisor, and administrator training, the efficiency of the distribution and replacement systems for program materials, and the ease of record keeping.

Incorporation and continuance. Installing new curricula does not necessarily lead to different instructional outcomes, a painful observation made by students of the massive curriculum reforms in the United States in the 1960s (Ornstein, 1982). Studies of incorporation suggest that innovations must go through a series of passages and cycles in order to become routinized within the system (Yin, 1979). Passages reflect significant changes in organizational structure that bring about increased support for the innovation. Cycles are organizational events that occur repeatedly during the lifetime of an organization and lead to a questioning of the innovation. The more cycles an innovation survives, the more likely it is to continue (Berman & McLaughlin, 1976; Rosenblum & Louis, 1981). Instructional program evaluations must be sensitive to the nature of these passages and cycles to avoid overinterpreting preliminary data that may be unstable. What occurs in the first year of a program may differ dramatically from that same program in its fifth year of existence.

Quality of teacher training. Innovations in developing countries have attempted to reduce the need for teacher content expertise because of the large numbers of underprepared teachers. Despite this trend, teachers continue to play an important role in the delivery of new programs to students. Noncompliance with the requirements of a new program on the part of the teacher, be it deliberate or unintentional, can undermine the most carefully defined program. Evaluators should examine the length, type, and quality of training provided to teachers who are to implement a new program. Matching of skills taught in the training with classroom practice is an indicator of training effectiveness. Self-reports by teachers of their compliance are unsatisfactory proxies for actual classroom observation. Fuller (see Chapter 2) reports that ethnographic studies of classrooms in developing countries are only beginning to appear.

Quality of supervisor and administrator training. Building principals and instructional supervisors play influential roles in instructional innovations, and their involvement should be assessed in the program evaluation. The responsibility of program implementation and reporting often falls to these individuals because they are the main contacts with the Ministry of Education personnel. Without their support, teachers may not receive program materials or implement them as intended. Monitoring the training they receive, as well as the impact of this training, will inform program designers about the quality of the implementation.

Efficiency of distribution and replacement systems. Distribution of educational materials in developing countries is a chronic problem. The lack of vehicles and/or fuel is one cause. Vehicles wear out and are not replaced, fail to be repaired, or have no gas. Even prior to distribution, the production system itself may break down or be inadequate to fulfill the production schedule. The evaluation of a program should include an examination of how well these systems work so that existing and potential problems can be recognized or anticipated.

Ease of record keeping. The capacity to keep accurate and up-to-date records on the instructional program is another element that the evaluation design should consider. This information should be transportable to the Ministry of Education or other central office. Summarizing and reporting of program data should be done on a regular basis so that this information is accessible for a variety of purposes.

The nature of outcomes in an instructional program varies by the needs and interests of stakeholders, the number and types of roles affected by the program, and the stage of the program at the time of the evaluation. With the diversity of stakeholders usually present in developing country programs, agreement on program outcomes may be difficult to achieve.

Learners and Their Characteristics

Studies of factors that affect school achievement in developing countries have included inputs of students' age, gender, nutritional status, and parents' social class. Fuller (see Chapter 2) observes that rarely have such studies examined student ability, prior knowledge, or level of cognitive development.

In developed countries there is growing evidence that instructional content, and the treatments that deliver it, are received and processed differently by different students. In some instances these differences are quantitative; young girls, for example, generally perform better on writing tasks. At other times the manner of attacking a task differs qualitatively; children with strong spatial orientation skills interpret verbal task directions more visually than other children.

New programs within developing countries are designed with the goal of producing a single best method that will be effective for a broad spectrum of students. But growing literature on the impact of individual differences on learning from instruction suggests that evaluators might begin to consider how instructional programs fare with students of different abilities, backgrounds, and learning or cognitive styles (Tobias, 1988). Careful selection of individual difference data can assist decisions makers in at least three ways. First, information documention how different students respond to the program as a whole, as well as to individual components, can lead to modifications or adaptations of the program for defined subgroups of students. Second, scores on individual difference measures can be used as predictor variables in the analysis of student achievement scores to provide more precise interpretations of program effects. Third, beyond rendering information about specific instructional programs, the collection of individual difference data as part of the evaluation design will enhance knowledge about the nature of the school population. Sorely lacking in most developing countries is student data that go beyond simple demographic descriptions. Four categories of student differences, (1) ability and prior knowledge, (2) cognitive styles, (3) gender, and (4) attribution of success and failure, are suggested as potentially relevant to instructional programs.

Ability and prior knowledge. Two powerful predictors of academic achievement are general ability and prior knowledge (Cronbach & Snow, 1977; Tobias, 1988). These characteristics have been shown to affect how long students take to master subject matter, the degree of support they need from a teacher, and their willingness to persist at a task. Acquiring general ability data allows the evaluator to determine the effects of the program on students with different ability levels. This could lead to prescriptions for modifications in the instruction to benefit a range of abilities. For example, lower-ability students may need more practice opportunity to master concepts or materials written at a lower reading level. Setting expectations about progress levels for students of differing ability levels would also result from these analyses.

The lack of standardized achievement or ability measures normed on primary students within developing countries prevents a convenient assessment of these characteristics. Formal assessment often does not occur until students have left the primary school. Evaluators may be confined to the use of instruments created in developed countries and normed on children who are not representative of those in the country of interest.

At the secondary level, the picture is somewhat more optimistic. In West Africa, for example, the West African Examination Council has created examinations for ninth- and twelfth-grade completers that assess mastery of content in the basic subject matter areas. Subscores on these exams could be useful in profiling the entry characteristics of students in new instructional programs that emphasize specific subject matter.

Gender. The problem of educational equity for the sexes plagues all developing countries. Fewer girls than boys begin school and a higher percentage of them drop out. There are both economic and cultural reasons for this discrepancy. Further, there is evidence of differential achievement between boys and girls in the same class—possibly due to developmental differences, but possibly due to subtle differences in the way teachers treat boys and girls in the classroom (Boothroyd & Chapman, 1987).

Cognitive styles. Another characteristic that has been shown to be influential in students' perceptions of instruction and their academic performance is cognitive style, generally defined as an individual's characteristic way of perceiving, processing, storing, and retrieving information. Two dimensions that are characteristic of many cognitive style instruments are the degree to which they assess a student's proclivities for (1) abstract over concrete thinking, and (2) action over reflection (Kolb, 1979). Cognitive styles appear to influence many aspects of performance in instruction. Students whose style requires highly structured, sequential processing will perform optimally when a task is broken down into small subtasks that can be accomplished in short periods of time. Those with a more reflective style are optimally productive when instructional conditions allow them a great deal of autonomy, when independent investigation is encouraged, and when self-imposed task definitions are acceptable. An example of the power of styles can be seen in considering one familiar instructional technique, small-group work. Highly action-oriented students are impatient with small-group work because they perceive it to be inefficient and slow moving. Alternatively, reflective students may need the long processing time fostered by discussions in a group setting to convince themselves that all options have been explored. Although cognitive learning styles have not been studied as extensively in developing countries, cross-cultural research by Witkin and Goodenough (1981) on field independence styles demonstrates their universality.

Attribution of success/failure. Students attribute their success or failure on academic tasks to different sources. Attribution theory (Weiner, 1983; Kukla, 1978) posits that the degree to which students ascribe the causes of their own past success or failure in school to ability, effort, task difficulty, or luck will differentially predict what kinds of subsequent choice and performance behaviors they are likely to exhibit. Attributions of success/failure to task difficulty and luck represent external sources. Internal sources are ability and effort.

Williams (1988) argues that attribution variables exist in a reciprocal relationship with performance. Attributions, by definition, reflect personal interpretations of successful or unsuccessful performance. But a change in attribution can often improve performance, causing, in turn, a consequential modification of attributions. There is therefore a circularity of events: (1) individual attributions influence choices of tasks; (2) task characteristics (e.g., difficulty) influence success or failure; and (3) success or failure will be personally interpreted by the student, thereby updating the individual's momentary attributional judgments. Cultural context may also affect an individual's attributional perspective. A program that requires a disciplined, self-directed student may fail if students perceive that external sources, rather than their own efforts, will account for success or failure. Assessment of attributional characteristics could explain student response to program structure or components.

This cursory summary of selected learner characteristics emphasizes the complexity of attempting to interpret the impact of an instructional program on students. In developed countries such analyses have led many to conclude that forms of individualized or adaptive instruction provide the optional solution to diversity.

Unfortunately, evaluators often must compromise on the types and quantity of learner characteristic data captured within a program evaluation. Reading level may be assumed when it should be assessed. Indicators of general ability or achievement may be unavailable. Teacher perceptions may substitute for a more reliable assessment of student learning style.

Evaluators in developing countries typically have less student characteristic data available to them because students have not been studied as comprehensively as their counterparts in developed countries. Databases containing ability, achievement, and personality data do not exist, so evaluators must literally "start from scratch" with school populations. The investment of resources in this direction, on at least a sample of the students involved, may yield at least three forms of payoff. First, such data may help to more precisely explain observed achievement in other program outcomes such as affective responses. Second, the examination of student differences often can suggest inexpensive modifications in programs to yield a better fit with a broader range of students. Third, the collection of such data may help stakeholders form a more comprehensive picture of their student population, which can be referred to when designing other programs.

Teachers and Principals

Teachers and principals are crucial to instructional program evaluations because of the centrality of their respective roles in delivering classroom instruction and managing the school. When new programs are introduced, it is usually the teacher who is asked to change. It is the teacher who undergoes training, grapples with unfamiliar materials, and attempts to implement new methods with students. Despite efforts to minimize the role of the teacher as information provider, in programs in some developing countries a teacher's influence over the amount of student progress toward objectives can be substantial. As classroom managers, teachers can foster or inhibit a task-oriented atmosphere. Principals can use their authority to oversee classrooms to ensure that teachers are following the prescribed curriculum. If laissez faire, principals communicate that a program is unimportant or fail to apply appropriate incentives. The actions of teachers and principals together will determine the quality of the intervention.

Beyond their instructional roles, both principals and teachers typically acquire additional responsibilities during a program evaluation. The design may require that teachers and principals record classroom or school-level information in a systematic way for the duration of the evaluation.

Because these responsibilities will be new for many building-level educators, training in how to fill out forms and monitor the completion of these forms will be important. Similarly, observation of teacher and principal classroom behaviors as a data source may be a new phenomenon for the schools in developing countries. Those who are about to be observed must be readied for this experience.

Because so much depends on the perceptions and performances of teachers and building principals, their roles in the evaluation process are particularly crucial. It is these individuals who must implement the new materials or teaching approaches. They must record certain types of information for the evaluators. They are interviewed to provide perspectives on student affect and achievement. They must undergo training to prepare to implement the program and, subsequently, be observed and interviewed about the effects of the program. Factors accentuating the difficulty of placing such expectations on teachers and principals in developing countries are the lack of adequate preparation of teachers, concerns and anxieties about new programs, and a defined role definition for principals.

Lack of preparation. In developing countries the teaching force is often underqualified and underprepared to assume an instructional role. In Liberia, for example, less than half of the teachers hold a baccalaureate degree. Many of them are products of that country's own educational system in which more than 50 percent of the students fail the 12th-grade examination. Teachers themselves are weak in the basic skills they are to foster in their students., As a result, teachers and principals may be willing but unable to comply with tasks expected of them in the evaluation process. An example occurred in Liberia when a group of teachers were asked to complete a survey. The evaluators estimated that the survey would take 20 minutes to complete but most teachers needed 90 minutes or more, even with assistance from a Peace Corps worker.

Anxieties and concerns. Teachers and principals may feel threatened by new programs that demand more accountability. When a new program challenges the normal patterns of attendance, work styles, or parental involvement in the school, teachers and principals are affected. The progression of teachers' concerns about new programs in developed countries range from fears about survival in the program (i.e., can I fit into this new approach?) to concerns over student performance (i.e., is this program a good match for Johnny?). It seems that in the early phases, teachers are likely to worry primarily about themselves and their own security; later they will develop concerns about the impact of the program on their students (Hall, George, & Rutherford, 1977). How less well-trained teachers in developing countries respond to innovation in their classrooms is not well documented, but evaluators should be sensitive to indications of these concerns. If achievement data from a classroom is highly skewed, for example, it may suggest that a teacher has misrepresented actual achievement in order to present himself or herself in a positive light.

Role of the Principal. Little cross-cultural research has been done to validate that the continuum of concerns demonstrated by teachers in developed countries is reflected in the concerns of teachers from developing countries. Similarly little is known about the attitudes and concerns of school principals toward new programs or their behaviors during implementation. In developed countries, principals are especially powerful during times of change and implementation of new programs. Pravica and McLean (Lundstrom, 1983) found that principals can foster disequilibrium, raise alternatives, and stimulate discussion about innovation. Fuller (see Chapter 2) argues that the actual management practices of principals in developing countries is unclear. Proxies of these practices, such as length of training or years of experience, substitute for more direct measures, such as observations. He summarized studies in which there was some indication of higher student achievement in schools where headmasters had attended more training or had more teaching experience, including studies done in Egypt (Heyneman & Loxley, 1983), Indonesia (Sembiring & Livingstone, 1981), and Bolivia (Morales & Pinellsites, 1977). In most of these studies, however, experience or training may have been confounded with other attributes, such as leadership ability.

One role that is seen as increasingly important among principals in developed countries is that of instructional leader. Weber (1988) defines instructional leadership as setting academic goals, organizing instruction, hiring, overseeing and evaluating teachers, protecting instructional time and programs, creating a climate for learning, and monitoring achievement and evaluation programs. In developing countries the principal or headmaster of a school is less likely to be perceived as an instructional leader than as a classroom teacher, building administrator, community spokesperson, liaison with the Ministry of Education, or parent. Few of them have been trained to assume any of the instructional leadership roles described by Weber.

If the program requires principal leadership in order to be effectively implemented, measures of day-to-day indicators of leadership behavior must be constructed that allow evaluators to monitor ways in which principals actually support or hinder the implementation of new programs. Principals might be asked to complete logs of their daily activities to provide evaluators with the means to determine time spent on the various program-related tasks. If baseline data were available on principals in program schools prior to the implementation of the program or on a control group, comparisons of time spent on instructional, management, and other tasks could result.

Subject Matter

In developing countries curriculum goals for elementary and secondary education often are defined at a national level. Curriculum goals for mathematics, science, social studies, and other areas are compiled by teams consisting of Ministry of Education personnel, school people, and university faculty. While subject matter domains may be carefully delineated in national curriculum guides, they are rarely followed in the day-to-day activities of the classroom. There are three explanations for the failure to implement national curriculum goals. The first is the lack of teachers' subject matter knowledge. Teachers cannot teach concepts they do not know. Second, there are few materials to support the curriculum available to teachers. Teachers who are underprepared are not likely to elaborate upon what is offered in textbooks. The way that a textbook or teacher's guide presents information is thus a powerful determinant of how students will receive it. Third, the lack of accountability in schools reduces teachers' motivation to comply with curriculum goals.

FINAL COMMENTS

In this chapter the argument as been made that evaluations of new instructional programs in developing countries must be responsive to six instructional components including the political context, treatments, outcomes, learner characteristics, teachers and principals, and subject matter. These six elements are inherent in all instructional programs. The *context* may be a centralized, politicized Ministry of Education that attempts to reconcile donor interests with self-defined needs and priorities in program development. At the local school level, community norms may dictate practice more than published curricula or other government policy because of the lack of adequate supervision to enforce government mandates.

The new program is operationalized through an *instructional treatment*, which reflects the design team's philosophy about how best to reach the school children of a county, a region, or nation. A common philosophy is that programs should reduce dependence on teachers' subject matter knowledge and pedagogical skill, owing to the underqualified teaching force in many of these countries. Evaluators must take a close look at the compliance of teachers to their assigned roles under new programs. If the shift is dramatic, so too might be the level of resistance.

How to define program *outcomes* is a general problem faced by all evaluators, regardless of context. They must grapple with establishing the *criteria* to be used in reviewing the program, selecting the *indicators* that best assess these criteria, and establishing *standards of performance* for these indicators. Increased student achievement, greater efficiency, and improved attitudes toward learning are familiar criteria in instructional program evaluations. The complexity of these three indices is enhanced in developing countries because of the different, and sometimes competing, priorities of multinational stakeholders coupled with the logistical problems of large-scale data collection efforts in countries with poor communication and data handling capacities.

As central to the program as those who implement it are those who receive it. *Student characteristics* are not easily captured in settings that have inadequate record-keeping systems and lack of history of student assessment. To make the picture murkier, instruments used in one country may not be transportable to others because of language or differing cultural conventions.

Teachers and principals, crucial implementors of new programs in schools, may face demands from several sources in program evaluation. The first is the program implementation itself, requiring them to assume new roles and carry out new tasks. The second source is the evaluation design itself, which may envision teacher and principal both as objects of observation and as recorders of data.

The choice of *subject matter* and its mode of presentation within the program are typically intended to reflect national curriculum goals at the elementary or secondary level. Evaluators can perform an important service in assessing the appropriateness of content for the intended target population. Are illustrations and examples meaningful to students? Is the sequence logical? Another focus should be the degree to which the subject matter presentation reduces the draw on the teacher's own knowledge base.

Models of frameworks to guide evaluation of new programs, like the one discussed in this chapter, should have as their primary goal the improvement of educational quality. Unfortunately this goal may be masked by the effort required to implement the evaluation. The complexities inherent in evaluating new programs in developing countries, of data collection, or the political liabilities associated with reporting unfavorable results, can shift the attention of the evaluator from concerns about quality of the program to undue attention on the logistics of the evaluation design and implementation.

REFERENCES

Berman, P. (1981). Educational change: An implementation paradigm. In R. Lehming & M. Kane (Eds.), *Improving schools: Using what we know* (pp. 253–286). Beverly Hills, CA: Sage.

Berman, P., & McLaughlin, M. W. (1976). Implementation of educational innovation. *The Educational Forum, 40*, 345–370.

Boothroyd, R. A., & Chapman, D. W. (1987) Gender differences and achievement in Liberian primary school children. *International Journal of Educational Development, 7* (2), 99–105.

Chapman, D. W., & Boothroyd, R. A. (1988). Evaluation dilemmas: Conducting evaluation studies in developing countries. *Evaluation and Program Planning, 11,* 37–42.

Cousins, J. B., & Leithwood, K. A., (1986). Current empirical research on evaluation utilization. *Review of Educational Research, 56*(3), 331–364.

Cronbach, L. J., & Snow, R. E. (1977). *Aptitudes and instructional methods.* New York: Irvington.

Dick, W., & Carey, L. (1985). *The systematic design of instruction* (2nd ed.). Dallas, TX: Scott, Foresman.

Flanders, N.A.E., Werner, E., Elder, R. A., Newman, J., & Lai, M. K. (1974). A minicourse on interaction analysis. San Francisco: Far West Laboratory for Educational Research and Development.

Fuller, B. (1986). Is primary school quality eroding in the Third World? *Comparitive Education Review, 30,* 491–502.

Fuller, B. (1987). What school factors raise achievement in the Third World? *Review of Education Research, 57* (3), 255–292.

Gagne, R., Briggs, L., & Wager, W. (1988). *Principles of instructional design* (3rd ed.). New York: Holt, Rinehart, & Winston.

Giacquinta, J. B. (1973). The process of organizational change in schools. In F. N. Kerling (Ed.), *Research in education I* (pp. 178–208). Itasca, IL: Peacock.

Goldhammer, R. (1969). *Clinical supervision: Special methods for the supervision of teachers.* New York: Holt, Rinehart & Winston.

Government of Liberia (1986). *The feasibility of integrating programmed learning with conventioal instruction in Liberian primary education* (Report). Monrovia: Ministry of Education and Tallahassee: Florida State University, Improving the Efficiency of Education Systems Project.

Government of Liberia (1988). *Liberia education and human resources sector assessment* (Report). Monrovia: Ministry of Education.

Hall, G. E., George, A., & Rutherford, W. L. (1979). Measuring stages of concern about the innovation: A manual for the use of the SoC Questionnaire. Austin: The University of Texas.

Heyneman, S., & Loxley, W. (1983). The effect of primary-school quality on academic achievement across twenty-nine high- and low-income countries. *American Journal of Sociology, 88,* 1162–1194.

Hord, S. M., & Hall, G. E. (1986, April). *Institutionalization of innovations: Knowing when you have it and when you don't.* Paper presented at the annual meeting of the American Educational Research Association, San Francisco.

Kolb, D. (1979). Student learning styles and disciplinary learning environments: Diverse pathways for growth. In A. Chickering (Ed.), *The future American college.* San Francisco: Jossey-Bass.

Kounin, J. S. (1970). *Discipline and group management in classrooms.* New York: Holt, Rinehart & Winston.

Kukla, A. (1978). An attributional theory of choice. In L. Berkowitz (Ed.), *Advances in experimental social psychology: Vol. 11.* New York: Academic Press.

Lundstrom, K. V. (1988). *The relationship between school context variables and the continuation of a planned curriculum change*. Unpublished doctoral dissertation, Minneapolis, University of Minnesota.

Morales, J., & Pinnellsiles, A. (1977). *The determinant factors and the costs of schooling Bolivia* (Working Paper No. 4–77). La Paz: Universidad Catolica Boliviana.

Ornstein, A. C. (1982). Innovation and change: Yesterday and today. *High School Journal, 65*, 279–286.

Rosenblum, S., & Louis, K. S. (1981). *Stability and change*. New York: Plenum.

Ross, A. S. (1984). Practical problems associated with program evaluation in Third World countries. *Evaluation and Program Planning, 7*, 211–218.

Sembiring, R., & Livingstone, I. (1981). *National assessment of the quality of Indonesian education*. Jakarta: Ministry of Education and Culture.

Sjoberg, G. (1975). Politics, ethics and evaluation research. In M. Gutentag & E. Struening (Eds.), *Handbook of evaluation research, vol. 2* (pp. 29–51). Beverly Hills, CA: Sage.

Snyder, C. W., Jr., & Nagel, J. (1986). *The struggle continues: World Bank and African Development Bank investments in Liberian educational development (1972–1985)*. McLean, VA: Institute for International Research.

Tobias, S. (1987). Learner characteristics. In R. Gagne (Ed.), *Instructional technology* (pp. 37–67). Hillsdale, NJ: Erlbaum.

Weber, I. (1988). Instructional leadership. *Newsletter from the North Central Regional Education Laboratory, 1*(2), pp. 1–4.

Weiner, B. (1983). Some methodological pitfalls in attributional research. *Journal of Educational Psychology, 75*, 530–543.

Williams, M. (1988). Determinants of choice and learning in a learner-controlled computer-based tutorial. Unpublished doctoral dissertation proposal, University of Minnesota, Minneapolis.

Witkin, H. A., & Goodenough, D. R. (1981). *Cognitive styles: Essence and origins: Field dependence and field independence*. New York: International Universities Press.

Worthen, B., & Sanders, J. (1987). *Educational evaluation: Alternative approaches and practical guidelines*. New York: Longman.

Yin, R. K. (1979). *Changing urban bureaucracies*. Lexington, MA: Heath.

10

Monitoring Implementation

David W. Chapman

Seemingly good programs encounter unexpected difficulties. Anticipated outcomes fail to materialize. Program managers, participants, and evaluators, in discussing a program in which they all shared, appear to be talking about entirely different events. Possible explanations for these experiences are that the program was not implemented fully, was implemented incorrectly, or was not implemented at all. Potentially effective programs may be discredited due to negative evaluation results derived not from the ineffectiveness of the program concept, but from a failure to consider whether the treatment was ever delivered at all. Consequently, there has been a growing interest in procedures for monitoring levels of implementation as part of program management and evaluation.

Innovations go through stages as they move from initial conception to full functioning—from design, through adoption, to implementation, and finally maturation. Attention in this chapter is on implementation, the extent to which a program is actually used. Implementation differs from the decision to adopt the program; it is not the same as planned or intended use (Fullan & Pomfret, 1977; Wooster, 1988). In actual practice, the monitoring of implementation is often overlooked. Program managers typically give primary attention to monitoring the flow of inputs and evaluating outcomes; they give less attention to monitoring what actually happens within the program (Imboden, 1980). In part, this indicates an assumption of the part of program designers and funding agencies that once a program is adopted it will be implemented as designed. In part, it may reflect a lack of consensus about the essential characteristics of the program being implemented. However, it also may reflect managers' recognition that they are evaluated primarily on their ability to commit inputs on schedule and, only to a lesser degree, on program outcomes—which may not be apparent for a long time. Hence, managers may have less interest in monitoring implementation than in making sure that the resources flow so that the project stays on schedule (Baum & Tolbert, 1985). Finally, the lack of attention to implementation, particularly in developing countries, is due to the obstacles to devising effective monitoring systems, given the difficulties that characterize those settings (Ross, 1984; Chapman & Boothroyd, 1988b).

This chapter argues the importance of monitoring implementation, identifies six purposes that monitoring implementation can serve in program management and evaluation, and presents a model of the influences affecting the implementation of large-scale educational programs. Particular attention is given to special problems encountered in monitoring program implementation in developing countries. Fielding new programs in developing countries poses particularly severe problems for implementation—unreliable communications, poor transportation, inadequately trained personnel, and often, limited staff to monitor program activities. There is a greater risk in developing countries, then, that considerable time and money is expended evaluating projects outputs when, in fact, important project components have not yet occurred.

REASONS FOR MONITORING IMPLEMENTATION

Monitoring implementation has six possible purposes within project management and evaluation—to assure that the plan is being carried out; to detect needed changes in the program design; to identify logistical weaknesses that threaten program success; to train; to police; and to provide an incentive to implementers. While monitoring activities may be undertaken to serve more than one of these purposes, it is unlikely monitoring would serve all these purposes simultaneously. Indeed, some of the purposes are in conflict with each other. Further, the manner in which monitoring might be undertaken differs, depending on the purpose to be achieved by the monitoring activity. It is important, then, that the purpose of a particular monitoring activity be established to help ensure that the appropriate monitoring strategies are employed.

The most common reason for monitoring is to assure fidelity of the program as it is implemented with the program as it was designed. This application generally is grounded in a belief that following the program design maximizes the probabilities of achieving intended program impacts. It assumes that the program design sequence provided careful, thoughtful, and comprehensive analysis of how inputs should best be organized to achieve the desired outputs.

A second reason for monitoring implementation is to detect needed changes in design. The need for changes is indicated when implementation is not occurring as anticipated—often because planners did not correctly identify the interplay of program components with the external context in which the program is being implemented. The monitoring activity offers a means of identifying the source of the problem. In that respect, monitoring can be viewed as an extension of the planning process, as project activities can be calibrated and adjusted to adapt to circumstances that were not fully anticipated or incorporated in the original plans.

A third reason is to detect logistical weaknesses in program implementation. Here the issue is not a weakness in design, but a weakness in providing the logistical support to ensure that the design is adequately tested. The success of many large-scale educational programs is contingent on cooperation of agencies and individuals who may not be part of the program itself, who may not share the same degree of commitment to the program, but who provide support services essential to program functioning. For example, a World Bank education project in West Africa depended on private booksellers for the national distribution of textbooks. The system collapsed, in part, because booksellers failed to remit the funds to the government on a timely basis and the intended national revolving book account failed to revolve (Snyder & Nagel, 1986). The program failed in part due to implementation problems outside of the program manager's control.

Fourth, monitoring implementation sometimes is undertaken as a covert means of training field staff who are supposed to be implementing the program. The monitoring activity becomes a means of in-service training as supervisors use the opportunity of monitoring to train personnel who may not have fully grasped the program concept or strategy or who do not have the skills to perform their role within the program. This informal training is a useful supplement to more formal pre-service training activities, since the supervisor can tune the training to the actual circumstances the member faces.

Fifth, monitoring is sometimes used to police program implementers. In this role, a message is conveyed that individuals found not to be implementing the program may face a sanction or punishment (specified or unspecified). This often is the message underlying the Inspectorate (a unit of the Ministry of Education responsible for ensuring compliance with ministry policies and rules). Generally, this role is incompatible with monitoring as a training intervention. The training role works best in an atmosphere of openness—when implementers feel free to admit their confusion and ask the questions necessary to resolve their prob-

Figure 10.1
Factors Associated with Level of Implementation

```
                   PROGRAM FACTORS

           clarity of program characteristics
                specificity of intended outcomes
                adequacy of resources
                   administrative support
                      supervision


CONTEXTUAL FACTORS
     cultural characteristics                ---->>>    LEVEL OF
     community support                                  IMPLEMENTATION


            INDIVIDUAL FACTORS

                     adequacy of training
                  adequacy of incentives
            prior experience
```

lems. In the "monitoring-as-policing" role, implementers tend to mask their unsureness and try to present themselves in the most favorable light. The policing function, then, operates as a negative reinforcement. Consequently, the policing function generally is appropriate only when implementers have received adequate training and there is little doubt about their ability to implement, given adequate motivation.

Finally, monitoring activities sometimes are built into a program to signal the importance of a program to those charged with implementing it. Monitoring serves as a form of incentive. This use of monitoring plays on the "Hawthorne Effect," in which participants in a program or study have been found to increase the speed or quality of their work in response to the apparent interest of higher management levels in their welfare. Monitoring sends a signal to first-line implementers that what they are doing is important enough for their efforts to be carefully watched.

A MODEL OF THE FACTORS ASSOCIATED WITH IMPLEMENTING LARGE-SCALE INSTRUCTIONAL IMPROVEMENT PROGRAMS

The purpose of monitoring implementation is more than to assess the level of implementation. The activity needs to identify the factors inhibiting and, alternatively, those facilitating implementation. In order for that to occur, those responsible for monitoring need some framework that identifies key factors to consider in the monitoring process.

Figure 10.1 presents a model of the influences on level of implementation of large-scale educational innovations that have particular relevance in developing countries. The model suggests that level of implementation is a function of program factors, individual factors, and contextual factors. Program factors include clarity of program characteristics, specificity of intended outcomes, adequacy of resources, administrative support, and adequacy of supervision. Individual factors include implementer's personal characteristics, adequacy of training, adequacy of incentives, and implementer's prior experience. Contextual factors include community support and larger cultural factors. While each of these components will be discussed, the discussion begins with a brief review of the theoretical underpinnings of the model. The model is grounded in systems theory at the organizational level and draws from social learning theory at the level of individual behavior.

General systems theory emphasizes the relationships among system components, between the system and its environment, and between one system and another. The theory posits that components of a system are interrelated and that changes in any one subsystem have implications for the operations of other subsystems. These relationships are iterative and reciprocal. The systems approach is particularly useful for analyzing complex systems such as those that operate in the education sector. Since the complexity of both learning processes and systems of education administration make the imputation of simple, unidirectional causality inappropriate, and since the external bureaucratic and economic contexts of education are so complex, systems theory provides a useful conceptual scheme for thinking about education change and people's and organizations' adoption of those changes (Windham, 1988).

From a systems perspective, the extent to which a new program is implemented depends, in large part, on the impact that changes required to implement that program would have on other subsystems already in place. While innovation and change are vital processes to organizational growth and survival, the conservative nature of organizational structures inevitably leads to factors that are resistant to such processes, whether they are of benefit to the organization or not. New programs threaten the equilibria of relationships among subsystems. As the new program perseveres, new relationships are formed between the subsystem experiencing the primary change and other subsystems with which it interacts. As these changed relationships become regularized, the network of interrelationships operates to hold this new set of relationships in place until yet another innovation is attempted.

Implementation of a new program or procedure, however, ultimately relies on thousands of micro-decisions from the people who compose the system. New data systems, food distribution plans, and vehicle repair schemes only succeed to the degree that individuals who staff those activities allow them to. Hence, it is not enough to analyze change as establishing new equilibria among subsystems. It is necessary also to consider the dynamics that motivate people to change their day-to-day behaviors in the ways that support a new program. Social learning theory provides a useful framework from which to operate.

Social learning theory posits that behavior is a function of personal characteristics, prior experience, environmental influences, cognitive and emotional responses, and performance skills. From a social learning perspective, individuals' decisions to implement a program (e.g., a set of behaviors) is a function of the individuals understanding the desired behaviors, having the skills necessary to implement the behaviors, and believing that they are capable of effecting those behaviors. This belief in their efficacy to implement the target behaviors, in turn, comes from their prior experience with similar skills in similar situations. The lack of any one of these components can result in a failure to implement.

Implementation of a new program depends on individuals understanding the demands of the new program, having the skills with which to meet those demands, and having a positive appraisal of their ability to succeed. If program demands are not clear to the potential implementers or, if clear, appear to place demands on the potential implementers that exceed their self-assessed abilities to perform effectively, they engage in coping or avoidance behavior that can undermine program success. These behaviors often take the form of a failure to implement or a failure to implement correctly. Within social learning theory, it is potential implementers' cognitive evaluation of a new program and their role in it that determines their willingness to support implementation.

The model also draws from innovation theory, particularly as it places the implementation phase within a larger framework of decisions that concern the design, adoption, and maturation of a project. Innovation theory is less well developed than the previous two theoretical perspectives (Scheirer & Rezmovic, 1983). Nonetheless, considerable research has sought to identify stages of implementation and the factors that affect movement through the stages (Hall & Loucks, 1977).

The determination of the need for an innovation, the design of the program to bring that innovation about, and adoption of that program can be understood as discrete stages that precede the implementation phase. Each of these stages is subject to its own set of pressures and politics. Indeed, one problem facing program managers trying to encourage implementation is that considerable political support and program resources already may have been committed to ensure success at these earlier levels, without adequate regard or attention to needs of first-line implementers. It is assumed that once a decision to adopt a program is made, that first-line implementers can be ordered to implement, or alternatively, that they will share the designers' and adopter's enthusiasm for the innovation and be eager to implement. Often overlooked is the possibility that first-line implementers—often teachers and headmasters—may evaluate their self-interest in very different ways than national-level planners evaluate the national interest. What is good for a country may not necessarily be good for any particular individual. Those asked to carry the most direct cost of implementing an innovation may not be the primary benefactors of that innovation once it is operating. For example, national implementation of a new primary school curriculum based on programmed instruction in Liberia was shown to improve student achievement, but resulted in more work for teachers. Some teachers complained that this interfered with their ability to engage in supplemental income producing activities—to hold a second job (Kelly, 1984; Chapman & Boothroyd, 1988a).

Efforts to conceptualize and measure implementation generally take one of two forms. Implementation studies using a *fidelity perspective* explore the extent to which actual use of the innovation corresponds to intended or planned use (Leinhardt, 1980; Hall & Loucks, 1977; Gross, Giacquinta, & Bernstein, 1971; Naumann-Etienne, 1974). The key features used to assess correspondence are gleaned from the program being implemented. Studies based on an *organizational change perspective* assume that implementation involves a mutually adaptive process between the user and the institutional setting (Berman & McLaughlin, 1976; Shipman, 1974). Both may change as a function of implementation. Studying that process requires the researcher to observe both the innovation and the organizational context over time.

Most donor-funded education programs in the Third World tend to operate from a fidelity perspective, focusing on the correspondence of intended with actual use. Both donors and host governments are under pressure to justify their education investments; they are reluctant to admit their planning may have been flawed; and, they tend to lack mechanisms for undertaking major alterations once a project begins.

The proposed model of factors associated with implementing educational programs has roots in all three of these theoretical perspectives. It is intended as a practical framework to assist policy makers, project managers, and evaluators in designing systems to monitor implementation in large-scale educational programs. While the model has relevance in countries spanning a wide range of economic and social development, attention in this chapter is paid to its application in Third World contexts. In the following section, each of the 10 components of the model will be discussed.

PROGRAM FACTORS

Clarity of Program Characteristics

Monitoring implementation requires, first, a clear idea of what program components and behaviors constitute appropriate implementation.

Consequently, central to the task of monitoring implementation is determination of the behaviors or events that will signal successful program functioning. Conventional wisdom is to specify the important characteristics of the treatment (e.g., the program) and examine the extent to which those occur. In practice, this strategy is the victim of three problems. Large-scale educational programs generally have multiple stakeholders—groups with a legitimate interest in the program but who may vary in the aspects of the program they regard as most important and in the criteria they use to judge the program's success (Chapman & Windham, 1986). When programs have multiple stakeholders, groups may vary as to what they think is the important issue to monitor, the reason they think monitoring is important, and the outcomes they most value.

Second, large-scale education programs often have multiple objectives. When this occurs, each particular objective tends to get diffused as singularity of purpose gives way to multiple goal pursuit. Objectives may compete. Some objectives may be achieved at the expense of others, either because the pursuit of some is deferred until others are realized or because the ends being sought are in competition for the same resources.

Third, program plans differ in the clarity and specificity of key components. During the planning process, specifics of program operations sometimes are left vague or intentionally obscured as a means of eliciting wider political support. At high levels of abstraction, agreement among disparate groups is easier to achieve. Ambiguity allows interested persons and groups to project their own intentions and needs on a program plan. People can share support for generalized goals while holding very different notions about the specific outcomes they really want a project to achieve. Once the program is adopted and implementation is underway, specific choices signal the real intent of program managers and disagreements begin to surface.

If implementation is not progressing well, clarity and consensus about program goals is an area for early attention in the monitoring process. The question facing those monitoring implementation, then, is what events, characteristics, or behaviors signal that a program is being implemented correctly? On what basis can fidelity with original program design be claimed if the original program is not clear?

Separate from the problems posed by multiple or ambiguous program characteristics are the dilemmas encountered when programs differ in the extent to which the determination of specific activities to meet program goals is purposefully decentralized and left to the discretion of first-line implementers. In decentralized programs, differing notions about what constitutes appropriate activities are not indicative of a flaw in implementation, but rather is an intended feature. Nonetheless, decentralization of program specifications poses a serious challenge for those charged with monitoring implementation.

How a program is monitored depends heavily on the specificity with which the treatment is prescribed. These differences can be envisioned as a continuum ranging from highly detailed treatments at one extreme to treatments that are specified in only general concept at the other. While highly prescribed programs may be easily matched against a template of expectations, programs designed to implement more general concepts may leave considerable discretion to field staff running the program. Such programs are expected to be operationalized in different ways, in response to personal and situational factors that may differ from site to site. Examples illustrate the continuum.

Example one describes a highly elaborated treatment. Project Advance is a program sponsored by Syracuse University that offers selected college credit courses in secondary schools in New York and nearby states where they are taught by secondary school teachers under the supervision of university faculty (Chapman & Wilbur, 1976; Wilbur & Chapman, 1978). Secondary students completing these courses can receive both high school and college credit for their work. The courses have been carefully developed through a systematic process of instructional design.

High school teachers of Project Advance courses must use prescribed textbooks, follow a prespecified syllabus, and generally move through the course content at a comparable speed. This is essential, since the credibility of the program depends, in part, on being able to show that high school students enrolled in Project Advance courses performed as well as college students enrolled in the same courses at the university.

Example two describes a generally unspecified treatment. The New York State Teacher Center program was funded by the state legislature to create professional development centers for teachers across New York state (Pruzek & Boothroyd, 1987, 1988). Teachers within each participating district could determine what activities their center would sponsor. Some centers emphasized formal content-oriented, in-service training programs; others used the money to create computer laboratories, peer mentorship programs, faculty research grants, and personal growth activities. No common core of activities was mandated. Indeed, the New York State Education Department, which distributed the funds on behalf of the legislature, was interested in encouraging a wide variety of strategy. The primary emphasis in funding was that teachers be involved in designing and running the teacher center in their district, that there be wide teacher participation, and that the services be positively received by the teachers. Within those constraints, individual centers could vary widely.

Example three is a program that contains both highly specified and unspecified activities. In the Improved Efficiency of Learning (IEL) and its successor, the Primary Education Project (PEP) in Liberia (West Africa), a combination of programmed teaching (grades 1 through 3) and programmed instructional materials (grades 4 through 6) were developed and employed to instruct students in five subject areas. The IEL materials operationalized the national primary school curriculum by providing clear learning objectives, programmed instructional materials, and structured classroom activities. This approach was judged to be particularly appropriate for use by underqualified teachers since it shifted much of the responsibility for structuring instructional time from the teacher to the materials.

Teachers complained that the specification of activities was too detailed and interfered with their own creativity. In response, as part of its adoption as the national instructional system at the primary level, more instructional options were introduced in the upper primary grades. Teachers in grades 5 through 6 were allowed to combine use of regular textbooks with the programmed materials, increase the number of teacher-directed classes, and assign more out-of-class work. Teachers discussed examples of the options available to them at a summer workshop. However, teachers were generally left to their own creativity to determine the nature and mix of these supplemental activities during the school year. No teachers guides were available to assist teachers to combine programmed instruction with other pedagogical techniques.

The programs illustrated in these three examples place quite different demands on program managers and quite different challenges for those monitoring implementation. The range of acceptable program activities varies across programs; consequently, what constitutes proper and effective implementation differs. The greatest challenge is in monitoring implementation of programs in which there is a wide range of activities that might constitute fidelity to the intended design.

Specificity of Intended Outcomes

Just as programs differ in the clarity and specificity of the treatment, they can also differ in the clarity and specificity of the intended outcomes. Implementers need to know what outcomes they seek and, in programs that seek multiple outcomes, the priorities among the outcomes. First-line implementers need to understand the logical linkages in project design—how project activities are expected to lead to intended outcomes; they need to know for which of the outcomes they will be held responsible. It is this linkage of activities to outcomes that is often a weak point in the implementation process—largely because program planners themselves are sometimes unclear about the links. For example, managers of a program aimed at assisting a Ministry of Education improve its management of national-level education data argued that improved student achievement was an appropriate indicator of project success. While improved data management might result in more efficient allocation of resources and assignment of teachers, the improved data could not themselves be expected to improve teachers' classroom instruction in a way that would show as increased student achievement. The managers failed to clearly understand the model that would link improved national-level data with student achievement.

Adequacy of Resources

Presumably, planning for a program includes providing for the resources and material inputs necessary for program implementation. Nonetheless, problems in availability and flow of resources are often cited as a primary reason why a program was not implemented or was not implemented as intended.

Implementation problems are easily blamed on resource problems. However, it appears that problems are due as often to the difficulties of managing resource flow as they are to insufficient funds for implementation. Educational programs targeted at a particular problem or subsector activity are particularly susceptible to resource flow problems. Such programs are those designed to address one aspect of a larger set of problems—such as a national in-service teacher training program, a materials development effort, or upgrading of instructional supervision. If these programs fail to address the linkages of the target program with the larger system, resources that are necessary for project success but that are controlled by other subsectors or agencies may not be available in a coordinated way or may be withheld entirely. In-service teacher training may be of little use if the teachers, once trained, have no instructional materials with which to work. A textbook development project has limited impact if no system is available to get the developed materials to the schools.

Even when programs are designed in a more comprehensive manner, and efforts are made to plan more integrated projects, planners may incorrectly anticipate resource demand or problems in resource flow. For example, a World Bank effort to assist the Liberian Ministry of Education (MOE) develop a decentralized administrative structure by constructing regional education offices was judged unsuccessful, in part because the regional education officers, once in place, did not have gasoline necessary to get to schools (Snyder & Nagel, 1986; Government of Liberia, 1988). Implementation is best supported by project design that builds on regular and frequent reviews of resource flow and that allows for easy adjustment and reallocation of resources when such a need is indicated.

Administrative Support

Administrative support operates in three ways. At the most basic level, it refers to the efforts of administrators to handle logistics, manage the budget, align incentives, reduce outside interference, and keep a project running smoothly. Administrators' involvement, support, and enthusiasm generally are required to set the implementation process in motion. Once underway, administrators can influence implementation of a new program through: (a) their ability to articulate the goals and strategy of the program to teachers, students, parents, and other key audiences; (b) their ability to train and motivate teachers to implement the program; (c) the manner and extent to which they encourage teacher participation in addressing problems; (d) the manner and frequency with which they evaluate teachers' performance in the classroom; (e) the extent to which they encourage different approaches and the exercise of professional judgment; and (f) their competence in budgeting and accounting of material inputs necessary to the success of the program being implemented. These activities are essential to successful coordination of inputs and process. They are identified in virtually all innovation research as a necessary precondition of implementation (Waugh & Punch, 1987; Fullan & Pomfret, 1977; Havelock & Huberman, 1978).

However, in addition to their task performance, their personal sanction of the program and of the participants is important. Recognition, approval, and support of administrators has consistently been found to be a key factor in teachers' adoption of innovation, in both developing and developed countries (Chapman, 1983; Waugh & Punch, 1987; Fullan & Pomfret, 1977; Wooster, 1987; Wellman, 1987). For example, Wooster (1986), examining the relationship of support and involvement of the elementary school principal to teachers' implementation of a state-sponsored social studies curriculum in New York state, found that higher levels of principal support were significantly related to higher levels of implementation.

Kelly (1984), conducting an evaluation of a primary school curriculum project in Liberia, found evidence of a link between student achievement and headmaster behavior. Specifically, female achievement appeared to be higher in schools in which the principal took a strong position on not releasing girls from school to assist their mothers on market day. Female students in schools in which the principal was successful in this effort experienced more direct instructional time, which was reflected in higher achievement.

The third way in which administration support operates is through instructional supervision. Due to the importance assigned to this role, it is treated as a separate category within the model.

Instructional Supervision

The failure to implement instructional programs may be due to problems in instructional supervision. Instructional supervision is a subset of administrative support specifically concerned with helping first-line implementers–often classroom teachers and headmasters—to know what they are doing. The school principal (or headmaster) provides the most immediate instructional supervision in the school. Generally, there are then layers of district, regional, and central ministry administrators, all of whom have some responsibility to monitor school activities. In addition, many countries have an Inspectorate, a division of the ministry with particular responsibility to monitor school compliance with instructional and/or administrative regulations of the ministry. In some countries (e.g. Somalia), there are separate Inspectorates to monitor school administration and to provide instructional supervision.

Since most large-scale educational programs in developing countries are centrally imposed, instructional supervision in many programs is progressively delegated—from central program managers, through regional and district education officers, to school principals. One risk is that intermediate supervisors may be among the least qualified personnel to advise others on how to properly implement a new program. Those who serve as instructional supervisors may not have been part of the design or adoption process and may never have taught in the program.

Moreover, in developing countries, the effectiveness of administrators above the school level is open to considerable question for other reasons. Inspectors and district education officers in many countries are appointed on political grounds. They often lack school experience. They are not in a strong position to be offering advice to experienced teachers on how to improve their teaching. In many countries they do not have the transportation, logistical support, or motivation to visit schools. A study of 561 primary school teachers in Liberia, for example, found that over half of the schools represented had not received a visit from their district education officer in the previous year (Chapman & Carrier, 1988).

The principal is in the best position to influence the day-to-day activities of teachers and, consequently, is the best source of instructional supervision. Research has consistently found that the active support of principals increases the chances of successfully implementing a new program (Waugh & Punch, 1987; Berman & McLaughlin, 1976; Wooster, 1987; Wellman, 1987). The principal, however, while closest to the actual delivery of instructional programs, may suffer from the same isolation and lack of communication experienced by teachers. Consequently, the use of principals as monitors of implementation must be combined with mechanisms to ensure that principals can align their perceptions of successful project operation with project management.

There is accumulating evidence that headmasters' education and experience are related to student achievement. Higher student achievement has been found to be related to headmasters' teaching experience and number of training courses attended in Egypt (Heyneman & Loxley, 1983) and Paraguay (reported in Fuller, 1987). Higher student achievement in Bolivia was found to be related to length of headmasters' postsecondary schooling (Morales & Pinellsiles, 1977). In Indonesia, higher student achievement was related to headmasters' length of teaching experience and salary (Sembiring & Livingstone, 1981). While it is unlikely that salary is related directly to student achievement, it probably serves as a proxy for amount of training or years of experience (Fuller, 1987). These same variables are expected to influence a headmaster's ability to understand, support, and monitor implementation of new education programs.

INDIVIDUAL FACTORS

Personal Characteristics

Personal characteristics mediate how people respond to their environment, to other people, and to new experiences. They influence how people respond to incentive systems, authority structures, training, and new ideas. Some personal characteristics, such as educational background, are related directly to peoples' ability to implement a new program. Other personal characteristics are proxies for a participants' attitudes and values, which affect how they perform in a new program. For example, individuals from low-income backgrounds may have a different constellation of experiences that shape their evaluation of current events than might individuals from more affluent backgrounds. While substantial research exists on the impact of personal characteristics on program performance, broad generalizations are inappropriate, since the particular personal characteristics that may affect implementation are often a function of the unique characteristics of a program. Nonetheless, if problems in implementation are observed, the personal characteristics of participants is a key area to examine.

Adequacy of Training

To perform effectively in a new situation, individuals need to know what is expected of them, they must have the skills to perform those expected behaviors, and they must believe they can apply those skills successfully. Training should address all three of these components and should be supplemented with an appropriate program of instructional supervision.

If a program appears to be failing at the level of first-line implementation, adequacy of implementers' training is a key variable to examine. The further an innovation is from a teacher's prior experience, the greater the amount of training needed. At the same time, it is easy to blame poor performance too quickly on insufficient training. More training will not solve the problem if the training that is available lacks relevance, is of poor quality, or is inappropriately delivered. Training will not improve implementation if the real problem is misalignment of the incentive system or unanticipated negative consequences brought about by implementation. One role of the project monitoring process is to ensure that the training is appropriate to the tasks being demanded, adequate in amount, and properly delivered.

Adequacy of Incentives

New programs can have both direct and indirect costs to participants. Direct costs occur when, for example, the time commitments of a new program cut into participants' opportunities to hold supplemental employment. Indirect costs occur when a new program alters the status and authority structure in a way that causes some individuals to lose prestige. Presumably, however, new programs offer benefits to compensate for the costs—perhaps directly in the form of participant stipends, or indirectly, by providing new skills that give a participant a market advantage in the future. People evaluate new opportunities and programs in terms of the benefits they expect to reap through participation or support of a program relative to the direct and indirect costs of that support.

Problems in the design and operation of incentives are a primary reason for the failure to implement. The problems generally fall into five categories. First, program planners presumably design programs to achieve some benefits. However, the benefits may not accrue back to those who are expected to bear the costs of the program. The outcomes of a program may contribute to the good of the society as a whole, a particular subpopulation, or a future generation, but not directly regard those who are being asked to change their work styles, learn new skills, or alter their professional relationships with others. For example, a program designed to encourage female participation in education by increasing the number of female teachers in rural areas may offer clear long-term benefits to the society, yet not offer adequate inducement to encourage female teachers to volunteer to teach in rural areas.

Second, key incentives built into a program often are intended to encourage adoption by providing regards to those at a decision-making level. Incentives for those actually charged with implementing may be less clear. The assumption often is that once a program has been accepted, a set of directives to people already in the system will get it to operate. Nonetheless, success in the implementation of large-scale programs typically depends on thousands of micro-decisions by individuals. The personal payoff of implementing the project needs to be clear to each of them.

A third problem program planners encounter is that they make assumptions about what participants find rewarding that are not fully shared by participants themselves. In some cases it is because the participants do not see the value of the training, procedures, or system being offered. In other cases, they recognize the value, but regard it as of less value to them personally than what they gain by retaining the existing procedures or system.

Fourth, training alters a person's opportunity cost. Once trained, it is not unusual for a person to want to apply the new skills in a setting offering better compensation. For example, it is not uncommon for Ministry of Education staff, once trained in computer operations, to leave the MOE for better-paying opportunities in the private sector or more prestigious government agencies. One common response is to adjust the incentives to encourage those with particularly needed skills to remain on the job. The most common way is with a salary increase or a special allowance. This can lead to a second problem—incentives designed to support one goal may distort the larger incentive structure of an organization.

Finally, the pursuit of one goal may result in the creation of incentives that inadvertently operate as disincentives to some other goal. For example, in Yemen, the subsidies to teacher training students enrolled at the university were found to be greater than the salary a graduate would receive as a teacher (Government of Yemen, 1985). Enrollments in teacher training were high, yet retention in teaching was low. The system was effective in what it was designed to do—attract Yemenis into teacher training—but ineffective in achieving a larger national goal—which was to encourage Yemenis to enter and remain in teaching. In Liberia, national-level education management information system collapsed when the government instituted a student registration fee to offset a drop in the government budget for education. School personnel quickly learned that school fees could be retained for use at the school level by under-reporting actual enrollment—or not reporting at all (Government of Liberia, 1988). In the Yemen case, a direct incentive at one level operated as a disincentive at another. In the Liberian case, a policy intended to offset one negative event (a reduction in the national education budget) result in another. Monitoring implementation requires attention to the incentive structure to determine that it is adequate, but also to determine that it is operating in the manner intended and not yielding unintended outcomes and disincentives.

Prior Experience

New and innovative programs generally operate from a premise that a different configuration of behaviors, resources, and context can yield different and, presumably, more desired outcomes. Such programs confront participants with situations and demands with which they may have had little or no experience. Yet, experience is a filter through which people view events; people interpret new experiences by drawing on their prior experience with similar events. They judge their own capacity to meet the personal demands imposed by the change based in large part on their experience in similar situations in the past.

Two important functions of monitoring are to determine the extent to which the lack of prior experience inhibits implementation and to identify interventions that can help offset the lack of prior experience or previous negative experience. Monitoring can serve as a tool for helping to break an unreflective use of experience as the basis for responding to new program demands.

CONTEXTUAL FACTORS

Cultural Factors

Cultural factors are the constellation of values and attitudes that tend to characterize a group or nationality and that distinguishes it from other groups and nationalities. These attitudes and values shape the meaning people assign to their experiences. They play a large part in determining how people approach intellectual or cognitive tasks, form and sustain relationships with others, and approach their work.

People respond to new experiences, programs, and demands placed upon them from the perspective of their cultural values and norms. These values and norms shape what people find rewarding, how they relate to authority, the importance they attach to time, how they handle conflict, the importance they assign to family versus work pressures, and the efficacy they assign to individual action. Cultural differences, then, affect how people view the educational process and how they respond to encouragement and direction that would have them alter their practice.

Important aspects of educational and classroom experience differ across cultures. There is widespread evidence of cultural differences in how people view the educational process and differences in the rights, obligations, and prerogatives they assign to various roles within that process. For example, Bae (1987), using multidimensional scaling techniques, found meaningful differences between Korean and American elementary school teachers' conceptions of effective teaching. Clarity of presentation, questioning, pacing of instruction, and teacher–student rapport were more closely related to effective teaching for American teachers than for Korean teachers, while availability of materials was more closely related to effective teaching for Korean teachers than for American teachers.

Similarly, Chapman and Kelly (1981), investigating the dimensions of teacher behavior and classroom characteristics used by Iranian and American high school students in evaluating their classroom experiences, found similarities in the dimensions used to evaluate courses. However, students in the two cultures differed on the dimensions they used to evaluate teachers. The activities of teaching and classroom management most directly under the teachers' control differed markedly between cultures (e.g., opportunities for student participation, pace of coverage, and overanswering).

While cultural differences can be observed in how teachers view teaching and in how students regard teachers, those differences also can be an important factor in how teachers view and respond to innovation and change. A recent study by Chapman and Carrier (1988) investigating the underlying dimensions that characterize Liberian primary school teachers' concern about adopting a new national curriculum helps illustrate the point. The study was grounded in the Concerns Based Adoption Model developed by Hall, George, and Rutherford (1977). During January, 1988, 461 Liberian primary school teachers completed a survey based on the Stages of Concern Questionnaire by Hall et al. as part of their participation in an in-service workshop to prepare them to teach the new curriculum. (The IEL curriculum is described in more detail in Chapter 4). The factor structure found in the Liberian teachers' data differed meaningfully from the structure expected on the basis of previous research using the Stages of Concern Questionnaire with American teachers. Liberian and American teachers differ in the way they evaluate the risks, consequences, and rewards of implementing a new program. These differences, in turn, have consequences for teachers' willingness to implement a new program and how that implementation should be monitored.

Those charged with monitoring implementation need to recognize the potential influence of cultural considerations. These cultural considerations are particularly acute when a program, curriculum, or instructional materials are developed by people from one culture for use by people in another—a common event in projects funded by donor agencies and using expatriate technical assistance personnel, who may not fully understand the person, social, and work norms that operate within a society. At the same time, it is important to recognize that there can be cultural differences as significant within a country as between countries. For example, the geographical boundaries of many Sub-Saharan countries cut across tribal boundaries—which for many residents forms a more primary reference group. In Liberia, for example, 16 languages from three major linguistic groups are spoken in the country, indicative of the multicultural environment. Such a multiplicity of cultures poses yet another dimension for those charged with monitoring implementation.

Community Support

Through education in most Third World countries is a responsibility of the government and most key school decisions are highly centralized, the support of the local community can play a powerful role in determining the extent to which new educational programs are implemented, and once implemented, the degree to which they are successful. In many important ways, the local community controls the incentive system closest to teachers' and principals' daily activities. Community members interact with school people in the market place, share with them in the operation of community life, and in some communities, directly contribute food, housing, and salary supplements to their maintenance.

The extent to which the community is willing to support homework assignments, contribute money for special causes, and tolerate teacher absenteeism sends an important message to school personnel. At the same time, parents in many Third World countries are intimidated by school personnel. Lacking formal education themselves, many parents do not understand how schools work or what activities signal an effective school. They often are not sure what expectations they can reasonably hold, what demands they can place on the school, or what authority they can invoke if answers to their questions are not forthcoming. Hence, many parents do not know how to determine if school funds are being spent efficiently and whether school staff are doing an effective job. School people, enjoying their status in the community, may discourage parent involvement or see it as an intrusion on their prerogatives.

Ministries of education in some countries have actively sought to increase parent participation in the education system as a means of encouraging greater community financial contributions to the schools (Strudwick, 1986). Liberia is experimenting with the use of radio to build community support for new educational programs. Short radio spots explain the purpose and activities of a national primary education project, describe what a properly functioning school should look like, and suggest how community resources might best be mobilized to improve school quality (Government of Liberia, 1988; Burke & Cowell, 1988).

An important issue to consider in monitoring implementation, then, is the extent of local community support. This, in turn, relates to the extent community members are kept informed and included in the planning and activities of the schools.

SUMMARY

Assessing the level of program implementation is not necessarily difficult if intended characteristics of the program are well defined and data on actual program performance are readily available. Often, however, intended program characteristics are poorly articulated, key audiences disagree about what aspects of a program are important, and data on actual program performance is lacking. Moreover, the monitoring process itself sometimes is used for multiple and even competing purposes. These problems tend to be exacerbated in developing countries, given the complex interplay among host government, donor agency, school, and local community personnel, and the problems of transportation and communication within the field settings where actual implementation is occurring.

Even then, assessing the level of implementation, by itself, is seldom helpful unless the reasons implementation is encountering difficulties can be identified in a way that allows for design of an appropriate intervention. To identify factors inhibiting implementation requires some conceptual map of the possible influences on implementation that can guide those charged with monitoring program progress. This chapter offered a model of the influences affecting the implementation of large-scale educational programs, with particular attention to its application in educational programs in developing countries. The model identifies 10 organizational, individual, and program factors that influence implementation and that should be examined as part of an implementation monitoring activity.

REFERENCES

Bae, H. (1987) *A cross-national study of teachers' conceptions of effective teaching.* Unpublished doctoral dissertation, School of Education, State University of New York at Albany.

Baum, W. C., & Tolbert, S. M. (1985). *Investing in development: Lessons of World Bank experience.* New York: Oxford University Press.

Berman, P., & McLaughlin, M. W. (1976). Implementation of educational innovation. *The Educational Forum*, 40(3), 345–370.

Burke, R. C., & Cowell, R. N. (1988, July). The feasibility of using radio broadcasting to support education in Liberia. Tallahassee: Florida State University, Improving the Efficiency of Education Systems Project.

Chapman, D. W. (1983). Career satisfaction of teachers. *Educational Research Quartely, 7*(3), 40–50.

Chapman, D. W., & Boothroyd, R. A. (1988a). Evaluation dilemmas: Conducting evaluation studies in developing countries. *Evaluation and Program Planning, 11,* 37–42.

Chapman, D. W., & Boothroyd, R. A. (1988b). Threats to data quality in developing country settings. *Comparative Education Review, 32*(4), 416–429.

Chapman, D. W., & Carrier, C. A. (1988). *The dimensions of teacher concern about adopting an innovation: The case of Liberian primary school teachers.* Albany, NY: State University of New York at Albany, School of Education.The Evaluation Consortium.

Chapman, D. W., & Kelly, E. F. (1981). A comparison of the dimensions used by Iranian and American students in rating instruction. *International Review of Education, 27,* 41–60.

Chapman, D. W., & Wilbur, F. P. (1976). Project Advance—college courses in the high school classroom. *New York State Personnel and Guidance Journal, 11*(1), 28–37.

Chapman, D. W., & Windham, D. M. (1986). *The evaluation of efficiency in educational development activities.* Tallahassee: Florida State University, Improving the Efficiency of Educational Systems Project.

Fullan, M., & Pomfret, A. (1977). Research on curriculum and instruction implementation. *Review of Educational Research, 47*(1), 335–397.

Fuller, B. (1987). What school factors raise achievement in the Third World? *Review of Educational Research, 57*(3), 255–292.

Government of Liberia. (1988). *Liberia education and human resources sector assessment.* Monrovia: Ministry of Education.

Government of the Yemen Arab Republic. (1985). *Yemen education and human resources sector assessment.* Sana'a: Ministry of Education.

Gross, N.,, Giacquinta, J. B., & Bernstein, M. (1971). *Implementing organizational innovations.* New York: Basic Books.

Hall, G. E., George A., & Rutherford, W. L. (1977). *Stages of concern in adopting an innovation.* Austin: University of Texas.

Hall, G. E., & Loucks, S. F. (1977). A developmental model for determining whether the treatment is actually implemented. *American Educational Research Journal, 14*(3), 263–276.

Havelock, R. G., & Huberman, A. M. (1978). *Solving educational problems: The theory and reality of innovation in developing countries.* New York: Praeger.

Heyneman, S., & Loxley, W. (1983). The effect of primary-school quality on academic achievement across twenty-nine high- and low-income countries. *American Journal of Sociology, 88,* 116 2–1194.

Imoden, N. (1980). *Managing information for rural development projects.* Paris: Organization for Economic Cooperation and Development.

Kelly, E. F. (1984). *Evaluation of the Improved Efficiency of Learning Project in Liberia, Africa: Overview and peculiar problems.* Albany, NY: State University of New York at Albany, The Evaluation Consortium.

Leinhardt, G. (1980). Modeling and measuring education treatments in evaluation. *Review of Educational Research, 50*(3), 393–420.

Morales, J., & Pinellsiles, A. (1977). *The determinant factors and the costs of schooling in Bolivia* (Working Paper No. 4–77). La Paz: Universidad Catolica Boliviana.

Naumann-Etienne, M. (1974). *Bringing about open education: Strategies for innovation.* Unpublished doctoral dissertation, University of Michigan, Ann Arbor.

Pruzek, R. M., & Boothroyd, R. A. (1987). *A statewide evaluation report on New York state teacher resource and computer training centers, 1986–1987.* (Report submitted to the Division of Teacher Certification). Albany: New York State Education Department.

Pruzek, R. M., & Boothroyd, R. A. (1988). *A statewide evaluatio report on New York state treacher resource and computer training centers , 1987–1988* (Report submitted to the Division of Teacher Certificaiton), Albany: New York State Education Department.

Ross, A. S. (1984). Practical problems associated with program evaluation in Third World countries. *Evaluation and Program Planning, 7,* 211–218.

Scheirer, M. A. & Rezmovic, E. L. (1983). Measuring the deg ree of program implementation: A methodological review. *Evaluation Review, 7*(5), 599–633.

Sembiring, R., & Livingstone, I. (1981). *Natinal assessment of the quality of Indonesian education.* Jakarta: Ministry of Education and Culture.

Shipman, M. (1974). *Inside a curriculum project.* London: Methuen.

Snyder, C. W., Jr., & Nagel, J. (1986) *The struggle continues: World Bank and African Development Bank investments in Liberian educational development (1972–1985).* McLean, VA: Institute for International Research.

Strudwick, J. (1986). A proposal for research in strengthing local education capacity: Indonesia and Botswana. Tallahassee: Florida State University, Improving the Efficiency of Education Systems Project.

Waugh, R. F., & Punch, F. F. (1987). Teacher receptivity to systemwide change in the implementation stage. *Review of Educational Research, 57*(3), 237–254.

Wellman, L. (1987). *Factors relating to the implementation of the New York state curriculum for English as a second language in secondary schools.* Unpublished doctoral dissertation, School of Education: State University of New York at Albany.

Wilbur, F. P., & Chapman D. W. (1978). *College courses in the high school* (Monograph). Reston, VA: National Association, of Secondary School Principals.

Windham, D. M. (1988). Proposed agreement among Shanxi Provine, Beijing Normal University, and the State University of New York at Albany, School of Education. Albany: State University of New York at Albany.

Wooster, J. (1986). *The effect of three variables on teacher implementation of a centrally imposed curriculum.* Unpublished doctoral dissertation, State University of New York at Albany.

11

The Role of Education Management Information Systems in Improving Educational Quality

David W. Chapman

One of the highest-priority issues in many international educational development projects is the improvement of the collection, analysis, and use of quantitative data in decision making. This priority emerges from the convergence of five trends—(1) the explosive growth of the education system in many countries; (2) the increased complexity of education systems as ministries of education have undertaken more complex programs and pursued multiple objectives; (3) the increased financial pressures experienced by many governments, which has created pressure for more efficient resource allocation procedures; (4) increased donor demand for quantitative data to meet their own pressures for accountability; and (5) the availability of low-cost technology for handling large amounts of data.

This chapter examines key issues in the design and implementation of education management information systems (EMIS), with particular attention to the use of information systems in improving educational quality. This chapter begins with a discussion of ways that management information systems can contribute to improving educational quality. It is followed by a brief review of Third World experience with EMIS that suggests that despite the potential for contributing to quality enhancement, the EMIS record has been mixed. Key issues encountered in specifying data needs and selecting indicators are then examined. It is argued that a narrow (versus a broad) spectrum data system is the most appropriate design, but should incorporate a series of techniques for expanding the information utility, including the use of derived indicators and common coding schemes. Particular attention, then, is given to three key problems that confront EMIS designers—accommodating the need for multi-level data analysis, low data quality, and political resistance to improved information.

THE ROLE OF DATA SYSTEMS IN IMPROVING EDUCATIONAL QUALITY

Improved education data have been argued to be necessary input to resource allocation, project implementation, and planning decisions that face educational managers. Educational management information systems, in turn, have been advocated as means of ensuring that the necessary data are available when they are needed. Yet, while data systems have been touted as necessary inputs to better decision making, evidence of their positive contribution to improved educational quality often has been harder to document. One reason for this is the failure of observers to understand the role of information in decision making—as a necessary but not a sufficient ingredient. If observers expect better information to drive decision making, they will be disappointed—and render similarly disappointing judgments about the role of EMIS in educational development.

Quantitative data, as provided by a management information system, can play three roles in educational development. Such data are important in determining the nature and extent of the problems facing an educational program or system; they are used in the political process as justification for the difficult decisions that need to be made; and, they are a necessary ingredient in guiding the allocation of the resources that are available. Whether or not they operate in these roles depends, to a substantial degree, on the political context in which educational development activities operate, management capacity of the education sector, and type and usefulness of the data collected. These considerations, then, must weigh heavily in designing an EMIS.

Political Context

Resource allocation and planning decisions in education are always made within a larger social and political environment. Data managers often fail to realize the complex determinants of choice faced by educational decision makers. Even if decision makers accept the analyst's data, they still must interpret the data for themselves in terms of the larger social or political system within which they operate (Windham, 1988). In that respect, quantitative data are a necessary but never a sufficient basis for policy formulation. If this relationship is not understood by decision makers, it can lead to unfair claims that the EMIS is of little relevance. If the relationship is not understood by data system managers, it can lead to intense frustration as they see their work ignored or only selectively accepted.

On the other hand, incentives in developing countries to use objective data are weak. The failure to use data may not be due to lack of availability (though that may be a problem), but to a decision process guided by other criteria. The ability of decision makers to secure necessary political support, implement policy, or compete for resources may be tied more directly to personal, familial, or tribal interests that need to be accommodated if the decision maker is to be judged successful within their local context. Furthermore, confronted with incomplete or untimely data of questionable accuracy, decision makers have ample cause to be skeptical of relying too heavily on quantitative information.

Management Capacity

Even if individual decision makers support the use of more objective data in policy and resource allocation decisions, overall management capacity of government can severely limit the utility of these data. Weak management capacity is a product of rapid system growth, at rates faster than personnel could be trained for the positions to which they are assigned and faster than systematic procedures for communication, program monitoring, and decision making could be implemented. It has been identified as a major constraint to educational development in many Third World countries (Government of Somalia, 1985; Government of Yemen, 1986; Government of Liberia, 1988; World Bank, 1988). Weak management capacity has a nonrecursive effect—it constrains the ability of even strong managers by limiting the information available to them and, at the same time, it undermines the capacity of the system to collect better data. Improving data is a precondition of strengthening management capacity but it does not by itself necessarily improve decision making when the underlying problem is one of inadequate staff training or an inability to implement policies once they are made.

Usefullness of Data

Finally, the effectiveness of an EMIS depends heavily on the type, timeliness, and relevance of the data collected. In many respects, these factors are the easiest to influence and, consequently, have received the most attention in the EMIS literature (Ad Hoc Committee on the Use of Microcomputers in Developing Countries, 1986; Imboden, 1980). While an appropriate EMIS design is essential to an effective system, one risk is that attention to efficient data collection and analysis displaces concern for data use.

Data can be used to improve educational quality in four principal ways: by providing data that is used directly to secure or allocate resources, by constraining bad decisions, by detecting inefficient resource use, and by supporting mechanisms that offset the impact of resource loss. The most common argument for improved quantitative data is to provide needed information to decision makers faced with complex resource allocation and planning decisions. Student enrollment projections, for example, provide a basis for determining teacher demand, adjusting intake to teacher training institutions, ordering textbooks, and estimating the need for new facilities. Data on student achievement by school provides the basis for targeting interventions to assist weak schools, such as teacher training, special educational programs, and improved supervision.

Equally common in practice is the use of data by political or professional adversaries to oppose a policy. Data may be used more often by critics of a policy to head off a decision they regard as unfavorable than by policy makers in formulating that policy in the first place.

The efficacy of data in this role is that presenting a positive plan may require a coherent weave of data, while an attack on someone else's plan may require a focus on only one dimension of that plan. Hence, the use of data as an attack strategy contains a certain efficiency—selective data use can discredit an entire plan by attacking only a selected aspect. Proponents of a plan are put on the defensive for the entire plan, while opponents need only to concentrate their attack (and their data collection) on a much narrower set of issues. The reverse is also true. A poor or self-serving plan can quickly be discredited by highlighting and publicizing the more egregious dimensions of self-interest.

Data also can contribute to enhancing educational quality when it is used to detect inefficient resource use. Educational expenditures often are demand driven, triggered by system expansion without attention to resource availability. Moreover, spending more does not ensure that a need is being met. For example, increasing the size of the teaching force may do little to improve educational quality or access and may actually lower educational quality if teacher salaries are diverting funds that would be better used for instructional materials and school maintenance. With information on teacher demand and an effective system of teacher assignment, the efficacy of such expenditures can be examined.

Finally, data can sometimes help offset resource loss. As severe financial conditions beset the education sector, governments have cut, delayed, or frozen teacher salaries at present levels, even in the face of high inflation. Education ministries have tried to offset the brunt of these cuts by more propitious use of nonmonetary incentives—such as advanced training or preferential future assignments for teachers who remain in the system or who accept less desirable current assignments (see Kemmerer & Thiagarajan, 1988). Many of these nonmonetary incentives presuppose a data system capable of tracking teacher assignments and matching teachers with incentive opportunities.

Better information on the education system will not itself improve education quality, but quality improvement efforts within complex social and political contexts are unlikely to succeed unless decision makers have an objective basis for assessing the dimensions of the issues they face and the probable consequences of the alternatives available to them. To help ensure the usefulness of data, an EMIS needs to emphasize three characteristics. First, education information systems should be developed from a realistic assessment of what types of decisions can be based on objective criteria. Second, data must be collected at a sufficient level of detail to support meaningful planning. For example, if data on teacher qualifications, ethnic background, or family ties would meaningfully constrain teacher assignment, this information must be included in the collection and analysis. Third, data need to be collected and analyzed in a manner that makes them available in the decision process at the time they are needed.

Before proceeding to a discussion of EMIS design, it is useful—and humbling—to review the dominant trend of experience with EMIS in developing country settings. The brunt of experience suggests EMIS have made a contribution to improved planning, but not necessarily in the ways or with the same consequences anticipated by information system advocates. The experience already gained with EMIS helps ground the discussion of EMIS design issues that follows.

PRIOR EXPERIENCE WITH EMIS

While the potential of EMIS is compelling, efforts to develop and implement data management systems have a mixed history of success. A review of the research on information management systems in developing countries for rural development (Imboden, 1980), energy (Burchfield, 1986), and education (Brodman, 1985; Ad Hoc Committee on the Use of Microcomputers in Developing Countries, 1986; Gaal & Burchfield, 1988; Dhungana & Butterfield, 1988), supports a series of generalizations about EMIS development.

1. There is an inevitability about the move to computer-based information management in education. Government officials, educators, and donor agency officials recognize that efficient information management is a necessary condition for continued social and economic development. Information is a currency of exchange and increasingly a precondition of political and financial support across ministries, among governments,

and with international donor agencies. Even in countries with little history of information collection or use, government officials appear to recognize the importance of strengthening their management information systems. The failure to do so has progressively serious consequences as competition for national and international resources heightens. While success with EMIS is mixed, it is unlikely that failure to successfully implement a management information system would be accepted as an adequate reason to abandon the effort, given the current pressures.

2. Decision makers frequently are unable to specify in advance what information they need in planning, policy formulation, and project monitoring activities. This task then falls to "information experts" who construct the information system based on their own judgments of what is needed. The information specialists design the system in a vacuum and it ends up being irrelevant from the standpoint of political users' perceived needs (Imboden, 1980).

3. The inability of data systems to provide timely, relevant, and accurate data is cited by decision makers as the main reason for their nonuse of quantitative information.

4. Case studies of EMIS implementation and use indicate that the more successful information management systems are those that emphasize lower levels of technology, local participation in all stages of system development, and that respond to clearly articulated information needs. Unfortunately, most current EMIS initiative in the Third World continues to emphasize high technology and expatriate leadership, often with little meaningful local participation.

5. Information systems are most useful at the planning stage—decision makers have little ability to react to the information provided or to alter policy or practice once those have been implemented.

6. The introduction of a data management system is nearly always preceded by a formal needs assessment, required by the donor as justification for the investment. However, the design of data management systems generally is not based on an analysis of the management system that really operates within a ministry. Management of a project or a ministry is normally a complex structure of numerous levels of decision making with various degrees of delegation of power. Educational managers often do not have the authority to make decisions based on the information provided. The list of management tasks that information systems are supposed to address often has no relationship to the managerial tasks that actually are performed in the project (Imboden, 1980).

7. Data management systems often are presented as an evaluative tool, a means of monitoring program effects. Case studies show that what is being managed are inputs and in some cases physical targets. Project management is not responsible for project effects and goals and therefore is not concerned with their management. Most often, no one has the authority or clear responsibility to manage outputs and goals, and they tend not be be managed.

8. The absence of an identified user for the information system is a major reason for the failure of that system. Intended users frequently do not know how to interpret and use quantitative data, so they ignore them. Some potential users are excluded by restrictions on or confusion about who may have access to the data.

9. Information systems are often overdesigned in terms of the information that is really required by decision makers. Ministry personnel need hard information on inputs and outputs that generally is easily obtainable. In terms of effects, decision makers require information on general trends, but no hard evidence. Donor agencies often express an interest in effects and goals, however, information from data systems is used by those agencies to a surprisingly limited extent (Imboden, 1980).

10. Incentives in developing countries to use objective information are weak. Managers within ministries tend to be rewarded for securing additional funds. Careful data analysis may reveal problems that might delay the funding of additional projects.

11. In many countries, more data is collected than is analyzed or used. Many developing (as well as developed) countries are characterized by duplication of information gathering activities, lack of coordination among data gathering efforts, and a failure of data managers to anticipate how data from one sector could be of interest to decision makers in another sector. Non-use of data is often attributed to the very limited interpretation of the masses of data that get collected.

12. Outside technical assistance often is counter-productive to the development of a data system since key steps in planning and implementation are done by outsiders rather than local staff. Outside assistance should be limited to specific short-term assignments and should be restricted to offering advice and not include the execution of a task.

These findings suggest that EMIS have not been a panacea for educational decision makers. However, the problems encountered are often a product of EMIS managers failing to adequately understand or accommodate the political and social realities of the settings into which information systems are introduced. The next section, then, turns to a consideration of selected issues in EMIS design.

DESIGNING AN EMIS

An EMIS is an overall system for providing relevant and timely information to decision makers. These systems can be in the service of a particular program or project, an administrative department, or an entire government agency. At all of these levels, the quantitative data available through an EMIC has four primary uses: describing the status of a program or system; identifying trends; monitoring the progress of particular programs or projects; and developing projections for use in planning. The relative importance assigned to these four uses will have ramifications for how the information system should be designed, the type of personnel and staff training required, and the position of the information system within the organization.

The most pressing need for many education ministries is for current, reliable, and accurate information *describing the status* of the present education system. Ministries of education in several countries report that they do not have accurate counts of the number of schools, students, or teachers currently in the system (Government of Liberia, 1988; Government of Yemen, 1986). Even in countries with a longer history of collecting these types of basic descriptive data, the quality of these data often are low or highly variable.

To the extent that descriptive data are collected systematically, summarized, and reported on an annual basis, the yearly reports can serve as the basis for *identifying trends* in the education system. This is accomplished by generating data in comparable form and definition for each year to permit comparisons across time.

Trend identification represents a direct extension to the use of descriptive data. Identification of historical trends are less threatening than projections because they usually are confirmation of what people already realize, though the data may add a sense of dimension and degree that was not fully appreciated at the more intuitive level. Further, historic trends to not necessarily convey the same urgency to action carried by projections, since trends refer to the past. Nonetheless, they foreshadow the future and provide stimulus for discussions that descriptive data alone may not provide.

While descriptive data are the most basic need, *project monitoring* is more often the reason an information system is actually introduced. The implementation of information systems, particularly computer-based systems, is frequently through the urging and financial support of donor agencies. Their motives often are related to their need to monitor, or have the host government agency monitor, the progress of the projects they fund. Hence, the introduction of microcomputer-based information systems is generally through project-linked funding. There are distinct advantages to starting an information system in this way. The project parameters, key policy questions, and people involved are more narrowly defined, and system implementation is more manageable. Moreover, project-linked information systems provide an incremental way to introduce EMIS to the larger ministry. Project use provides a demonstration of management information systems (MIS) to the larger audience of ministry personnel and allows operational problems to be detected and corrected while the system still operates on a small scale. Project-linked information systems often are better funded than general Ministry of Education (MOE) activities, since they have donor support and the donors are more likely to continue funding to ensure success of the activity.

The development of *projections* is the application most directly useful to planning, yet it is the least frequently done. Projections are about future events. Since the events have not yet occurred, there is the possibility that decisions and actions can be undertaken to alter their course. Projections, then, hold open the possibility of intervention to shape future events—a possibility that is not as clearly contained in the analysis of historic trends. In this sense, projections are a basic ingredient to planning. Yet two factors may inhibit their use. Decision makers may not have the technical expertise to understand fully how projections are developed or how they are to be interpreted as a basis for action. They may not understand about the degree of probability and error generally associated with predictions. Even when they do, interventions often involve negotiation, conflict, and political risk that may not be attractive to the decision maker. In either situation, projection data may not be sought.

For example, a recent study of major education reports in Somalia over the last 10 years found that only donor-sponsored studies provided projections on key educational variables; ministry-sponsored studies reported only descriptive data on past system performance (Gaal & Burchfield, 1988). Somali ministry officials reported, however, that they did not refer to donor studies when formulating educational policy; they referred only to MOE studies. This was attributed, in part, to ministry officials not understanding how the projections were calculated or how they could be used. The MOE studies to which they did refer were not as informative, but local ministry personnel understood what the numbers meant and how they were derived. For *them*, the local studies were more informative, though they conveyed less information.

BROAD VS. NARROW SPECTRUM SYSTEMS

EMIS are nearly always designed in situations of ambiguity about what information will be needed or how it will be used. At the same time, these systems are criticized for not providing relevant information in a timely manner. Decision makers often are faced with decision situations that arise suddenly and revolve around issues that were not anticipated, yet require immediate action. The lack of relevant data to address the question, even after a ministry has invested heavily in a data system, is judged as a failure of the data system (rather than as poor planning or weak vision on the part of the decision maker).

In an effort to blunt such criticism and to be more responsive, information system managers often move to a broad spectrum data collection strategy in which large amounts of data are collected against the possibility that unexpected questions might arise. As those questions emerge, the data with which to formulate a response are then already available. This approach to information management is widely described as a "decision support system" and is a relatively common approach among public sector agencies in more industrialized countries.

However, the experience of many developing countries is that the collection of a great deal of data without a clear plan for its use tends to be counter-productive. Case studies show that far more data is collected than is ever analyzed or used, physical retrieval systems (codebooks, data tapes, discs, output) are poor, and the availability of massive amounts of data overtaxes the capacity of information center staff—who are unable to service the information requests even though the data may be available (Imboden, 1980; Chapman & Dhungana, 1988). Too much data can swamp a data system—leading to the charge that the data system is not responsive, not timely, and ineffective. Not having the data might be a more protective position than having it and being unable to produce it in a useable form when it is needed.

A major decision, then, for MIS designers is the extent to which the data system is to be *broadly focused* to service as yet unanticipated data needs or *narrowly focused* to concentrate attention on those data already recognized as important. This is a continuum, not a polar choice, and both extremes hold risks. However, experience with EMIS in developing countries reflects an irony—the dynamics of information use often push a data system toward a broad spectrum approach, which ultimately can lead to non-use or collapse of the system.

The alternative is to start smaller and to focus on fewer, more clearly defined information needs, but to do it in a way that allows incremental system expansion over time. Within this strategy, data sets are conceived as modular—each modular addresses a self-contained set of questions. These modules, in turn, can be linked together to support construction of a broader set of derived indicators and to address a wider set of questions. (These techniques are discussed in the next section.) By starting small, a data system may not develop the political constituency of satisfied users that some believe is necessary to EMIS success. By contrast, starting big may result only in more users and less satisfaction.

COMPONENTS OF AN EMIS

An EMIS consists of components: (1) a specification of data needs; (2) selection of appropriate indicators; (3) a procedure for collecting, coding, and storing the data; (4) a system for analysis (manual or computer-based); (5) personnel trained to conduct the analysis; and (6) personnel who can interpret the information after it has been analyzed and relate the results back to the questions and policy issues under discussion. If any one of these components is missing, the usefulness of the EMIS will be severely limited and the effort to develop it will be wasted. The following discussion addresses selected key issues encountered at each of these points.

SPECIFICATION OF DATA NEEDS

Specifying data needs is a first step in designing an EMIS. A common misunderstanding in specifying data needs is over the nature of the decisions to be made. There is a need to distinguish between questions that are essentially empirical—those that can be resolved by referring to data–and questions that are, at root, normative judgments that can be resolved only by the exercise of personal or collective judgment. Empirical questions address such issues as which educational treatments are related to higher student achievement, positive attitudes, or greatest long-term economic benefits. Normative questions are moral in nature and concern what a person or society *should* do. Such questions are resolved only when a person or group with the appropriate authority, stature, or prestige renders a decision. Normative deliberations can sometimes be informed by data, such as how many people might be affected by a policy, but ultimately, normative questions are resolved through individual or collective judgment.

Misspecification about the nature of the decisions under discussion leads to confusion about data needs, as managers make essentially empirical determinations without realizing the potential relevance of data or, alternatively, seek data when the issue can only be resolved by the exercise of normative judgment. When empirical questions are treated as normative, program managers may make resource allocation decisions without attention to the appropriate data on the relative consequences of alternative courses of action. When normative questions are treated as empirical, serious resource misallocations occur when people "chase data" in response to questions that, in reality, can only be resolved by the exercise of judgment.

Even when empirical questions are recognized as such, mangers may not be in a political position to rely entirely on objective data in rendering a decision. Third World decision makers operate within organizational structures and traditions that place more emphasis on personal or familial ties than on objective data. Effective education information systems must be developed from a realistic assessment of what types of decisions can be based on objective data. This is not to imply that important data needs should be ignored because they have negative political ramifications. Rather, data managers must understand that offering information on politically sensitive topics may not result in users taking action and that it may foster hostility toward the data system itself and those charged with its management.

Actual determination of what types of data to collect can be formulated as responses to three questions: What data are necessary to meet program reporting requirements? What data are desired as input to resource allocation, planning, and policy discussions? And, what level of precision is appropriate and necessary?

The use of an EMIS to help meet existing reporting requirements is the most credible beginning point for a system because it addresses a function MOE project managers and government officials already perform. Project managers understand the reporting function and reporting requirements generally are already specified. Servicing report requirements is an attractive beginning point because the EMIS is viewed as reducing an aspect of workload that managers often view as unappealing.

Designing an EMIS in anticipation of policy questions that the data should address is more important, but also more difficult. Decision makers often are unsure of the policy questions they will face, unaware of the analytic strategies available to them, and unfamiliar with how data can help them address the problems that do arise. They are unable to specify the data they need.

Forces outside the Ministry of Education often dictate the issues that take on unexpected urgency. By the time the urgency is apparent, there is little time for new data collection or even analysis of the data that may already be collected. Unable to anticipate the issues, officials frequently do not have the appropriate mix of policy analysis skills represented in the staff people available to them.

Compounding the dilemma is the reluctance of many policy makers to engage in proactive policy analysis or to encourage this on the part of their staff. Probing data to examine implications of alternative policy scenarios often is interpreted as implying criticism of present government policies. Such actions hold political risks and frequently are discouraged, if not viewed as outright subversion.

Equally important as specifying data needs is specifying what level of precision is necessary and appropriate to the decisions to be made. Data is expensive to collect and maintain, especially in countries characterized by poor communications and transportation systems, limited history of data provision and use, and high levels of reporting error. As precision increases, so do the costs. Given the limited resources that characterize many projects, serious decisions need to be made about how much accuracy is necessary.

Many management decisions are made in response to general trends; high degrees of precision are unnecessary. Timeliness matters more than precision. Information is needed quickly and decisions are preempted with the passage of time. Commitments to courses of action come early and sometimes are irreversible. Information system managers, then, need to monitor the trade-offs between the value added by continued analysis versus actual benefits of getting the data in use (Chambers, 1981). Two principles must guide the selection of what data to collect: (1) knowing what is not worth knowing, and (2) recognizing the degree of accuracy required (Chambers, 1981). More data does not always assure a better decision; order of magnitude and direction of change may be all that are needed or will be used.

Unfortunately, many data system managers fail to understand this trade-off. The pragmatic approach of "rapid assessment" is offensive to many data analysts, whose training emphasized caution. They may fear that the lack of precision will be the basis of a future criticism of their work. Indeed, decision makers' criticism that data are not sufficiently relevant or timely are interpreted as a demand for *more* rather than *better* data, which may only serve to further slow the system.

SPECIFICATION OF INDICATORS

Once data needs are specified, those data must be operationalized as a set of indicators. Indicators are the proxies used to represent the underlying reality of a system or program. They are the measures used to represent individual and system performance along dimensions judged important in planning and resource allocation (Chapman & Windham, 1988; Windham, 1988). For example, test scores are commonly used as an indicator of academic achievement, increased annual earnings sometimes serve as an indicator of program impacts, and student retention may serve as an indicator of the internal efficiency of a school system.

As proxies, indicators represent a necessary oversimplification of the underlying reality. The appropriateness of particular indicators is judged in terms of their fidelity with the underlying reality they represent, the extent to which the indicators are relevant and understandable by the data users and, the extent to which data on these indicators can be collected and analyzed in a cost-effective manner. A full discussion regarding the development, use, and interpretation of indicators is provided in an excellent monograph by Windham (1988). Two issues are of special relevance to the present discussion—the formulation and use of derived indicators and the use of common coding schemes to link data sets.

Derived Indicators

Storage and retrieval capacity of the information system limits the number of first-order indicators—those on which data is collected directly. However, these first-order indicators can be combined to form a series of second-order, or derived, indicators—such as student/teacher ratios, unit and cycle costs, attrition cost index, and textbooks per student ratios—that expand the utility of the data set. These second-order indicators need not be stored in the data base, but can be calculated as they are needed.

Common Coding Schemes

A data set, understood within an EMIS, is a set of information about the education system—results of a national school enrollment study and results of the latest national census are each data sets. A data base consists of several data sets. Within a data base, the data sets can sometimes be combined, if sufficient information exists on which to combine them. For example, if the census data on population by age group for each district can be combined with school enrollments for each district, important new questions about school location can be answered that could not be answered by either set alone.

The purpose of using a common coding scheme is to provide the basis for linking data sets that concern the same schools, villages, or individuals but that were collected at different times or by different agencies. To the extent that any given person, school, or village has a unique code number and information about that person or location appears in two data sets, microcomputers can be used to link those data together.

Use of a common coding scheme dramatically increases the usefulness of data collected about a school. It allows the data to be used to investigate questions and relationships well beyond those underlying the reasons for the separate data collections. It enhances the efficiency and cost-effectiveness of data gathering, since data collected for one purpose can serve other analytic purposes as they are merged with other data sets.

In developed countries, these coding schemes are developed by government and their use mandated—such as social security numbers—or are initiated by private agencies and adapted for common practice through more informal means—such as the use of Educational Testing Service codes to designate colleges and universities in the United States. In developing countries, government generally needs to take the initiative in designing and mandating an appropriate coding scheme.

Implementing the scheme requires considerable cross-department and cross-agency cooperation, since the value of the system is only realized as all groups are using exactly the same codes. There must be one group responsible for maintaining the coding scheme, and changes in coding schemes (as new schools are built, new towns formed) have to be introduced simultaneously at all participating ministries. A common coding scheme is expensive to get started. Until school personnel understand the system and know the correct code designation for their school, someone in the data collection agency has to look them up manually.

PROCEDURES FOR COLLECTING, CODING, AND STORING DATA

A majority of the error in national education data is introduced during collection and coding phases by data providers who do not understand what is expected of them, believe that providing the requested information will be detrimental to their interests, or make arithmetic errors in reporting (Chapman & Boothroyd, 1988). These problems persist due to proper incentives at the school level for reporting data, the use of poorly trained personnel for data transcription and coding, and weak or nonexistent verification procedures. Since a considerable literature discusses issues of collecting, coding, and storing data in computer-based information systems, the reader is directed to other sources. (See Babbie, 1986; Ad Hoc Panel on the Use of Microcomputers in Developing Countries, 1986).

SYSTEMS FOR ANALYZING DATA

In most countries, the rapid growth of the education system long ago outstripped the capacity of manual data systems. This resulted in delays or breakdowns in quantitative information flow or in a switch to a computer-based system. Until recently this meant a mainframe system. But mainframe systems carried their own problems. High cost, complicated programming requirements, unreliability of the equipment, and delays in or unavailability of servicing all contributed to a healthy skepticism about reliance on high technology. Any disruption could incapacitate the information flow within the ministry. Consequently, the use of mainframe computers for information management frequently was backed up by a manual system that could be used if the mainframe ceased to function. This precaution, although necessary, tended to undermine users' confidence in the computer as a reliable source of information. Too often the computer was unavailable when analyses were needed. Staff realized that if they relied on the computers for essential information on the conduct of ministry affairs, serious consequences could follow if the equipment was unable to function. Thus the use of computers, rather than enhancing MIS efficiency, sometimes reduced it, to the extent that a parallel manual system needed to be maintained.

The advent of microcomputers provided a low-cost alternative that was less sensitive to environmental conditions (than a mainframe), more portable, which allowed it to be moved when electricity was off to parts of a city, and easier to operate. Powerful data management and analysis software that did not require knowledge of computer programming languages were widely available.

The low cost permits redundancy and dedicated use. Several comparable machines can be purchased for the cost of one mini or mainframe system. If a microcomputer breaks down, the ministry is still able to get the data it needs. Equally important is dedicated use. When a mainframe is purchased, it is justified in terms of its multiple uses across ministries. Analysis of national education data competed with the data analysis demands of other sectors and frequently received a lower priority. The low cost of microcomputers has made it more feasible to dedicate a computer to a particular project, bureau, or ministry for its exclusive use.

Five criteria should guide selection of hardware—compatibility, redundancy, versatility, simplicity, and durability. Compatibility means that software and auxiliary hardware that operate on one machine can be operated on another. Non-compatibility has proven to be a serious problem in many countries, as different ministries and even different departments within the same ministry order different equipment due to preferences of a donor who is financing the equipment, the persuasion of a local computer dealer, cost, or simple ignorance about the importance of compatibility as a criteria in equipment selection. This can result in development of parallel or competing information systems that cannot be linked or shared. One example is that in Somalia, the Ministry of Education was provided with Wang microcomputers through a United States Agency for International Development (USAID) contract, the choice dictated in part by the desire to be compatible with the type of equipment used by the USAID mission and in part by the availability of servicing. However, the only major local computer training program for government employees in the country used IBM compatible equipment.

Redundancy assumes compatibility. Redundancy, discussed earlier, means having more than one hardware system that can be used to access and analyze a given data set. If a microcomputer breaks, work can continue on another computer until it is fixed. Versatility refers to the ability of the equipment to be adaptable to a wide range of settings. Microcomputers have a strong advantage over mainframe systems because they can be physically moved to accommodate changing work patterns, staff configurations, and information needs. However, even within microcomputers, some systems have greater versatility than others. Simplicity refers both to the ease with which the hardware can be operated and maintained and the "user friendliness" of the software that is available to be run on the system. Data analysis depends more on the software than the hardware—programs are available that offer considerable analytic power yet do not require complex programming skills and can be mastered by users with relatively little technical computer training. Finally, durability refers to the resilience of the EMIS system to the harsh physical settings in which they occasionally are used. The difficulties and delays experienced in getting computer equipment repaired makes durability a major consideration in the long-term success of EMIS efforts.

One risk in the early stages of EMIS is that the system is overwhelmed by requests for new and different types of data analyses. It is important, then, that clear mechanisms be established for setting priorities for data analysis. The criteria for determining access and priority might include how clearly the analysis is related to policy issues under discussion, the time frame in which the information is required, the ability of the official requesting the analysis to interpret and use the results, and the amount of staff and computer time that will be tied up in conducting the analysis. To help reduce pressure on the system, some EMIS managers have been successful in developing a system of standard report formats for areas in which there are routine reporting needs. This frees staff for responding to special reporting and analysis needs.

PERSONNEL TRAINED TO CONDUCT THE ANALYSIS

Some studies of management information centers suggest that information systems give rise to a new elite—people who derive their power from being gatekeepers of information (Imboden, 1980). That pattern, however, is not consistently true of the education sector. Brokering information access into personal power comes only if quantitative data become sufficiently important in the decision process, a situation that in many places has not yet occurred. Special knowledge of computers results in prestige, but not necessarily enhanced personal power. At present stages of development in Africa, for example, the problem is just the reverse—attracting and retaining skilled personnel in the face of increasing competition for those personnel from the private sector and other more prestigious or better-paying sector agencies. Training of staff in information management and computer operations dramatically changes their opportunity cost of working in the Ministry of Education.

The staff turnover that characterizes EMIS operations has three implications for EMIS design. First, staff training has to be continuous— not just to accommodate new developments in information management, but to compensate for staff turnover. Continuous training has budget implications that frequently are overlooked in initial EMIS planning. Secondly, documentation of data (codebooks, output, etc.) has to be good enough to allow new people to maintain the work flow without disruption. If a new staff member cannot make sense of a previous year's data, the value of the data collection is jeopardized. Finally, ministries of education need to assure operation of an adequate incentive to retain personnel once they are trained. This can be complicated, since salaries competitive with the private sector are generally outside civil service pay scales.

Once personnel have been selected and trained, there are three primary patterns for organizing EMIS staff. They can be assigned to work on issues pertinent to a particular level of the education system. For example, one person may do all analysis of secondary school data. Presumably one advantage is that this person is aware of the different types of data across one level of the education system. Secondly, staff members can be assigned to issues—for example, one person in charge of enrollment tracking, another person in charge of teacher supply data. The advantage here is that a person builds experience and expertise in collecting and analyzing a particular type of data. Supposedly, this person is better aware of the various data sources that relate to a set of issues and how to link those data sets across years. Finally, the staff can be organized into "issue teams"—in which a team of analysts are assigned to issues as they become important. This approach provides a broader skill mix, but may trade off detailed knowledge of the various relevant data that address an issue. The choice of staff assignment pattern will be a function of staff size, individual strengths and expertise, and user demands on the information system.

DATA INTERPRETATION

Proper interpretation often is the stumbling block of an information system. Effective EMIS needs policy analysts who can develop projections, design and test simulations, interpret the implications of emerging trends in the data, and present those findings clearly to others in positions of authority. Successful analysis at this level requires advanced training in such areas as economics, planning, and evaluation. Those who have such skills face two dilemmas. First, in countries with limited management capacity, people with such skills often move quickly into prominent administrative and political positions. They quickly become too busy to be involved as a staff person in policy analysis or day-to-day EMIS management.

Secondly, policy analysis that links data back to action too often is in the service of officials more interested in justifying a course of action chosen for political reasons than openly examining alternatives in pursuit of the best choice. Many ministries discourage freelance policy analysis, often imposing restrictions on who can access data or receive study results. This pattern, in turn, tends to discourage policy analysts, who feel their contribution is being ignored or given inadequate attention and, as such people leave for other opportunities, it exacerbates the shortage of ministry personnel capable of relating EMIS output back to the decision context of the education sector.

KEY ISSUES IN UTILIZATION

The remainder of this chapter discusses three issues of particular importance in determining the extent quantitative data from an EMIS will be useful or used. These include the potential political resistance to improved information, the threat posed by low data quality, and the need to accommodate multi-level analysis and interpretation of data.

Resistance to EMIS

Effective information systems are not necessarily popular innovations. Decision makers may view information systems as intruding on their autonomy as their decisions need to be justified in terms of more objective data to a wider circle of others. They enable a level of accountability that may operate against the interests of individuals who have found ways to exploit poor information flow.

Special interests can exploit poor information flow when officials make administrative decisions that benefit some person or group that would not be supported by the data, were they available. To the extent data become available, officials' options for shaping decisions to favor themselves or some special constituent is curtailed as they need to justify their decision to others. For example, in some countries, ministry approval for school construction is seen as a form of patronage, a way to reward a village or secure political support. It generates construction contracts, employment for teachers, and community good will. Abuses are evident when some districts have multiple schools while other, larger districts have none. As the data on population and school location that would support a more systematic approach to school placement becomes widely available, decision makers often are constrained by their own fears that decisions based on self-interest may become more widely known.

The case of teacher assignment in one West African country illustrates how poor information can be exploited to the point that strong vested interests opposing improved information can emerge. Official appointment of a new teacher in that country requires 29 approval signatures from personnel across three different ministries before the teacher officially can be put on the government payroll. The difficulty of securing these signatures leads to hiring delays of up to a year. These delays pose serious problems for schools faced with teacher turnover as teachers die, relocate, or resign during a school year. To compensate for the bureaucratic delays, the MOE allows headmasters to hire replacement teachers on a provisional basis while they secure their full appointment. During the provisional period, the provisional teacher can receive and cash the paycheck of the teacher they replaced.

While the system was a reasonable adaptive response to an overly elaborated bureaucracy, it lead to another set of unanticipated problems. The teacher pay system in that country is tiered on the basis of education credentials. Provisional teachers with less educational background than the teachers they replaced continued to receive the higher salary of their predecessor. Those teachers have no incentive to update the ministry information because it would result in a salary cut. Consequently, many teacher replacements go unrecorded at the central ministry level.

However, of greater threat to the system was that headmasters would sometimes choose not to replace departed teachers and, instead, would collect and cash those paychecks themselves. Some MOE officials participated in the same scheme, supplementing their own income by not forwarding notices of teacher turnover to the Ministry of Finance and then cashing those teachers' checks.

The example illustrates how poor information flow can be exploited for personal gain. However, the situation created by the exploitation had a series of secondary consequences. National data on teachers' level of education and teacher preparation were incorrect, since the education level of those officially recorded as teachers did not necessarily correspond to the education level of those actually doing the teaching. Consequently, planning for education development was seriously constrained by a data system that bore little relationship to the underlying reality in the schools. For example, efforts to plan for in-service teacher training were hampered by the inability of program managers to secure accurate information on the dimensions of the training needs.

An improved information system, capable of cross-checking teacher salary information with other school data would pose a serious threat to this informal system that exploited poor teacher data. To correct and improve that data system would expose practices that would jeopardize individuals' financial situations and could expose some of them to criminal charges. Hence, strong financial incentives operated to resist an improved information system.

Data Quality

Primary attention to implementing data systems often has been on clarifying the policy issues that the data are intended to address and presenting the data to users and decision makers in relevant and useable ways. Frequently overlooked is the quality of the data that gets collected and stored. The sophistication of the subsequent analyses or output may further mask underlying problems with the meaningfulness or trustworthiness of the data (Chapman & Boothroyd, 1988).

Chapman and Boothroyd (1988) identify seven threats to data quality in developing countries—errors in reporting data at the school level; in transferring and summarizing data as they move through the collection system; in the treatment of missing data; lack of consensus about data definitions; the inability to merge data sets across departments or over time; errors due to low reliability and validity of data collection instruments; and errors introduced by the failure of analysts to understand the assumptions of their analytic programs. Of these, school-level errors in reporting appear to be one of the most serious.

For example, research on data quality in 35 classrooms in Yemen found a 56 percent discrepancy in student enrollment between school records and the official enrollment reports submitted to the ministry by these schools (Chapman & Boothroyd, 1988). There was a discrepancy of over 25 percent in reported enrollment due to errors in transferring data from school reports to the ministry summaries. Yet, a study of school enrollment in two regions of Somalia indicated that arithmetic errors in school and regional enrollment reports accounted for less than 1 percent error. In Somalia, however, substantial discrepancies (23 percent) were detected between the number of schools reported to exist in the regional education reports and the number submitting a MOE school report form (Chapman, Gaal, & Burchfield, 1988).

The causes and direction of reporting error varies by country. In Liberia there are financial incentives at the school and district level for under-reporting student enrollments (Government of Liberia, 1988). The under-reporting occurs to mask the retention of student registration fees by the headmaster or country education officer. Some of the retained money is used for operation expenses of the schools and the ministry, while some of it is diverted for personal use. In Nepal, on the other hand, there are financial incentives for over-reporting enrollments, since the Ministry of Education subsidy to each school is based on a school's reported enrollment.

For example, a study of data quality in Botswana and Somalia found that school headmasters and MOE officials regarded 10 percent error in national education data as acceptable but estimated that the actual error was closer to 19 percent.

Level of Aggregation

Most educational programs occur within some group context—classrooms, schools, districts. MIS managers face a series of decisions about the level at which data will be collected, analyzed, and stored. Their decisions frequently are shaped by technical concerns for system capacity. The constraints posed by the physical storage and analytic capacity of the data system lead some data system managers to store data only after it has been aggregated to classroom, school, or district level. In their efforts to solve a storage problem, they may create two equally serious but less apparent problems.

First, the same indicator can take on different meanings at different levels of analysis. For example, family income and parental employment may serve as proxies for socioeconomic status of the family when considered at the individual level of analysis. It may serve as an indicator of community resources when aggregated across a community. Similarly, student test scores may indicate individual accomplishments. When aggregated to the school level, test performance may reflect the competitive milieu of the school.

Second, aggregation tends to loose detail that forecloses the opportunity to answer certain types of questions. When test item responses are collapsed into a total score for an individual, internal consistency reliability of the test cannot be computed. When test scores are recorded only as classroom or school averages, the equity of student achievement across gender, age, or ability groupings can no longer be examined. When those same test scores are recorded only as regional totals, student achievement as a function of school characteristics cannot be examined.

Data systems designed to support the monitoring and evaluation of specific educational programs generally need to retain information at the individual and classroom levels. Systems designed to support national education policy formation often aggregate to the school level. But, even in national policy deliberation, the issues of greatest relevance regard the distribution of students, teachers, and educational materials at a level where individual information still is necessary. This means that the data storage system must be expanded (often not economically or logistically feasible), important policy issues are not addressed (leading to further charges of EMIS irrelevance), or alternative ways are found to handle data.

A common practice is to collect data in the greatest detail at which it is available and aggregate it at progressively higher stages of the education system. In theory, this ensures that detailed data are available to "back up" schools, district, and regional summaries. In practice, the strategy can backfire. For example, when headmasters are expected to complete complex school report forms (e.g., student enrollment by gender, by age group, by grade) that collect data that are not used, school-level resistance to future data requests builds.

This chapter examined key issues in the design and implementation of computer-based management information systems with particular attention to their role in improving educational quality in developing countries. EMIS can help decision makers assess the nature and extent of problems facing the education sector, guide the allocation of increasingly scarce resources, and provide justification in support of decisions made on other, more political grounds.

Better information on the education system will not itself improve education quality, but quality improvement efforts within complex social and political contexts are unlikely to succeed unless decision makers have an objective basis for assessing the dimensions of the issues they face and the probable consequences of the alternatives available to them. To help ensure the usefulness of data, an EMIS should be developed from a realistic assessment of what types of decisions can be based on objective criteria, data must be collected at a sufficient level of detail to support meaningful planning, and data need to be collected and analyzed in a manner that make them available in the decision process at the time they are needed.

It was argued that a narrow (versus a broad) spectrum data system is the most appropriate EMIS design for a developing country, but it should incorporate a series of techniques for expanding the information utility, including the use of derived indicators and common coding schemes. The data system also should be designed to accommodate multi-level data, since the same indicator can take on different meanings at different levels of aggregation. Even with attention to these design features, EMIS managers must recognize and continuously monitor threats to data quality, many of which occur even before the data is entered into the computer system. Finally, it was pointed out that effective information systems are not necessarily popular innovations; the availability of better data may limit managers' autonomy in decision making. Efforts to improve educational information need to address political as well as technical issues if better data are to result in an improved education for children.

REFERENCES

Ad Hoc Panel on the Use of Microcomputers for Developing Countries. (1986). *Microcomputers and their applications for developing countries.* Boulder, CO: Westview Press.

Babbie, E. (1986). *The practice of social research.* Belmont, CA: Wadsworth.

Brodman, J. (1985). *Microcomputer adoption in developing countries: Old management styles and new information systems, a case study of microcomputer adoption in Kenya and Indonesia.* Cambridge, MA: Harvard Institute for International Development.

Burchfield, S. (1986). *Improving energy data collection and analysis in developing countries: A comparative study in Uganda, Liberia, and Sudan.* Washington, D.C.: United States Agency for International Development, Bureau for Africa.

Chambers, R. (1981). Rapid rural appraisal: Rationale and repertoire. *Public Administration and Development, 1,* 95–106.

Chapman, D. W., & Boothroyd R. A. (1988). Threats to data quality in developing country settings. *Comparative Education Review, 32*(4), 416–429.

Chapman, D. W., & Dhungana, M. (1988, March). Education data quality in Nepal. Paper presented at the annual meeting of the American Educational Research Association, San Francisco.

Chapman, D. W., Gaal, A. H., & Burchfield, S. (1988). Education data quality in Somalia. Albany: State University of New York at Albany; The Evaluation Consortium.

Chapman, D. W., & Windham, D. M. (1988). *The evaluation of efficiency in educational development activities.* Tallahassee: Florida State University, Improving the Efficiency of Education Systems Project.

Dhungana, M., & Butterworth, B. (1988). Status report: Education management information systems research initiative in Nepal. Tallahassee: Florida State University, Improving the Efficiency of Education Systems Project.

Gaal, A. H., & Burchfield S. (1988). Education management information systems research initiative in Somalia: Status report. Tallahassee: Florida State University, Improving the Efficiency of Education Systems Project.

Government of Liberia. (1988). *Liberia education and human resources sector assessment,* (Report). Monrovia: Ministry of Education and Ministry of Planning.

Government of Somalia. (1985). *Somalia education and human resources sector assessment* (Report). Mogadishu: Ministry of National Planning.

Government of the Yemen Arab Republic. (1985). *Yemen education and human resources sector assessment* (Report). Sana'a: Ministry of Education.

Imboden, N. (1980). *Managing information for rural development projects.* Paris, France: Organization for Economic Co-Operation and Develpment.

Kemmerer, F., & Thiagarajan, S. (1988). *What is a teacher incentive system?* Tallahassee: Florida State University, Improving the Efficiency of Education Systems Project.

Windham, D. M. (1988). *Indicators of educational effectiveness and efficiency.* Tallahassee: Florida State University, Improving the Efficiency of Education Systems Project.

World Bank (1988). *Education in Sub-Saharan Africa: Policies for adjustment, revitalization, and expansion.* Washington, D.C.: The World Bank.

12

Going to Scale: Why Successful Instructional Development Projects Fail to Be Adopted

Frances Kemmerer

Much has been written about why successful projects fail at or beyond the threshold of wide-scale implementation. The homely truths of lack of political will and appropriate human and material resource capacities typically provide the rationale for an honorable if disappointing (and for those most personally involved devastating) retreat from years of investment. The outstanding questions are:

1. How can instructional innovation that is successful—that is, demonstrably superior to conventional practice—fail to pass the tests of political acceptability and resource capacity?
2. How do the characteristics of successfully diffused projects differ from the characteristics of projects that have not been implemented?
3. How can developmental projects be redesigned to increase the probability of successful diffusion?

Since implementation failure can be caused either by divergence of goals of incompatibility of goals and means, the chapter begins with a review of the ways in which project success is defined by different stakeholders in a project over the project cycle. Next, the characteristics of successfully diffused innovations are examined in the interest of identifying means of enhancing the probability of diffusion success. Finally, the differences in definition of success and the attributes of successfully diffused innovations are used to redefine the project cycle to ensure that political considerations and capacity issues are addressed.

Since, the rubric *project* is used to describe many different types of investment in developing nations (building programs, technological experimentation, and the introduction of new technologies are all classified as projects), some delimitation is in order. For the purposes of this chapter, the term project is used to refer specifically to the introduction of new educational technologies. A new educational technology is defined, in turn, as a unique combination of human and material resources designed to improve student learning (Thomas & Kemmerer, 1983; Heinich, Molenda, & Russell, 1985).

PROJECT SUCCESS: A CASE OF MULTIPLE REALITIES

Definition of project success is likely to vary both with the stage of the project (identification, design, development, evaluation, and diffusion) and relationship to the project (host country representative, donor, technical expert, host country participant, potential adapters). While the summative evaluation of the project and the projection of diffusion costs are properly developmental activities, they are classified as a separate stage for the sake of clarity.

Project Identification

Project identification may grow out of a host country/donor's ongoing discussions about quality enhancement of an educational subsector, a crisis in a subsector, or the desire, on the part of the donor, to introduce a new and potentially powerful instructional technology. As the idea for the project emerges, both the host country representative(s) and the donor are interested in maximizing visibility and impact. What each set of actors means by these terms, however, may be very different.

In the best of all possible worlds, host country representatives and donors agree both on the specification of system deficits and the means to address them. In the worst-case scenario, host country nationals may agree to a particular project not because of conviction toward intrinsic merits but because of system need for resources. In this event, system maintenance and institution building are seen as the long-term solutions to observable system weaknesses, such as rote teaching, poor examination results, or lack of supervisory support for teachers. From the perspective of the host country then, quality enhancement may not necessitate system change but system enrichment. If this is true, donor funds, regardless of the specific project purpose, will be seen as a substitute for national resources.

Project success from the donor's perspective is likely to be defined very differently. The donor is typically not interested in system maintenance but rather in system change. Inefficiencies are seen as the result not only of underinvestment but also of misallocation of existing resources. The purpose of the project is to develop an alternative use of resources in the interest of improving efficiency. For these reasons, the worst-case scenario, where the host country representative and the donor disagree profoundly on the need for basic system change, is likely to be the rule rather than the exception.

On the one hand, vested interests virtually guarantee a conservative institutional bias, a bias that favors certainty and resource aggrandizement to uncertainty and efficiency (Tornatzky, Fergus, Avellar, Fairweather, & Fleischer, 1980). Donors committed to development, whether working in more or less technological advanced nations, are, on the other hand, forced into the role of change agent by virtue of the relative size of the resources at their disposal and the recipient's poor capacity to support larger institutions. Further, the donor is typically not interested in financing system maintenance. The purpose of the innovation is to increase the efficiency of government investments in schooling. Robert Jacobs, the USAID regional advisor for southeast Asia in 1967, summarized the position of the donor thus:

The stark fact is that the kind of problems faced by educators in developing countries . . . can never be solved by traditional approaches. But these problems are in a sense self imposed. They are problems simply because educators in these countries insist on traditional classrooms with standard equipment, on the goal of having a qualified teacher for each 35 students, on bound textbooks that are costly to produce and difficult to keep up to date, on the instructional methods whereby one student performs while his classmates sit idle and passive, and all other outmoded features that countries which are exporting educational expertise are trying to replace in their own systems. (Cited in Cummings, 1986, p. 4)

However diverse the host country and donor perspectives may be, the differences often are not clear until well into the project development stage, or at a point where a decision must be made about diffusion since neither the host country representatives nor the donor has any incentive to reveal their true preferences; the host country representative is required to identify means to finance recurrent system costs and the donor may be obligated to commit a certain percentage of his or her agencies' resources to education.

Project Design

The initial agreement to design a project may be specific (to a particular technology) or general (identification of the problem). A design team, typically financed by the donor, will be tasked with either fleshing out the original proposal or conceptualizing an approach to the problems identified in the system. In the eyes of the experts, often international consultants, project success is a technical matter of configuring a particular technology or a combination of technologies to the local environment (language, teacher skills, curriculum, etc.). The consultants may or may not have first-hand knowledge of the system or access to detailed information on how the sector actually functions as opposed to how it is designed to function. Lack of information at this stage can lead to overestimation of the human resources (quantity of individuals and skills of individuals) that the host country is willing or able to commit in the development stage and overestimation of infrastructure capacity (enabling capacities such as management, training, printing, distribution, communication) and, therefore, underestimation of project costs.

During the design stage, the host country representative, regardless of his or her initial motivation for agreeing to the project, is likely to argue for maximizing the number of ministry units and schools that will be involved in the project in order to spread the resources more evenly through the system and thereby reduce resistance to the innovation. At the same time, the donor will try to contain the number of participants and minimize the layers of bureaucracy between the project team and the schools. The compromise will be dictated by the total funds available for the project.

Project Development

Once the project begins, the definition of success for the host country representative continues to be project visibility. At this stage, visibility means the observability of the acquired resources and the absence of substantive negative feedback on the quality of imported or indigenous personnel, the quality of the lessons produced, or the way in which the resources have been allocated among ministry units or schools.

The donor typically shares these concerns but they are dominated by the requirement to keep the project on schedule. Delays in the schedule of deliverables, for whatever reason, require either the reallocation of the remaining funds or costs overruns. Meeting the schedule of deliverables thus becomes the prime constraint on the decisions made by the experts hired to develop the innovation. In order to stay on schedule, personnel and infrastructure issues will be downplayed. The technical experts will substitute their own time for local counterpart time if the skills or commitment or number of those assigned to the project have been overestimated. At the same time, project funds will be used to compensate for the infrastructure weaknesses that have been discovered. For example, project funds might be used to pay for the travel of supervisors who otherwise would be unable to visit the schools or to ensure the delivery of necessary materials and services (Kemmerer & Wagner, 1986).

The commitment of additional time or other scarce project resources for infrastructure support are matters of only secondary concern to the developers. Their definition of success rests on feeding the information from the formative evaluation back into revision of the materials already developed and forward into the design of the materials not yet developed. Success lies, first, in finding the appropriate fit between lesson content and the preparation and experience of the teachers, on the one hand, and the national curriculum, on the other, and second, in minimizing the trade-off between the quantity of the lessons developed and their quality.

The local counterparts (as distinguished from project participants—typically school personnel) are likely to view success at this stage of the project in terms of monetary rewards (increased salary and allowances), training, and future career mobility. This is particularly true if participation in the project is a promotion rather than a lateral transfer. The local counterpart to the chief of party, for whom the benefits of participation are less obvious, might define project success in terms of greater responsibility. His or her interests, therefore, will lie in minimizing negative reactions to the project either by attempting to share resources or by disassociating himself or herself from project goals if these goals appear threatening to others.

For school personnel, the benefits of participation in terms of training, materials, and contact with other educationlists generally outweigh the costs of more frequent attendance at school and in the classroom (Thiagarajan & Pasigna, 1985). Generally, even those who object at the start have been won over by the end of the project development stage (Imhoff & Christensen, 1986). Nonetheless, project teachers' invidious comparison of their efforts to the average level of effort provided by teachers in conventional schools or their salaries to those of supervisors has proved a problem in more than one project (Cummings, 1986).

Summative Evaluation and Planning for Diffusion

As the developmental phase draws to a close, three activities take priority. These are the summative evaluation, publication of the evaluation results, and the design and costing of diffusion.

The typical summative evaluation measures the value added by the innovation as compared to "conventional practice" or to the "traditional approach." Either is problematic but for different reasons. In the first instance, comparison to conventional practice, it is not clear what the innovation is being compared to since non-experimental schools differ widely in resources (teacher attendance, textbooks, facilities, etc.). In the second instance, schools characterized by the full use of the "traditional approach" (mature teachers, supervisors, textbooks, and materials) are also experimental since the creation of such schools is included in the project design.

While the comparison of two treatment groups to a control group represents a valid research design, it is not an appropriate test given the context. The absence of schools with the traditional complement of resources indicates that the government does not have the resources and infrastructure strength necessary to support "traditional schools." If this is the case, it can be argued that the appropriate evaluation question is not whether the innovation is more efficient than the traditional approach but whether the new approach produces the same (or greater) gains in student achievement at a lower (or the same) cost than does the conventional approach under the same infrastructure conditions.

While this test appears to be unduly harsh, it is likely that many innovations such as programmed teaching and interactive radio (when radio is used for all subjects) are more cost-effective than current practice since they reduce the need for pre-service teacher training from years to weeks and eliminate the need for bound textbooks.

Comparisons of innovations to "what if" situations, as well as marketing programmed teaching and interactive radio as complements to rather than substitutes for teacher training (and, in some cases, textbooks) is, however, virtually dictated by the fact that neither the donor nor host country representative were willing to reveal their preferences for institutional growth or change in the project identification and design stages.

The summative evaluation, which is a technical exercise, and the presentation of the findings to an intentional audience of technical experts are at any rate probably more important to the donor than to the host country representatives, counterparts, and participants. Evaluation results are unlikely to persuade ministry officials, who have been only tangentially related to the project or who are opposed to it, that the new approach is efficacious.

The projection of costs and the design of the implementation schedule are generally based on an analysis of the costs of the material inputs and the time necessary to produce them. Rarely are the costs (in time and money) of increasing managerial and infrastructure capacity or making the transition from one system approach to another taken into consideration (Kemmerer & Wagner, 1986).

Diffusion

The decision to implement the project on a larger scale is, by definition, essentially political since it deals with the allocation of scarce national resources. The decision makers must take into account not only the monetary costs and benefits but the societal costs and benefits. At this stage, the social calculus may have less to do with the innovation's potential for improving student learning than it has to do with who stands to win and who stands to lose within the ministry. For the host country representative then, project success is defined by the active support of the constituency favoring implementation of the new technology. If the donor has promised support through the diffusion stage, the nature and amount of support itself will become an important factor in the ministry decision making.

Once the decision has been made to implement the project, decisions of success mirror those of the development stage. Host country nationals and donors look for minimal negative responses and improvement of test scores, technicians attempt to maintain the integrity of the innovation, and adopters focus on the relative ease of difficulty of usage in terms of effort demanded.

To the extent that this description of the typical project cycle is correct, it is clear that definitions of success vary both among project participants and over the life of the project. This means that even if the host country representative and the donor begin with an identical goal—to increase student learning—political pressures or simply concentration on the technical elements of project activities may well force their interests to diverge. Host country nationals will increasingly focus on the political issues related to changing resource allocation patterns, and the donor on technical issues.

As will be seen in the next section, this divergence of interests over time constitutes a threat to both a favorable implementation decision and to successful adoption.

THE CHARACTERISTICS OF SUCCESSFUL INNOVATIONS

The central conclusion of the literature on innovations, that adoption is dependent on the nature of the innovation itself, appears obvious (Solo & Rogers, 1972). In fact, however, diffusion of a practice as apparently advantageous and straightforward as boiling drinking water has failed, at times, because the wrong approach was used. In Peru, for instance, an attempt was made to convince the sick of the superiority of germ theory to local beliefs that dictated that the healthy should take cold food and only the sick cooked foods. However admirable the decision to work with the sick, it represented a poor choice in terms of diffusion since they had marginal status in the village and the effects of boiling water on health were not observable. As a result, the innovation failed (Rogers, 1983).

Examination of countless experiments of this type in fields as diverse as agriculture and mental health suggests that successful adoption of a technology is dependent on at least six factors:

1. Comparative Advantage. The innovation is perceived by the adopters as representing a comparative advantage to the technology it supersedes. (Rogers, 1983)

2. Compatibility. The innovation is considered compatible with the values, perceived needs of the adopters, and existing patterns of doing things. (Rogers, 1983; Thiagarajan, 1985)

3. Flexibility. The innovation is straightforward rather than complex, and, therefore, can be readily understood and tried by the adopters. (Rogers, 1983; Foster, 1974; Thiagarajan, 1985)

4. Observability. The results of the innovation are readily observable. (Rogers, 1983)

5. Enabling Conditions. The institutional structures necessary to support the innovation exist (and are operable). (Foster, 1975)

6. Efficiency. The marginal costs of diffusion are low. (Cummings, 1986; Foster, 1974; Kemmerer & Wagner, 1986)

In sum, if the innovation appears advantageous (whether it is, in fact, or not), represents only a small change in conventional practice, does not violate folk beliefs, is not expensive to the adopter, and produces readily observable benefits, it is more likely to be adopted than not.

It is probably safe to conjecture, however, that innovations are much more difficult to diffuse through social institutions than through direct contact with potential local users. Social institutions, like ministries of education or health, tend to be protected by strong gatekeepers and to have limited contact with the potential clientele. This suggests that it is not enough to convince a high-level ministry official of the relative advantage of a new educational technology; the heads of the units needed to support implementation of the innovation, leaders of teachers unions, and local opinion leaders may also need convincing.

Moreover, the task is likely to be exceptionally difficult because the new technology, more often than not, requires change in both belief and institutional structures. Yet these structures have developed and concretized around the ideal that requires a professional teacher (in the normal school sense), professional supervisors (evaluators and master teachers), bound textbooks, and age-graded classes. Thus, both beliefs and organizational arrangements conspire to prefer the status quo to change.

For example, one implication of programmed teaching and interactive radio is that expensive pre-service training is not necessary. This has obvious advantages in terms of both the hiring of teachers (local individuals can be hired at a salary level that provides an incentive) and balancing investments in teacher and material resources (the costs of pre-service teacher training can be reinvested in educational materials). Viewed from inside the ministry, however, adoption of the new technology may be equated to settling for less. It matters little whether the educationalists from developed nations see their own teacher preparatory programs as inadequate and anachronistic. What matters is that in developed countries, pre-service training remains the principal route to teaching, teachers typically continue to carry the burden of instruction, and teacher professionalization is still being pursued. This suggests that substantial external incentives are required to make change possible.

Compatibility with existing structures, however, is only one aspect of what is meant by fitting the innovation to the local environment. Comparability with teacher practice is a more critical issue. To the extent that educational technologies represent a continuum from rote to discovery methods, then it is likely that the closer the teacher perceives the new technology to be relative to practice then the more likely he or she is to adopt it. If, for instance, the dominant teaching mode in the host country is teacher lecture/student recitation, then a technology that is based on routinized procedures such as programmed teaching might be more acceptable to potential users than one in which the teacher is uncertain of his or her rule in the instructional process (Thiagarajan, 1985).

In the United States, for example, where substantial efforts have been made to integrate computer usage into classroom instruction, research has shown that the computers are most frequently used for remediation or enrichment rather than for routine teaching/learning activities. A number of studies have suggested that this is because the students quickly surpass the teachers' mastery of both hardware and software (Becker, 1988). In short, teachers do not use computers for instruction because they do not have the expertise to feel comfortable with them.

Unfortunately, not enough research has been done to indicate whether preference for the familiar leads to adopter bias toward soft rather than hard technologies in education. Hard technologies clearly have an offsetting advantage in terms of observability. State governments in the United States, for example, have been willing to provide substantial subsidies for hardware and software purchase with only limited demonstration of effectiveness of the use of computers for general instruction.

Yet the standard of observability dictates that the *result* of the innovation, not the innovation itself, is perceivable and the idea of the innovation is readily communicable (Rogers, 1983). The value of the new educational technologies like programmed teaching and interactive radio lies in their potential for increasing the amount of classroom time actually devoted to teaching/learning, in the short run, and improved achievement, in the long run. The immediately observable results are, therefore, changes in student and teacher behaviors, not higher graduate rates, achievement, employability, and so on. Moreover, these changes tend to be observable only to the community in which the participating school is located and are rarely even the focus of summative evaluations. The evaluations *assume* changes in behavior, which may be why the effect sizes of the treatments are typically small; behaviors such as irregular attendance patterns take a long time to correct and, in the case of students, cannot be controlled by the school. Since the results of educational innovations are not immediately obvious, there is a clear need to make them so through intensive publicity and demonstration to key decision makers and potential adopters.

Ease in communicating an idea suggests that the idea can be applied with little difficulty. Educational innovations, however, like other innovations in social institutions, tend to be packaged. To produce the desired results at the least cost it is necessary for adopters to accept all rather than part of the package. Radio math, for example, is not likely to have the desired results if the teacher only uses the radio lessons that cover the content which he or she finds particularly difficult. This suggests that most educational technologies are not trialable in the same sense as are new fertilizers or medications. Teachers must have the support necessary to adopt the entire technology and feel comfortable using it. This may require short on-site supervision by the principal and a relatively slow diffusion rate.

Adopter enthusiasm, favorable summative evaluation results, and commitment to wide-scale implementation cannot overcome inadequate managerial, printing, distribution, supervision, and training capacities needed for going to scale. In many countries, the reason why "conventional" schools have not become "traditional" schools is because of the expense and difficulty of actualizing the necessary enabling structures. Books are not printed on schedule because of interministerial competition for the government press; printed books are not delivered because the ministry has too few trucks and the roads are difficult to negotiate during certain seasons; and supervisors do not visit schools for want of allowances. For successful diffusion, the innovation then must be either exceptionally self-reliant or the weaknesses of the system addressed during project development (trainers trained, alternative systems of printing and distribution, and maintenance, in the case of hardware, put in place, and a system of project management devised and tested).

A basic requirement for successful diffusion is that costs generated by transition between instructional systems, use of the new technology, or infrastructure weakness are not shifted forward to teacher adopters. Asking adopting teachers to bear the cost, for example, of radio maintenance provides less of an incentive for taking care of the equipment than it does for not repairing the malfunctioning radio. If teachers then try to pass the cost on to their students, the new technology is likely to be rejected by the community. At the same time, the ministry itself may be unable to absorb the extra costs of the innovation. Yet, as indicated earlier, the typical cost analysis for diffusion is generally limited to calculation of the marginal cost of the innovation, all else equal. Necessary transition expenditures and infrastructure repair or redesign falls under the ceteris paribus assumption and, consequently, are not explicitly addressed. In any event, since the cost analysis is typically undertaken at the end of the developmental cycle, the information would come too late, leaving the donor with a decision to either commit new funds to see the technology through diffusion or simply run the risk of diffusion failing for want of the proverbial nail. Windham's (1983a-d) analysis of the diffusion costs of the Improved Efficiency of Learning Project (IEL) at the end of the development cycle indicated that the costs of implementation of IEL were not competitive with the costs of providing primary schools with textbooks. This led to an enormous eleventh-hour effort on the part of the project staff to redesign materials in light of the information he provided on costs, the average number of actual school days, and enrollments (Cummings, 1986; Thiagarajan, 1985). The point is that this could have been avoided by providing the contractor with better information at the beginning of the project.

While the characteristics of successfully diffused projects are difficult to replicate in an educational project because of the bureaucratic nature of educational systems and the relatively poor observability of short-run results, it seems clear that a great deal more could be done to fit the innovation to the local system. How this might be accomplished is discussed in the next section.

Redefining the Project Cycle

Comparison of the definitions of success in the typical project with the characteristics of successfully diffused innovations indicate that successful implementation of a new educational technology demands, at a minimum, changes in the sequencing of some activities and introduction of others. In some instances, this will add substantially to developmental costs. The additional costs, however, may make the difference between diffusion success and failure.

If a recent assessment of the educational subsector in which the innovation will be introduced is not available, basic but detailed information on the absorptive and management capacities (including both project and information management capacities) of the ministry, teacher characteristics, the educational task, classroom resources, and infrastructure performance is required *prior* to actual start of the project. The difference between formal descriptions of how the educational system works and actual performance suggests that school and classroom observations should play a large role in the assessment. The school and classroom observations need not be formal in the sense of the use of lengthy and expensive observation systems but they must be able to yield the necessary information on patterns of teacher attendance, typical classroom practices, and so on.

This information can then be used by the design team to do the following:

1. Select and fit the innovation as closely as possible to conventional practice to capitalize on comparability and trialability.

2. Identify infrastructure weaknesses and develop strategies to actualize the infrastructure as it has been designed, or develop alternate permanent systems of distributing materials or supervision (e.g., principals pick up materials, principals are trained as instructional leaders, etc.).

3. Select development sites on the basis of observability (city centers), as well as on the basis of political and technical considerations.

4. Develop strategies for presentation of the innovation to opinion leaders (teacher unions, teacher training personnel, etc.) and potential adopters.

5. Specify the types of training necessary for information management and project management during diffusion, and plan for integration of training into the developmental cycle.

6. Identify the least-cost site for printing, the number of pages that can be cost-effectively produced, and the replacement rate of printed materials. If the project involves radio, identification should include the least-cost site for broadcasting, the number of hours that can be cost-effectively produced, and the reception range of the broadcast.

7. Estimate the marginal cost of the innovation and all transition costs. Assess the absorptive capacity of government to incur the extra costs.

8. Design formative evaluation to provide feedback not only on materials but on teachers and student behaviors, training in project management, and infrastructure improvement schemes.

If the sector review thus provides the opportunity to obtain the information necessary to ground the technical and cost issues, it also provides the basis for addressing political concerns. Discussion of the findings of the assessment in an inter-ministerial forum permits both donor and Ministry of Education personnel to frankly discuss their preferences for change or institution-building. Work done by the United States Agency for International Development (USAID) Improving the Efficiency of Educational Systems Project in a number of developing countries suggests that such discussions increase the probability that a coalition favoring and ready to support change will be formed. The support of such a coalition not only changes ministry incentives for committing the necessary resources to development but makes those in the ministry who support reform less vulnerable to political pressure to maintain the status quo (Kemmerer, 1988).

Once development is underway it is difficult to maintain the level of inter-ministerial interest in subsector reform captured at the time of the review. Yet it is clear that involvement must be maintained at all levels of the educational system if the decision to implement is to be favorable and diffusion proceed on schedule. Project design should, therefore, include a well-researched social marketing plan. The objectives of the plan are first, to keep the attention of the policy makers focused on subsector problems and the technical issues related to development of the innovation, and second, to provide a strategy for increasing the observability of the innovation to potential adopters.

All too often, the social marketing aspects of technology transfer projects are left to the contractors. This represents a poor choice since the donor agency, not the contractor, represents a source of future funds to the ministry and since once the development stage begins, contractors are viewed by ministry officials as employees. The role of contractors in social marketing is by definition a decidedly limited one; namely, demonstrating the innovation to potential adopters.

To summarize and conclude, successful projects may fail at implementation either because project personnel ignore warning signals that delivery systems and other types of infrastructure support are inadequate or because little attempt is made to market the innovation. To increase the probability of diffusion of new instructional technologies in developing countries, project design must be based on the premise that successful adoption of the new technologies demands change in orientation and practice at all levels of the educational management and delivery systems. The need for structural change combined with the relatively poor observability of the results of instructional technologies in the short run suggests that either extraordinary incentives must be provided for system reform or more attention paid to the social marketing, which is to say, the politics, of implementation.

REFERENCES

Becker, H. (1988). *The impact of computer use on children's learning: What research has shown and what it has not shown*. Baltimore, MD: Johns Hopkins University, Center for Educational Research on Elementary and Middle Schools.

Cummings, W. K. (1986). *Low-cost primary education: Implementing an innovation in six nations*. Ottawa, Canada: International Development Research Centre.

Foster, P. J. (1974). Reflections on the Waigani Seminar. In J. Brammall and R. J.

May (Eds.), *Education in Melanesia.* The Research School of Pacific Studies, the Australia National University, and the University of Papua New Guinea.

Heinich, R., Molenda, M., & Russell, J. D. (1985). *Instructional media: And the new technologies of instruction* (2nd ed.). New York: John Wiley.

Imhoof, M., & Christensen, P . R. (Eds.). (1986). *Teaching English by radio: Interactive radio in Kenya.* Washington, D.C.: Academy for Educational Development.

Kemmerer, F. (1988, November). *The use of information in inducing, tracking, and monitoring change.* Paper presented at the World Bank and U.S. Agency for International Development Conference on Education Policy Adjustment: "Raising School Quality and Efficiency," Washington, D.C.

Kemmerer, F., & Wagner, A. (1986, June). *The limits of the use of educational technology in developing countries.* Paper prepared for presentation at the International Conference on Economics of Education: "Tackling New Policy Issues," Dijon, France.

Rogers, E. M. (1983). *Diffusion of innovations* (3rd ed.). New York: The Free Press.

Solo, R. A., & Rogers, E. M. (Eds.). (1972). *Inducing technological change for economic growth and development.* East Lansing: Michigan State University Press.

Thiagarajan, S. (1985). *Factors that contribute to inefficiencies in primary schools in developing nations: A survey of the literature.* (Project Report for USAID Honduras No. 522–9105). Washington, DC: United States Agency for International Development.

Thiagarajan, S., & Pasigna, A. (1985). *Final contractor's report: Improved Efficiency of Learning (IEL) Project* (Final report to the U.S. Agency for International Development, Contract No. AID/AFR–C–1494). McLean, VA: Institute for International Research.

Thomas, J. A., Kemmerer, F. (1983). *Money, time, and learning* (Final Report to the National Institute of Education, Contract No. 400–77–0094). Chicago, IL: University of Chicago.

Tornatzky, L. G., Fergus, E. O., Avellar, J. W., Fairweather, G. W., & Fleischer, M. (1980). *Innovation and social process: A national experiment in implementing social technology.* Elmsford, NY: Pergamon Press.

Windham, D. M. (1983a, January). *Cost issues in the Liberian Improved Efficiency of Learning (IEL) Project* (Report No. 1). Monrovia: Ministry of Education.

Windham, D. M. (1983b, March). *Internal economies in the Liberian Improved Efficiency of Learning (IEL) Project* (Report, No. 2). Monrovia: Ministry of Education.

Windham, D. M. (1983c, June). *The relative cost-effectiveness of the Liberian Improved Efficiency of Learning (IEL) Project* (Report No. 3). Monrovia: Ministry of Education.

Windham, D. M. (1983d, September). *Cost estimates of the Revised Improved Efficiency of Learning (IEL) Project* (Supplemental Report to the IEL Cost Analysis Project). Monrovia: Ministry of Education.

13

Language Issues and National Educational Systems: Experiences in African Developing Nations

Jerry L. Messec

Most instructional interventions assume that students and instructor share a common language, a shared basis of formal communications through which instruction can be delivered. In many developing country settings this assumption is not met. Language differences between home and school, between students and teachers, among students, and language switching between grades represent major barriers to student attainment and efficient flow through the education system. Yet, in cases in which national self-identity and educational policy intersect, the loss to educational efficiency may be assigned only secondary importance.

The language policy of a country is a key point around which efforts to maximize educational efficiency may come into conflict with a nations' efforts to reflect a heritage, express an identity, or appease political forces. It is a point at which educational interventions must be carefully linked to the larger political, social, and economic framework of a country. It is also a point at which the brunt of the compromises to be made (if any) more likely will fall on the designers of instruction than on the political leadership.

This chapter examines some language issues that confront educational decision makers in developing nations. The consequences of language choices, whether such choices are clearly articulated from top governmental levels in support of explicit development goals or whether they are unstated and evolving from past colonial and present political experiences, can be shown to affect both the internal and external efficiency of educational systems. This chapter proposes no solution to the complex

Table 13.1
First and Last Languages Ranked by Economic Power, 1978 (GNP in U.S.
Millions)

LANGUAGE	GNP
English	2,938,850
Russian	965,520
Japanese	836,160
German	811,960
French	565,220
Chinese	448,550
Spanish	400,970
Arabic	219,590
Italian	218,320
Portuguese	210,340
- - - - - - - - - - - - -	- - -
Sinhalese	2,720
Albanian	1,920
Icelandic	1,880
Nepali	1,850
Khalkha	1,470
Khmer	570
Somali	470
Lao	300
Dzonkha	120
Divehi	20

Source: *Europa handbook: A world survey*. (1978). London, England: Europa Publications.
Note: The GNP of officially multilingual states has been allocated to the language that
    dominates the state's institutions (e.g., French in Belgium).

language choices facing developing nations who are attempting to develop national educational systems, but discusses the recent history of
language use in several African nations, the modern language choices
(implicit and explicit) of these nations, and the possible effects of these
choices on national educational systems. Language issues in Somalia are
given special attention, both because of the language problems presently
causing inefficiencies in the educational system and because of the author's experiences in that country.

LANGUAGE ISSUES IN AFRICA

The astounding complexity of languages across Africa excites the lin-
guist and confounds those involved in the complex process of development. However one looks upon development, history offers many
examples for the argument that linguistic homogeneity offers greater
competitive efficiency (Fishman, 1974). As Table 13.1 shows, those countries heading the per capita gross national product list are also those

Figure 13.1
An Example of Linguistic Complexity in West Africa

SINGLE UNIT: GOLA

GOLA, own name egola mie. LANGUAGE (or Dialect Cluster?).

Spoken by: GOLA, call themselves gola, called GULA by the MENDE.

Where spoken: Western Liberia, between Rivers Moa and St. Paul; also on the left bank of the St. Paul.

Number of speakers: 150,000 (about 8,500 in Serra Leone).

The GOLA consist of several sections, calling themselves:

den gola (from the GOLA name for the St. Paul river);

toldil (toodii), south of the den gola on the left bank of the river;

tege gola, on the right of the river, adjoining the den gola on the west, the KPELLE on the east;

senye gola, north of the tege;

mana gobla (gobla gola), on the right bank of the St. Paul as far as River Loffa;

kenbaa gola, on the right of the St. Paul;

pio gola, also on the right bank.

Nothing is known of dialectal differences within GOLA.

Source: Adapted from Laponce, J. A. (1987). *Language and their territories*. Toronto: University of Toronto Press.

countries where some resolution of linguistic complexity has been accomplished.

Resolution of linguistic complexity rarely has been the case in African countries. Even in the few countries that are officially linguistically homogenous countries, modern sector activities are conducted—at least in some part and frequently almost totally—in one of the languages that functions as an "international language" or what Fishman, Ferguson, & Das Gupta (1968) have called a "language of wider communication." This should not suggest that any vernacular ("mother tongue") language is structurally inadequate to serve as a modern sector language, but simply indicates that most have not had the opportunity to develop as such.

The number of languages in use across the African continent is unknown, a situation due both to the difficulties of conducting field research and to the enormous problems faced by researchers in sorting out dialectal, tribal, and ethnic names. In the West African area alone (Cameroon to Senegal), an estimated 500 to 1000 languages (or dialects?) are spoken (Armstrong, 1982). Figure 13.1 suggests the dimension of these problems; seven subgroups of Gola (Egola Mie) speakers in one area of western Liberia are identified, but dialectical differences are unknown.

Even this example of linguistic diversity, however, does not truly reflect the complexity of language use in rural areas in Africa. To do so, one would need also to list the use of regional languages for special functions (such as religious or social events) and the use of area lingua francas (common or commercial languages for speakers of different languages). To this list one might need to add other pidgin languages and the use of a national or international language.

In some countries, the choice of an international language has been a way of avoiding conflict among speakers of competing local languages. On the other hand, some colonial languages may not have remained dominant in the modern sector (i.e., the decline of Italian in Somalia) because they may not be seen as powerful avenues of access to international education and employment opportunities. In Asia, Indonesia is sometimes cited as a country in which a national language (Bahasa Indonesian) was afforded the opportunity to develop for modern sector use because of the perceived low utility of the colonial period international language (Dutch). African countries with English or French colonial pasts are almost certain to continue modern sector use of those languages. Because educational systems were normally well established in English and French colonies (they were of course very different systems), these languages remain as instructional languages in most countries—but not all. The perceived value of English and French in most countries has hindered the functional development of local languages and therefore their use in educational systems.

Spencer (1975) has pointed out that there seem to be three general steps in the functional development of languages.

1. *Graphization*. The development (usually alphabet adaptation with additional graphemes as needed) of a writing system.

2. *Standardization*. The emergence of a supradialectical norm, superimposed upon dialect variants, commonly a step or stage closely associated with graphization.

3. *Elaboration*. The process whereby the lexical resources are expanded to cope with the needs of increasingly complex social, economic, cultural, and technological domains, and the specialization of styles and registers for various fields. In the countries discussed in this chapter, some languages have not reached the first step of the process (i.e., some vernaculars in Liberia), while others have been written in widely accepted form but for some reason are not undergoing elaboration (i.e., Somali), such as the widespread use of a

Western language in the modern sector or the lack of publishing opportunities in-country for the language since independence.

Choice of an international language is usually dictated by the colonial history of African nations. Liberia and Sierra Leone are historically special cases in their modern origins, but their language past is not dissimilar from other African countries; that is, a Western language was established in the major urban area and dominates the modern sector, including national education. Table 13.1 attaches numbers to what both decision makers and citizens of developing nations already know. Knowledge of an international language affords access to modern sector activities and greatly increases opportunities for higher income. The collective state statistics shown in Table 13.1 may exaggerate the economic strength of national languages (they disregard unofficial state languages, such as Ukrainian and Georgian in the Soviet Union), but nevertheless they correspond well to the intuition of people in developing nations about the rankings of international languages. These 1978 figures should not be taken to suggest that the widespread use of French and English in former colonies may give way in coming years to the use of other international languages, such as Russian or Japanese, reflecting economic realignment in the postcolonial world. There are many powerful reasons (prior investments, cultural discontinuities, as well as the issue of new writing systems) why this could not happen without dramatic political changes.

It should be emphasized that linguistic competition is not limited to postcolonial African governments, but is a universal occurrence. Spencer (1975) emphasizes that language minority communities would impel themselves towards a "linguistic and cultural ghetto" if they were to insist on the sole use of their mother tongue. It is certainly clear to governments in developing nations (and elsewhere) that unlimited development of local languages for all functions does not promote nation-building efforts. The use of local languages, in fact, may be discriminatory in effect, as in the Bantu Education Act of South Africa which, by mandating the use of local languages, prevented access to the national languages of English and Afrikaans.

Somalia is sometimes noted as a nation fortunate in having a homogeneous language and culture. One language—Somali—is used (with dialectical variants) throughout the country, extending even into other countries in the region. This overlooks, however, the complexity of language use in Somali as a result of its colonial history, the late graphization of Somali, the low level of Somali language publishing, and the acceleration of donor and private sector activities using international languages (thereby hindering the elaboration of Somali). Language issues in Somali are in fact complex, not simple, and present a major obstacle to the development of a national educational system. Somali, as will be discussed below, is far from being a fortunate exception among African countries linguistically. It faces many of the difficult language policy choices now facing other African countries, and has as well a unique set of language issues as a result of its cultural and political history. These language issues are currently the source of significant inefficiencies in the education sector.

Each African country faces its own set of problems in implementing an educational language policy, but all face the economic, pedagogical, political, and linguistic consequences of their policy choices, whether such choices are made explicit or remain implicit. The immediate economic and pedagogical consequences of attempting to implement multilingual instructional programs should be carefully considered, as well as the political consequences within each country. The linguistic consequences (i.e., which languages will spread and which will not, which will proceed with elaboration and which will not) are of course closely tied to the national political situation in each country and may change rapidly with shifts in power groups.

Much has been written in developed nations concerning language issues, especially in the areas of bilingual or multilingual education. For African educational systems, however, comparisons with language issues in developed nations are frequently misleading. Native languages in developed countries are perfectly adequate for all needs, while most African languages are not (not due to any structural deficiencies, but rather as a result of the lack of opportunity for elaboration). Most African local languages have not reached the elaboration stage noted above because another lingua franca or international language has occupied the linguistic niche of access to the modern sector and technology transfer. The use of another language in developed countries is usually optional. Language policies thus may reflect political choices of specialized groups or communities. In most developing nations, however, such choices are not optional. Local languages share functions with other languages in a diglottic situation—language use is determined by situation. Figure 13.2 provides a schematic view of two languages (here French and English) in a common diglottic situation. Most commonly, vernacular ("mother") languages are used within families and local communities, and lingua franca (such as Swahili) or international languages (such as English) are used for all government activities, including education. As suggested above, however, the actual situation may be far more complex. A child may learn a first language (or dialect) from family, learn another regional language (or national lingua franca), study another national language in primary school, and learn (to some level of proficiency, "learn" being an undefined term) an international language for secondary or higher education. The costs to the education sector of

Figure 13.2
Degree of Knowledge and Frequency of Use

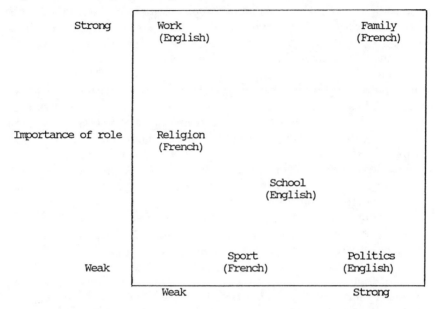

Source: Adapted from Laponce, J. A. (1987). *Language and their territories*. Toronto: University of Toronto Press.

this linguistic diversity may be great. These include the increased costs of training of multilingual teachers, the costs of producing multilingual instructional materials, and the costs of providing a relevant multilingual examination system (reflecting both linguistic diversity and range of language domain). Other costs to be considered are those resulting from the inefficiencies of retraining students in different languages at different educational levels—as well as the wastage attributable to language, not academic, problems. Considering the list above the precarious economic circumstances within which most ministries of education operate in Africa, the need for a coherent national language policy to permit the best use of resources is evident.

INSTRUCTIONAL LANGUAGES IN KENYA AND TANZANIA

Language policy decisions are never simple; they involve important linguistic, political, and financial consequences. Language policy choices thus can be traced to specific national development choices. The language policies of Kenya and Tanzania since their independence in the early 1960s illustrate how such choices lead to the creation of very different educational systems. These choices of instructional languages for national educational systems were made in order to achieve the development goals of each country.

Both Kenya and Tanzania were British colonies and began independence with very similar systems of formal education. This British educational structure has essentially continued in both countries, but the development strategies that each country chose have since resulted in different allocation of educational resources (Zuengler, 1985). Swahili is the national and official language in Kenya (ki = language, thus also: Kiswahili), and while language issues may appear less complex than those in Tanzania, which has approximately 100 vernacular groups within the three language families of Bantu, Nilotic, and Chushitic (Abdulaziz, 1971), the reality is not so simple. English is the language of Kenya's modern sector, but four major groups of vernacular languages are also important in the nation. Few Kenyans claim Swahili as their mother language, but most learn it instead as the national language.

Both Kenya and Tanzania began national independence with similar instructional language use in their British-based educational systems; Swahili served as the initial medium of instruction, followed by English in the higher grades. The systems began to diverge, however, by the time of their second development plans in the late sixties. Kenya continued to focus on meeting national high-level labor force needs, and English language instruction offered access to the modern sector technology required to meet those needs. Tanzania under President Nyerere, however, committed itself towards goals of socialism and broad-based rural development (Zuengler, 1985). Accordingly, the Tanzanian educational system changed to instruction entirely in Swahili as more appropriate for achieving those goals. The declaration of Swahili as the official language of Tanzania in 1967 represented a change in power for English and Swahili in that country and a clear national choice in development policy (Scotton, 1982).

Kenya's priorities of producing a high-level labor force led to the development of a system permitting local vernaculars ("dominant regional languages") and Swahili in the early grades (the first three primary standards), with a change to English as the language of instruction for all upper grades and higher education. Tanzania's priorities of rural development were better met by the use of Swahili throughout a system that recognized that primary education would be terminal for most students.

Competition between Swahili and English continues in Kenya, with English reportedly gaining in use. While Swahili serves as a lingua franca for low-status groups in Nairobi, increasing numbers of immigrants from rural areas are English-speaking as a result of passing through the national education system (Parkin, 1974). Unless national development priorities change, this triglottic (vernacular/Swahili/English) system will continue in Kenya, most probably with English spreading into Swahili domains in urban areas.

LANGUAGE AND EDUCATION IN LIBERIA

Language issues in Liberia concern the use of English as the sole instructional language for the national educational system as it prepares to expand into geographical areas dominated by many vernaculars and lingua francas. Sixteen languages from three major linguistic groups are usually reported to be used by groups within Liberia (Figure 13.1 suggests the complexity of the situation). A powerful social group, the Americo-Liberians, established the formal educational system with English as the language of instruction and, through their creation of the modern national structure, fixed English as the language of access to economic and political power. The 1980 military coup, which brought to power a vernacular speaker from outside the traditional Americo-Liberian group, has not resulted in any change in the exclusive use of English for national-level activities.

As elsewhere in Africa, a Western language has not *replaced* vernacular languages but rather has resulted in a distribution of functions across languages; vernaculars are spoken with families and communities and English is used for national affairs (including national education). Because Liberia is still in the process of attempting to implement a national education system (as are many African nations), many language issues may not yet be clearly perceived.

Liberia's new primary education initiative was planned entirely in English. When this program (which is materials-based and uses programmed learning and programmed teaching) is implemented in remote areas, it may be found that both teachers and students have not attained the level of English language competency necessary to use the instructional materials effectively. Even if the teacher does have minimal English competencies, the problems involved in teaching students new language skills while simultaneously teaching literacy and numeracy skills will need to concern Liberian educational researchers. During official school visits to rural—but not remote—areas, both students and teachers (with minimal English competency) can be observed using vernacular languages to discuss the lesson and their parts in it. To what extent teacher and student English competency levels match those required by the national curriculum as the system expands farther into remote areas may influence future language policy choices in Liberia.

Certainly the choice of an English-only system results in efficiencies in the production of instructional materials, the formal training of teachers, and the creation of examination systems. The costs to the national educational system of choosing to use other instructional languages at system entry level are probably prohibitive in Liberia today. Other language support strategies (information redundancies, graphics, vernacular feedback) may be considered as the system expands and further information is gathered by Liberian researchers.

SOMALIA LITERACY CAMPAIGN

The literacy campaign undertaken by the Somali government in 1973–1975 aimed at achieving widespread literacy based upon a common spoken language and the government choice of one national writing system. The campaign marked the end of a lengthy period of indecision about a suitable writing system for Somali. In addition to expressing a commitment to improving literacy in rural areas, it also marked a firm policy supporting the use of Somali as a national language of instruction. One of the first acts of the new military government, after coming to power (ending the period of parliamentary government) in October 1969, was to resolve the bitterly debated question of how Somali should be written. Many Somalis wanted to strengthen the cultural and religious heritage of Arab civilization by officially adopting the Arabic alphabet for written Somali; others wanted to promote access to modern Western culture by choosing the Latin alphabet. Still others urged the mandating of native, idiosyncratic scripts that had been devised to embody the genius of the Somali spoken language, long famous for its poetry and for the skill of its orators.

Before national independence in 1960, northern Somalia had been British Somaliland; the southern part had been Italian Somaliland. Italian and English thus competed for the role of international language. The newly independent nation made Arabic, Italian, and English co-equal written languages and designated Somali the official spoken language (Government of Somalia, 1984). Italian had the advantage of having the capitol city, Mogadisho, located within its domain, but English had the legacy of a better-established school system created in the north during the colonial period, thus producing an influential group of educated, English-speaking Somalis. Since national independence in 1960, both colonial languages have been used for government work, including education. During the postindependence parliamentary period (1960–1969), all official documents were bilingual in the two colonial languages (Somali was not yet written in a standard form). Important government posts were frequently held by two officials, one a speaker of English, the other fluent in Italian. During subsequent administrations of this period, however, more English-speaking northerners were appointed to important posts than Italian-speaking southerners. English increased in importance and began to replace Italian as the language of instruction in the south (Nelson, 1981).

A national committee was appointed in 1962 to evaluate the existing scripts for writing the Somali language. The committee recommended the Latin alphabet, but no steps were taken by the government to carry out these recommendations because of the strong objections of those favoring other writing systems (nine writing systems in all were considered by the committee). Following the military coup in 1969, the new government reconvened the committee in 1971 and tasked it with preparing textbooks, a national grammar, and a Somali dictionary (Nelson, 1981), even though there was as yet no official declaration of a national writing system.

In October 1972, the new military government announced the national language policy. Somali was the official language of Somalia and would be written in the Latin alphabet. Little adaptation was necessary for using the Latin system; double characters indicated phonetically long Somali (Soomaali) vowels and some of the Latin characters were designated to represent the glottal stop and other Somali consonant sounds (this had been worked out in the 1950s for literary journal use). An ambitious campaign (perhaps influenced by the Tanzanian mass literacy campaign launched in 1971) was soon announced to spread literacy in the new written language to all the Somali people, the great majority of whom lived in remote rural areas and were literate in no language (although they certainly did not—and would not—consider themselves "illiterate" in the common sense of that word).

A national planning group designed a two-phase literacy campaign, consisting first of an urban phase, followed by a far more difficult rural phase. The urban phase began in March 1973 and the rural phase in August 1974. The literacy campaign concluded in February 1975 (Bhola, 1984). At the beginning, it was declared that literacy was seen as part of a commitment to rural development. The objectives of the campaign were listed as eradication of illiteracy, public health improvement, animal health improvement, and a census of both people and livestock.

The question quickly arose of who, given the level of resources available and the large areas to be covered, would serve as the teachers in the national campaign. Government civil servants were considered for this task, but this plan was rejected. The planning committee at last decided to use intermediate and secondary teachers and students as the "soldiers" in this campaign, and schools were closed for this purpose (thus creating unusual enrollment "bubbles" in later years as students reentered the system). There was clearly a sense of national mission about the effort. Today, those who were involved in the literacy campaign as the student-teachers (many of whom now work in government ministries) still speak of the time with excitement and pride in their contribution, even though most are realistic in their estimates of literacy gains.

Many problems quickly emerged during the rural phase, as one might expect considering the gap that had developed between urban and rural life. Nomadic life was foreign to the visitors from the city, who were dependent upon their hosts for food and shelter, and the usual problems of understanding and toleration arose. In the remote rural areas, the arrival of representatives of urban life signaled the intrusion of central government—along with the fear of taxation of cattle herds, the basis of nomadic livelihood and wealth (suspicions were aroused by the human and animal census requirements—some volunteers recount being warned by their hosts not to attempt to count their herds).

Somali language instructional materials were minimal and many of the "teachers" themselves were scarcely familiar with the new writing system. Most of the volunteers (there were penalties for not participating) had little preparation and saw their task as one of supervising the memorization of written text. Estimates of low literacy levels in rural areas in more recent years certainly reflect the inability of the national system to sustain literacy in these areas, but also reflect the inexperience of the teachers and the lack of appropriate instructional materials for immediate rural needs.

The Somali literacy campaign of 1973–1975 was based on a decisive choice by a military government that had the authority to determine national language policy and to launch a national educational effort with a minimal investment of scarce resources. Plans were made for sustaining literacy classes, but these soon were abandoned as Somalia's economic crisis worsened in the early 1980s. The national education system has been unable to produce and disseminate the necessary Somali language instructional materials or to provide relevant training and incentives for the rural area teachers needed to carry on the literacy programs. These problems are, however, only part of the many language issues that have hindered the development of a national education system in Somalia.

LANGUAGE ISSUES AND THE SOMALI EDUCATIONAL SYSTEM

The literacy campaign in Somalia was based upon a widely supported policy decision regarding the official form of written Somali and was carried out with strong government and public support. Why then has the subsequent development of a national educational system been hindered by the lack of a coherent language policy regarding instructional languages?

Today Somali language is used for instruction in primary and secondary education (with English introduced in secondary grades). English is used for vocational and technical education. Italian is the medium of instruction at the Italian-assisted university (not in all faculties; the

College of Education—originally a USAID-funded teacher training college—uses English). Arabic language text is memorized in the Koran schools for preprimary age (and older) males. The employment patterns of Somalis in the nearby Gulf States and the frequent use of Arabic language in advertising and other printed media in Mogadisho today reflect the continuation of the country's historical and cultural ties to the Arab world.

The use of Italian at the university (lecturers are funded by the Italian government) presents a special problem. Somali students entering the university receive a brief course in Italian, but this is inadequate for understanding the lecturers. Somali instructors provide much help to students, but Somali language texts are not available and, as the elaboration process has not proceeded in Somali, there is much confusion about the Somali equivalent of both Italian and English technical terms. Messec (1986) prepared a technical dictionary of economic terms at the request of the university, working with faculty and government ministry officials to provide Somali standard terms in order to lessen this problem. Intraministerial and interministerial written communications suffer from the same problem of standardizing technical term translation. The one magazine published in-country on modern sector development (*Industrial Management Review*, published by the Ministry of Industry and Commerce) is in English with no Somali translations.

The *Somalia Education and Human Resources Sector Assessment* (Government of Somalia, 1984) notes the following language problems facing the Somali education system:

- loss of time and expense resulting from periodic need to retool in a different language prior to successive levels of education or training;
- instructional inefficiency resulting from use of language without student or, sometimes, teacher fluency;
- redundancy or inadequacy of curricular materials due to language shifts;
- weak fit between language of instruction and further study and/or work; and
- limited availability of means for teaching the various languages.

This study recommended that Somalia establish a "coherent, long-term policy for language use and language teaching." The study stressed the inefficiency inherent in the use of different languages at different educational levels and noted two underlying issues:

1. Is Somalia going to move to an all-Somali educational system through the university level? If not, where will the switch in language of instruction occur, and to what language? In deciding these matters, major considerations are:

- Internal access: Who will be able to enter the system or continue to the next level? Will entrants have been prepared linguistically by their prior schooling for the language of instruction at each level?

- Affordability: What are the costs of materials and text preparation or revision? Can use be made of existing materials?

- External access: Which language(s) will afford the greatest access to international commerce, technology, research, and scholarship?

2. Which of the three International languages (Arabic, English, Italian) is it practical to retain? What are the long-term priorities? Over the long run, what purposes will each serve?

A recent study (IEES, 1985) of primary and secondary school quality improvement again raised these issues and called for a national language policy to ensure the most efficient use of national resources. The Somali government, faced with severe economic problems and political conflicts, as yet has not developed a coherent language policy to reduce the current inefficiencies that exist throughout its educational system.

CONCLUSION

This chapter has discussed the complexity of language usage in African countries, the choices of national and international languages, and the use of instructional languages to support national development goals. In two of the countries discussed (Kenya and Tanzania), high-level policy decisions determined the language of instruction in the national educational systems. In another country (Liberia), the exclusive use of English historically by the modern state has resulted in the development of an English-only system that now will be expanded to serve the entire country. In Somalia, a new military government established a clear language policy in the late 1960s, but the present educational system suffers from the inefficiencies created by the use of different instructional languages at different educational levels, as well as the lack of Somali language elaboration as the result of increased donor activities using international languages.

From these examples it can be seen that a scale of language choices for educational systems exists (see Figure 13.3). This scale places the most efficient choice (monolingual, international language) at one end of the scale, moves to less efficient combinations of international languages, national languages, and vernaculars, and places the choice of all vernacular languages on the opposite end. It is apparent from the discussions in this chapter that the choice of instructional languages is not solely based on efficiency considerations. It might be observed, however, that in those cases in which explicit language policies have been established there appears to be better opportunity for both improved

Figure 13.3
Language Choices and Educational System Efficiency

Most Efficient	Less Efficient		Least Efficient
Monolingual	Bilingual	Trilingual	Multilingual
International Language only; no nationals, no vernaculars	International National	International(s) National(s) Vernacular(s)	Vernaculars only

efficiency and for achievement of system goals. Given this observation, educational decision makers should continue to gather and present more evidence for the creation of national language policies appropriate for their goals. An important part of this evidence, given the increased demands on educational systems and the decline of available resources, must be the costs that result from the language choices.

REFERENCES

Abdulaziz, M. H. (1971). Tanzania's national language policy and the rise of Swahili political culture. In W. H. Whitely, (Ed.), *Language use and social change* (pp. 160–177). London: Oxford University Press.

Armstrong, J. A. (1982). *Nations before nationalism*. Chapel Hill: University of North Carolina Press.

Bhola, H. (1984). *Campaigning for literacy*. Paris, France: United Nations Educational, Scientific, and Cultural Organization (UNESCO).

Europa handbook: A world survey. (1978). London, England: Europa Publications.

Fishman, J. A. (1974). *Advances in language planning*. The Hague: Moulton.

Fishman, J., Ferguson, C., & Das Gupta, J. (Eds.). (1968). *Language problems of developing nations*. New York: John Wiley.

Government of Somalia. (1984). *Somalia education and human resources sector assessment*. Mogadishu, Somalia: Ministry of National Planning.

Improving the Efficiency of Education Systems (IEES) Project. (1985). *Enhancement of school quality in Somalia*. Tallahassee: Florida State University, IEES Educational Efficency Clearinghouse.

Laponce, J. A. (1987). *Languages and their territories*. Toronto: University of Toronto Press.

Messec, J. (1986). *Soomaali-English English-Soomaali Technical Term Dictionary of Economics*. Tallahassee: IEES Learning Systems Institute.

Nelson, H. (Ed.) (1981). *Somalia: A country study*. Washington, D.C.: U.S. Government Printing Office.

Parkin, D. (1974). Status and language adding in Bahati. In W. H. Whiteley (Ed.), *Language in Kenya*. Nairobi: Oxford University Press.

Scotton, C. M. (1982). Learning lingua francas and socioeconomic integration: Evidence from Africa. In R. Cooper (Ed.), *Language spread: Studies in diffusion and social change*. Bloomington: Indiana University Press.

Spencer, J. (1975). Language and development in Africa: The unequal equation. In N. Wolfson & J. Manes (Eds.), *Language of inequality* (pp. 387–398). New York: Moulton.

Zuengler, J. (1985). English, Swahili, or other languages? The relationship of educational development goals to language of instruction in Kenya and Tanzania. In N. Wolfson & J. Manes (Eds.), *Language of inequality* (pp. 387–398). New York: Moulton.

14

Unmet Challenges: Educational Broadcasting in the Third World

John K. Mayo

The introduction of new media offers an educational system an un-equaled opportunity to review its goals, curriculum and methods of instruction. This is partly because the media are likely to be most efficient, both educationally and economically, when used in the context of change—to expand the educational system, to upgrade instruction significantly, to introduce new subjects or a new curric-ulum, to upgrade large numbers of teachers, or to reach beyond the present coverage of the school—in other words, to do something distinctly new.

Lerner & Schramm, 1967, p. 116

More than 20 years have passed since Wilbur Schramm and colleagues published their influential book, *The New Media: Memo to Educational Planners*. It reviewed the potential of various communication media for improving the cost-effectiveness of instruction. Schramm's analysis spanned the globe and included both formal and nonformal educational programs. His tone was forward looking and optimistic, reflecting the disposition of most development communication specialists in the 1960s. During those years, the "new media" were heralded as powerful in-struments of educational innovation and reform. However, neither Schramm nor his contemporaries claimed that the media *alone* were capable of producing systemic educational change. Rather, they viewed the mass media, and particularly radio and television, as "catalytic agents" and as the best means available for disseminating good teaching and helping fragile school systems cope with massive enrollment increases. Such notions were tested subsequently in a large number of experiments and demonstration projects, most of which received considerable amounts of international aid and attention (Emery, 1985). The results of these projects, and the lessons they hold for the future of all educational media in low-income nations, are the subject of this chapter.

Terms such as "educational media," and "instructional technology" are extremely broad. The connote different things to different people. In a generic sense, "educational media" are tools for extending or enriching teaching and learning, in or out of school. Included here are familiar classroom teaching aids such as textbooks, posters, projectors, and chalkboards, as well as the broadcast media and, increasingly, cassette recorders and microcomputers, which today permit learners to receive information across great distances of time and space. The term "instructional technology" is even more comprehensive. It encompasses the variety of media hardware listed above as well as procedures for designing, managing, and evaluating learning systems incorporating such media. The nature and power of such systems are discussed extensively in other chapters of this book.

The focus of this chapter is upon the broadcast media, specifically radio and television, for these technologies have made significant inroads within Third World educational systems in the past 20 years. They are the most broadly diffused and, in the case of classroom television, the most widely criticized of all the "new media" introduced to date. Millions of learners have received all or part of their education via radio or television; the total number is impossible to calculate with any precision. Furthermore, recent breakthroughs in satellite distribution and in cassette recording suggest that radio and television will continue to play an important role in the future, particularly within distance-learning systems. Other fast-evolving telecommunication technologies such as the telephone and the microcomputer are also performing essential training, administrative, and planning functions within many low-income nations, but for economic reasons they are unlikely to play a significant instructional role there until well into the next century.

Learning systems employing radio and television still require a considerable amount of research and development before they can be implemented effectively in one educational system, much less exported to another. Doubts surrounding their cost-effectiveness in Third World educational contexts stem from the fact that the services needed to support media systems have proven to be expensive and quite demanding. Similarly, the transfer and adaptation of program formats have been much harder tasks than originally anticipated. How have broadcast technologies been employed to date in schools and in out-of-school education programs in Third World nations? Under what circumstances or conditions have they improved the quality of instruction? What guidelines are there to guide future decision making in this area? Such questions are at the heart of this review. They will be addressed first by reviewing the factors favoring the use of radio and television in low-income nations. Historical patterns of media use will then be examined. The chapter will conclude by discussing the conditions under which media systems can be strengthened in the future.

FACTORS FAVORING THE USE OF MEDIA IN EDUCATION

The challenge of improving educational efficiency and effectiveness in low-income countries looms almost as large today as it did 30 years ago, when visionary leaders first considered introducing communication media in their nations' school systems. Coombs characterized the situation of that day as a "world educational crisis . . . born of the historic conjunction of five factors":

1. *The student flood*—the sharp rise in human expectations, compounded by a population explosion
2. *Acute resource scarcities*—the fact that supplies of teachers and buildings, equipment, and textbooks lagged well behind the rising demand for education
3. *Rising costs*—the inexorable upward trend of real costs per student, based largely on the fact that conventional education remains a highly labor-intensive activity
4. *Unsuitability of output*—the poor fit between what educational systems produced and the real needs of development
5. *Inertia and inefficiency*—the inability of educators to plan or otherwise adapt with sufficient speed to meet changing circumstances. (Coombs, 1968, p. 164)

Such problems persist, and they are by no means confined to the educational sector of poor countries. In many respects they are symptomatic of deep-rooted, structural inequalities historically associated with underdevelopment. Social and economic inequalities still stifle systemic change, and it is clear that reformers cannot expect education alone to solve all such problems. Yet, faith in education as a transforming force and as a path to economic growth and modernization has not diminished. If anything, it has grown as succeeding generations of leaders have concluded that investments in school as well as in other forms of education and training do accelerate development and social change. For this reason they have been receptive to innovative strategies that promise to increase educational opportunities and/or to raise academic achievement levels at costs governments can afford. Such receptivity also explains why media-based and media-assisted programs have grown in popularity over the years.

A second major factor favoring the use of media in human resource development has been their rates of commercial development and dissemination. The number of radio receivers per thousand population in the developing world now stands at 142 while the number of TV sets has reached 36 (United Nations Educational, Scientific, and Cultural Organization UNESCO, 1987). Whereas private access to the print media (33 daily newspaper copies per 1000) and to motion pictures (7 cinema seats per thousand) has not risen appreciably in Africa, Asia, and Latin America for over 2 decades, growth rates for radio and television exceeded 300 percent over the same period (UNESCO, 1985, 1987). The invention of the transistor made possible the manufacture of inexpensive, battery-operated receivers, and this made radio ownership a realistic possibility for people in even the remotest rural areas. Increasingly, television has also entered village life via small satellite earth stations and other sophisticated delivery systems (Hudson, 1984). Today radio and television vie with schools, families, and churches as socializing forces on the young, a fact that troubles parents and educators of many nationalities. One reaction to such fears is to blame the media for the perceived decline of traditional institutions and values, and to enact various forms of censorship to counteract such influence. More commonly, however, educational authorities have reacted positively and embraced the media as useful means for motivating and instructing learners no matter what their age or previous educational experience.

This chapter's terms of reference do not permit a systematic or comprehensive review of the literature on radio and television's contributions to education or on the criteria for selecting one medium over another. Others have proposed quite elaborate criteria (Reiser & Gagne, 1983; Romiszowski, 1974), although such efforts have been criticized for relying too much on "algorithmic, reductionist approaches" that apply to the "pedagogic requirements of the classroom . . . [but not] the real world, where finance, politics and the power of existing organizations all influence decision-making" (Bates, 1987, p. 2). Notwithstanding the above critique, enough "real world" media experiences have now accumulated to assist planners in making informed decisions regarding both the instructional capabilities and probable costs of alternative systems. Recognizing the need to design learning systems that meet each nation's unique historical circumstances and possibilities, planners must continue to rely as much on incomplete case studies and on intuition as on logical, step-by-step media selection procedures.

There is now ample proof that radio and television can play a variety of useful roles in the classroom as well as in less structured educational environments. They have proven to be particularly effective in enriching teaching and learning by providing resources that are not available in the local community or classroom; diffusing superior curricula and instructional methods quickly and on a broad scale; and meeting the educational needs of previously unserved groups, both in and out of school. Such attributes will be examined in greater detail in the next section.

When employed in a "live broadcast" mode, radio and television have a unique advantage over textbooks and other print media in that they can relate course materials to current circumstances and events in flexible and spontaneous ways. Furthermore, program presenters are frequently able to respond directly "on the air" to audience questions and concerns. Such feedback is particularly useful in reducing the isolation and loneliness distant learners often feel.

Radio has emerged as the instructional "medium of choice" within Third World nations because it can do much of what television can do, but for approximately one-fifth the cost (Jamison & McAnany, 1978). However, television may still be warranted for visualization of specific places, for detailed illustration or demonstration of complex processes, and for the teaching of artistic and craft skills. Televised instruction also permits the use of slow motion and time-lapsed cinematography as well as animation to illustrate physical principles and models.

Broadcasting remains the most cost-effective means for distributing live or prerecorded programs in most Third World nations, although audio and video cassette distribution systems are gaining in popularity. Cassette technology is particularly attractive when the number of learners is relatively small, when there is need for greater flexibility at the receiving end (as in distance-learning systems), or when programs are to be used repeatedly or reviewed in a detailed way. Most important of all, cassette recorders allow individual classroom teachers as well as distance learners greater autonomy in deciding which programs they will use and when they will use them. Such control has rekindled enthusiasm for television and mediated instruction generally in places where they have been abandoned for lack of the same flexibility. However, cassette technologies are relatively expensive for reaching large audiences, compared to broadcasting, and the logistical problems associated with their use in low-income nations have proven to be very difficult to overcome.

In concluding the discussion to this point, it is worth noting that comparisons of media attributes, costs, and effectiveness, whether in education or any other domain, depend ultimately on the goals and values that individual societies and their school systems espouse. What, in other words, do they hope to accomplish, and what are they willing to pay or sacrifice to achieve their objectives? These are critical questions in light of the extensive technology transfer activity that has characterized the dissemination and use of media within Third World educational systems to date.

Without addressing the general issue of technology transfer, three issues stand out with regard to low-income nations' historical reliance on imported media. The first is the *widespread but largely unchallenged belief that "new" communication media are desirable and that their use in education as well as other development sectors will help eradicate longstanding deficiencies and gaps.* Such an assumption is questionable given the uneven investment and distribution patterns found in most countries, whereby new information technologies have been found to benefit certain geographic regions or social classes at the expense of others (Webster & Robins, 1986; Goulet, 1977). A related and equally troubling assumption is that communication technologies carry no cultural baggage, are without historical context, and can therefore be transferred without much modification. Experience contradicts this view, too, and many Third World educational planners have learned this lesson the hard way.

The second issue concerns *the direct and indirect political consequences of technology transfers in communication.* To what extent do exporting countries retain control over key elements of their technology through licensing and patent agreements, maintenance and training contracts, and the like? How have such arrangements affected importing nations' ability to deploy new communication media as they see fit? Such questions are just beginning to interest communication development scholars (Samarajiva & Shields, In Press). They are complicated by the fact that communication technology projects typically have both hardware and software dimensions. As the hardware becomes more sophisticated, it may perpetuate importers' reliance on outsiders to install and maintain it. By the same token, imported media may create dependency on imported management and evaluation systems. In the content or software domain, the tendency toward outsider influence in education may not seem as great if it is assumed that authorities know what curricula they want to deliver and only are in need of the means to do so. Yet, there are dangers here as well. Because new media can place great pressure on course designers and content specialists to produce a sufficient number of lessons to fill ambitious transmission schedules, the temptation exists to import program series and to rely on program developers from overseas (O'Brien, 1976).

The third issue concerns *the difficulty media planners and scholars alike have had in assessing the true costs of technology transfers in communication.* To date, comparative cost-effectiveness studies have provided the most useful information on various projects, although such studies have been criticized repeatedly for failing to consider all the costs that media systems are likely to incur (Kremmerer & Wagner, 1986; Carnoy & Levin, 1975). In fact the debate among media advocates and critics over the true costs of educational media systems has intensified over the past decade, with no resolution in sight. Meanwhile, educational planners in need of reassurance and direction continue to make large capital outlays for communication hardware and software in the belief that such investments will pay off in the future. Alerted to the technology transfer issues noted above, it is instructive at this point to examine briefly the major educational tasks communication media have been expected to perform, and the extent to which they have fulfilled planners' expectations.

HOW THE MEDIA HAVE BEEN USED IN EDUCATION

In his excellent review of broadcasting in education, Bates (1984) contends that media usage typically falls along a continuum within formal academic settings. At one end of the continuum is "enrichment" programming; at the other "direct teaching and curricular reform." Standing apart, but in growing variety and number, are in-service training and a vast array of media-assisted correspondence courses set up to meet learner needs "at a distance;" that is, away from traditional centers of instruction. The objectives, operating procedures, and success of each of these strategies will be highlighted in this section.

Use of the Media to Enrich Education

The goal of enriching classroom instruction has been associated with new educational media even since radio was introduced on an experimental basis within British schools in 1924. School enrichment concepts and formats spread gradually to other English-speaking countries and eventually throughout the world. They are present today in virtually all Third World systems that follow the "schools broadcasting" model exported by Great Britain during the past 40 years. It is a model that embodies rather diffuse and nondidactic instructional strategies and that does not attempt to replace what classroom teachers are already doing. On the contrary, enrichment programs are intended to reinforce and to supplement existing classroom teaching practices by making available information and experiences that are beyond the reach (and budgets) of local schools. By providing appropriate examples and varied perspectives on established themes, as well as indirect access to cultural events of all kinds, enrichment programs tend to be valued as much for their motivational impact as for their effects on learning.

There is only limited and somewhat contradictory evidence upon which to judge the effects of enrichment programs on the quality of education in developing nations. In his review of media projects established to supplement formal school systems in Colombia (TV), India

(TV), and Thailand (radio), Schramm found that such programs were popular with teachers and that students outperformed their counterparts in traditional classes on various achievement tests. He concluded that:

Used as a supplement to classroom teaching, the media of instruction are effective. They work as well as other classroom teaching. Used in the right place, in the right way, for an appropriate purpose, they will improve on the classroom experience. (Lerner & Schramm, 1967, p. 194)

However, Lyle (1982) subsequently reviewed the status of 23 media projects that he and Schramm together had evaluated under UNESCO's auspices in 1967. Lyle found that many of these projects had withered away for lack of sustained support. Although classroom teachers noted the quality of the enrichment radio and television programs they had received, they had experienced difficulties integrating them into their daily classes. The problem was particularly acute in countries where teachers were not following a national curriculum. In such cases, enrichment programs too frequently were unrelated to the instruction students were receiving locally. Lyle's review documented a series of other classroom problems including:

- insufficient attention to broadcast reception problems, particularly in rural areas;
- inability of system planners to assess student and teacher needs in sufficient detail;
- failure to provide teachers with adequate scheduling information or guidance on how to integrate programs on a daily basis; and
- limited transmissions, which prohibits flexible or repeated use of the broadcast material.

Such problems are inherent to some degree within all educational broadcasting systems. How much autonomy will the classroom teacher enjoy vis a vis the use of material delivered from the outside? How can the classroom teacher be prepared and encouraged to meet the scheduling demands of mediated instruction? Bates (1984) provides useful answers to such questions in his review of enrichment broadcasting from developed as well as developing countries. He argues that the more such programs can be conceived as "learning resources" controlled by the teacher the better. To achieve such a status, classroom teachers will require:

- better day-to-day guidance on how to incorporate programs;
- additional pre- and in-service training on the goals, objectives, and formats of mediated instruction;

- adequate lead time to permit planning of integrated systems; and
- where feasible, provision of ancillary recording and replay equipment to permit greater flexibility at the receiving end.

Whereas the addition of cassette recorders has helped transform the status of enrichment programs from source-oriented to teacher-oriented "learning resources" in rich countries, comparable opportunities do not yet exist within the public educational system of most Third World nations. Furthermore, such technical upgrading will not be possible there for the foreseeable future. This fact underscores the importance of teacher training and other reinforcement strategies to the success of enrichment broadcasting in the future.

Use of Media for Direct Instruction

The appeal of media for direct instruction has been particularly strong in nations where educational needs are most acute and where conventional elements of education such as schools, trained teachers, modern curricula, and learning materials are in shortest supply. Here, unlike the enrichment strategies outlined above, media are expected to serve as "master teachers" and actually to replace classroom teachers in important ways. By the same token, such systems are often expected to diffuse new curricula and other innovations on a broad scale. Relying on carefully crafted lessons distributed from a central broadcast facility, educators pursuing a direct instruction strategy have sought, and frequently reported, learning gains well above national norms. Furthermore, by restraining teacher salary increases, they have been able to report cost-per-student ratios that are superior to alternative reform strategies and still within the means of most low-income nations.

The most recent and best-documented examples of media used for direct instruction are the nine "interactive radio instruction" (IRI) projects sponsored by the U.S. Agency for International Development (USAID) over the past 15 years. Development of the IRI model began in 1973, when the Institute for Mathematical Studies in the Social Studies at Stanford University launched an experimental project in Nicaragua to test the instructional effectiveness of radio as a means for direct instruction of primary mathematics. The 4-year Nicaraguan experience was followed by an equally ambitious language arts project in Kenya (1980–1985), by a primary science project in Papua New Guinea (1986 to present), by a community education program in the Dominican Republic (1982 to present) and by major adaptations of IRI materials in Thailand, Honduras, Lesotho, and Bolivia (Academy for Educational Development, 1988).

The IRI projects rely on carefully developed curricula and assume responsibility for the bulk of instruction children receive in specific subjects. Customarily, students receive a half-hour radio lesson each day followed by a set of activities directed by the classroom teacher. Throughout the broadcast lesson, pupils participate actively through a combination of oral, written, and often physical (clapping, raising hands, etc.) exercises. The projects generally provide no textbooks. Instead, one-page worksheets may accompany each lesson, although these, too, have been abandoned as a cost-saving measure in some instances. Use of other learning materials, such as textbooks, are often discouraged for the same reason. When illustrations are required, radio teachers simply ask their classroom counterparts to draw them on their blackboards. In the same spirit, classroom teachers and students alike are expected to provide stones, bottle caps, and whatever other locally available support materials are deemed necessary to reinforce concepts presented by radio.

In spite of the prominence given radio as a substitute for classroom teaching, local teachers were perceived to make a big difference as the original IRI experiments unfolded. The latter were responsible for seeing to it that pupils assembled for the broadcasts on time and that appropriate follow-up activities were conducted. To assist them on such tasks, the projects provided guides outlining what should be done in the classroom before and after each broadcast lesson. Teachers also were encouraged to intervene when they sensed students were having difficulties during the programs.

Formative evaluation plays a key part within the IRI model. Historically, most media projects have relied upon a "develop-tryout-revise" strategy to design and implement new curricula. Indeed, such a strategy was used initially by IRI project personnel to establish the format for Nicaragua's radio lessons. However, once daily broadcasting began, researchers realized they could not longer rely on traditional feedback methods; they were simply too cumbersome and required too much time. Needed was a means for obtaining precise and quick measures of student performance *and* a production schedule flexible enough to allow such information to be incorporated into future programs. In this manner they would be able to detect learning problems early, take remedial action, and thus enhance student achievement. Weekly tests, classroom observations, and teacher comments in time became the core of the IRI feedback strategy. Together, they helped the programs' designers shape all aspects of the radio instruction, from the speed, length, and vocabulary of each program segment to the weighting assigned each of the course's major concepts.

Evidence from a variety of sources suggests that when radio instruction is developed in as careful a way as it was in the IRI projects, it can have a powerful impact on student achievement (Imhoof & Christensen, 1986; Friend, Searle, & Suppes, 1980). Using effect sizes as a means for comparing relative as opposed to absolute levels of student achievement, the Nicaraguan and Kenyan projects each reported impressive learning trends attributable to direct radio instruction. The average effect sizes obtained in Nicaragua (.52) and Kenya (.45) signified gains from the 50th to the 70th and from the 50th to the 67th percentile, respectively. In interpreting these effect sizes, Anzalone (1987, p. 16) citing Walberg (1984) notes that "an effect size of .20 (equivalent to raising the mean from the 50th to the 58th percentile) is about average and one of .45 is considered large and exceeds about 84% of those typically found in educational research."

Additional cost-effectiveness data on the use of the media for direct instruction have been reported in recent years. They are based on measures of internal efficiency—reductions in school repetition and dropout rates, numbers of students being served, quality of instruction delivered compared to traditional alternatives, and so on (Jamison & McAnany, 1978). The evidence contained in such studies is mixed, due in large part, one suspects, to the variety of socioeconomic factors affecting such trends and the resulting difficulty at arriving at valid causal inferences concerning the influence of radio or any other innovation. Cost analyses and projections are equally difficult, due, in part, to the temptation of administrators to understate the "true costs" of technology systems by relying exclusively on inflated enrollment estimates and wishful thinking (Carnoy & Levin, 1975). In arriving at highly favorable ($.40) annual cost-per-student estimates for the Kenyan Language Arts Project, for example, Searle (1985) chose to ignore previous research and development costs and to assume that the number of participating schools, classes, and students would double, that reusable worksheets would be provided every student, and that an existing radio channel would be provided at no cost.

For cost and other reasons, projects incorporating media for direct instruction, such as the IRI demonstrations, have also experienced problems when they have sought to build upon their achievements and to gain a permanent place within their nations' educational systems. The pioneering IRI programs in Nicaragua and Kenya were not sustained beyond their pilot phases. In Nicaragua, political developments surrounding the Sandinista revolution foreclosed formal adoption of the Radio Math system, while in Kenya the Language Arts Project never was able to obtain a secure institutional niche. At the same time, common factors linked to these two projects may have made it more difficult for them to put down institutional roots. The teams that managed both projects were from outside the countries. They were composed of superbly qualified curriculum developers and radio producers. They had ample and independent budgets, and the backing of a large bilateral agency, USAID. To a large extent, the initial success of these programs also may be attributed to their leaders' ability to avoid the sorts of financial and political problems that have beset communication projects elsewhere. As a result, students were able to achieve the impressive learning gains noted above, and the projects' methods are now being applied elsewhere. Will these more recent applications be sustained beyond their pilot phases? Much will depend on established educational interests and local educators' willingness to accept the package of innovations associated with IRI. This, in turn, will depend on perceived costs—to the educational budget as well as to the workloads and status of existing institutions. Also important will be the continued support of classroom teachers and development of the technical and managerial skills necessary to keep a national system operating efficiently.

Use of Media to Reform Education

Confronted by enrollment bottlenecks, high dropout rates, antiquated curricula, poorly qualified classroom teachers, insufficient and unevenly distributed learning materials, and limited financial resources with which to expand or improve existing educational opportunities, it is easy to understand why politicians and planners worldwide have been attracted by the symbolism and perceived power of the mass media. In fact, the media's appeal to educators may stem as much from hope and from an appreciation of the technologies' influence in industrialized nations as it does from their proven instructional effectiveness to date in Third World countries (Anzalone, 1987; Arnove, 1976). The notion that instructional technologies, and particularly educational television (ETV), could help transform core elements of traditional school systems, reached its zenith during the late 1960s and early 1970s. During that period, governments in American Samoa, the Ivory Coast, and El Salvador launched national ETV programs whose goals far exceeded what had been tried anywhere before. Here television was installed as the cornerstone of sweeping educational reforms.

American Samoa (1964–1978). The ETV-based educational reform in American Samoa represented the U.S. government's attempt to redress its neglect of a territorial school system. Although universal education had been extended through high school in 1961, many Samoan teachers had no more than 9 years of schooling, and their command of English was judged to be quite poor. A study of the situation recommended that traditional, one-room schools (*fales*) be consolidated within "suitable buildings," and that the curriculum be revised to reflect the changing realities of Samoan life. Most importantly, the standard of English was to be upgraded via television instruction so that Samoan students eventually would have an easier time seeking employment on the U.S. mainland (Schramm, Nelson, & Betham, 1981).

The "bold experiment" mounted by a team of U.S. advisors in American Samoa began with a thorough revision of the territory's primary and secondary school curricula. Broadcast lessons were developed next. To insure full coverage of the territory's school system, over 6,000 programs were produced by the ETV production unit in less than 2 years, a rate that far exceeds what any other project has attempted before or since. The broadcast lessons accounted for approximately a third of students' classroom time, and most were accompanied by packets of materials to guide teachers' follow-up activities in the classroom.

Evaluation of the Samoan ETV experience was handicapped by the fact that baseline data were not collected at the outset of the project and 6 years elapsed before regular testing was introduced. Studies undertaken in succeeding years yielded mixed results. In their explanation of uneven and disappointing student achievement data reported at the end of the experiment, its evaluators concluded:

There is nothing in this evidence to say that television succeeded or failed, except that it did not accomplish the expected miracle. . . . Whether the Samoan students' performance on tests was good or bad is a relative matter. And we are sadly handicapped in trying to adjudicate it by the scarcity of test data from the years that would tell us most about the effect of the television curriculum. (Schramm et al., 1981, p. 145)

Subsequent reviews of the same Samoan data arrived at harsher conclusions. Noting that students in grades 3 through 12 achieved only 59 percent of U.S. norms after 7 years of ETV, Emery concluded that the system had failed "in direct correlation with grade, or increasing abstraction and conceptualization of knowledge" (Emery, 1985, p. 498).

Costs of ETV in American Samoa were also quite high compared to other media systems. By 1972, when approximately 8,100 students were enrolled in Samoa's ETV schools, the per-student cost (including a proportion of annualized capital costs) was about $166 per year. This fact, coupled with growing criticism of the system by secondary teachers and students, led to a sharp reduction of instructional broadcasts in the mid–1970s. By 1978, when broadcasting ceased to be a major force in Samoan schools, only one of the original six television channels provided by the project was in operation.

Ivory Coast (1971–1978). The use of television for educational reform in the Ivory Coast was stimulated by the government's decision to achieve universal primary education within a 15-year period. In 1970, only 54 percent of the nation's 7 through 12 year old children were enrolled in school. Whereas 25 percent of 7 year olds enrolled in first grade, by the fourth grade the percentage dropped to just 14 percent. By introducing television, Ivorian educators sought a rapid, cost-effective means for raising the quality of primary education, a policy that also would allow them to institute companion measures to raise promotion rates and reduce dropouts. Furthermore, the medium provided an opportunity to integrate different subjects, to upgrade the quality of instruction on a system-wide basis, and to train classroom teachers in a relatively inexpensive way.

Following years of planning supervised by UNESCO and French advisors, ETV broadcasting began to reach 447 first-grade classes (approximately 21,000 students) in 1971. More classes were added to the system each year, with the aim of eventually reaching all primary school pupils. By 1980, 15,635 classes were actually participating in the project, roughly 84 percent of all eligible students (Hawkridge & Robinson, 1982, p. 156). Broadcast subjects included French, reading, writing, mathematics, civics, moral education, environmental studies, hygiene, and physical education.

No integrated or long-term evaluation was conducted of ETV in the Ivory Coast, although a number of case studies were mounted over the course of the project. The latter noted the project staff's positive views regarding the ETV system's influence on the introduction of methods and attitudes, on children's activity level in the classroom, and on the overall quality of local teacher–student interactions (Lenglet, McAnany, & Grant, 1979; Grant, 1977; Kaye, 1976).

Achievement studies and teacher surveys conducted by researchers from the Laboratory of Experimental Pedagogy at the University of Liege, Belgium, rendered a less favorable judgment of the project. Although the Belgian team noted that ETV had equalized educational opportunities between urban and rural areas, they found that first- and second-grade students had great difficulty in mastering the curriculum. Whereas French speaking proficiency improved markedly, less satisfactory progress was achieved in the written language. Unfortunately, published reports of the Belgian studies are not available, so it is not possible to verify the team's conclusions or to conduct secondary analyses of their data. For the same reason, it is difficult to assess the importance or to generalize from the results of a large classroom teacher survey conducted by the same team in 1978 on the system's environmental programming. Teachers apparently were critical of the programs' pace and lack of follow-up, as well as their non-relevance to environmental problems experienced in the students' own communities (Hawkridge & Robinson, 1982, p. 164).

Unquestionably, the introduction of ETV in the Ivory Coast did coincide with a reduction of repetition and dropout rates, and unit costs per graduate were lower than under the traditional system (Kaye, 1976). Still, those costs (approximately $13 per student per year in 1976) apparently were not sustainable by the Ivorian government given the massive enrollment increases that occurred as part of the reform program. Perhaps for this reason more than any other, classroom broadcasts were suspended in 1978.

El Salvador (1968–1972). Educational reform emerged as a priority in the late 1960s when El Salvador's leaders realized that a comprehensive upgrading of their school system and the provision of new training opportunities were required if the country was to resolve its growing economic and social problems. Accordingly, a comprehensive 5-year reform plan was announced in 1968. It included: curriculum revision, teacher retraining, elimination of tuition in grades 7 through 9, double sessions to accommodate more students, and installation of a national ETV system. ETV was thrust immediately into the forefront of the reform because it exerted a powerful influence over the rates by which other innovations were introduced.

The Salvadoran reform was extremely successful in increasing student access to junior secondary school. In 1968 there were 19,104 students in grades 7 through 9. They, along with some 23,000 private school enrollees, constituted less than a quarter of the young people of eligible age (13 to 15) for the three grades. By 1973, more than 65,000 students were enrolled in public schools. The threefold increase in enrollment, brought on in part by the elimination of tuition fees, also resulted in a change in the average social background of students, with more students from poorer and rural homes able to register for the first time.

From 1969 through 1972, a research team from Stanford University's Institute for Communication Research administered general ability, reading, and achievement tests to three cohorts of Salvadoran students. Over their 3 years of junior secondary, students enrolled in ETV classes gained 15 to 25 percent more on the general ability measures than did their non-ETV peers. This advantage was unaffected when controls for socioeconomic status and for individual student characteristics were applied. On reading tests, ETV and non-ETV students gained about the same. Results on the achievement tests were mixed. ETV students generally gained more in mathematics; language arts gains were about equal; results in social science varied by grade; and in science, non-ETV students outperformed their counterparts in television classes (Mayo, Hornik, & McAnany, 1976)

The collection of learning data was supplemented by periodic surveys of student and teacher attitudes. High initial enthusiasm for the reform and for ETV declined as the project grew, particularly among teachers. Did the downward trend in teacher support belie the wisdom of spending so much time and money on ETV as well as on teacher retraining? The answer depends on how one considers the teachers' grievances. What seemed to account for the teachers' increasingly negative attitudes, and the strikes they produced, was not ETV or the reform program as such, but rather the poor working conditions (ever larger class sizes, grueling double sessions, lack of teaching materials) and low pay under which they continued to work.

Fixed costs of the ETV system were estimated to be $1.1 million. Of that sum, approximately $800,000 was the cost to the Salvadoran government; the remainder consisted of grants from USAID and other foreign donors. In 1972, when approximately 48,000 students were enrolled in the system, per-student costs were estimated to be $24.35, a figure less than one-sixth of Samoa's per-student student expenditures but almost twice that of the Ivory Coast. In a reanalysis of El Salvador cost data, Carnoy (1976) estimated El Salvador's ETV system costs at about $26 per student. He also observed that for an average class size of 30, this would translate into a cost of $780 per classroom per year, a figure equivalent to roughly 60 percent of the average teacher's salary ($1,300) at the time.

Considering the results and current status of educational reforms undertaken in El Salvador, the Ivory Coast, and American Samoa, it is easy to understand why most observers are now disillusioned if not flatly opposed to the use of television in the classroom. In a recent review published by the Harvard Institute for International Development, Anzalone (1987, p. 39) noted:

The overall impression is that the use of television can be expensive and that it contributes little (in some cases, nothing) to student achievement. Television often arouses strong opposition on the part of the teachers and sometimes resistance on the part of students. There is a striking lack of success in upgrading television use from an experimental phase to a permanent feature of national education.

Do such statements constitute a final verdict on the ability of television to contribute to the improvement of education in Third World countries? Are there any lessons that, if heeded, could justify some role for television in the future?

The three cases reviewed above shared many important characteristics:

- The countries were relatively small and could be served by a central broadcasting authority
- Each of the countries had a national curriculum judged to be inappropriate vis a vis development needs and priorities
- Two of the countries (El Salvador and the Ivory Coast) were experiencing severe enrollment pressures that could not be met by the traditional school system

• The decision to adopt television as the catalyst for reform was heavily influenced by outside funders and advisors

At the local level, ETV was intended in each instance to upgrade the quality of instruction by providing the core of new curriculum content. Because televised lessons reached all parts of the school systems simultaneously, classroom instruction was able to proceed at approximately the same rate—something that was impossible to achieve under the old systems. Of course, the fact that ETV was available throughout the countries did not guarantee that the lessons would be used properly, or that satisfactory learning would result. The critical task of incorporating televised instruction into school routines rested with the classroom teachers.

ETV in El Salvador, the Ivory Coast, and American Samoa provided information and new learning experiences for both teachers and students. Naturally, some classrooms adjusted to changed circumstances better than others. Based on the evidence, it must be concluded that in too many instances the televised lessons were only brief interludes in a continuing ritual of teacher lectures and student recitation. In others, new patterns of interaction apparently emerged in response to the stimuli provided from the outside. Still, in the view of most observers the creative potential of television was not realized in the three projects. The lack of stimulating, imaginative programming and the rigidity of the broadcast schedules probably account for most of the decline in the systems' popularity over time. Had more effort been devoted to the creative use of the medium and, specifically, to alternatives to the "talking head" style of television teaching, it is unlikely that support for ETV would have eroded. This conclusion is substantiated by the fact that language courses, which generally exhibited the most imaginative production formats across the three systems, consistently received high ratings from teachers and students.

In evaluating the three countries' educational reform experiences with television, one must also question whether the planners' economic and social goals were realistic, and whether they are the goals other nations seek. Introduction of the ETV systems was justified in part by the argument that they would eventually reduce costs per student, at least when compared to alternative reform programs. However, due to sharp increases in enrollment in El Salvador and the Ivory Coast, massive budget increases were required in education. By 1972, the final year of El Salvador's initial 5-year plan, the Ministry of Education consumed more than a third of the national budget. Other nations, facing economic problems and social pressures of all kinds, could not possible justify allocating so much money to education, at least in the foreseeable future. Furthermore, other groups may merit a greater share of the resources that have historically gone to school-aged youth. Indeed, as the ETV systems evolved in El Salvador, the Ivory Coast, and American Samoa, greater emphasis was placed on the needs of the adult populations for in-service training and other forms of distance education. The lesson here is that no matter how compelling the case may be for reform, particular educational innovations such as ETV must be considered within a political framework and alongside competing social needs and objectives.

Use of Media for Distance Education and Training

"Distance education" is a relatively new label for teaching and learning activities that have actually been going on for a long time. According to Perraton (1984a), distance education is "a process in which significant proportion of the teaching is conducted by someone removed in space and or time from the learner." Correspondence and extension courses have been conducted for decades in countries where people have sought alternatives to traditional residential courses *and* where they have had access to reliable mail service or other forms of two-way communication to make such alternatives possible. Interest in such programs has peaked in recent years because more "students" from more countries are engaged in a greater variety of distance education and training programs than ever before, and because the programs themselves are employing the mass media in many different ways.

Television and radio's roles vary widely within distance learning systems, but generally these media are not the primary means of instruction. Students' learning customarily is centered around print material, and two-way communication between the student and sponsoring institutions is maintained via written correspondence. Instructional links are strengthened when local tutors are provided to resolve student problems related to self-study materials, homework, or other written assignments. Still, there are clear advantages to incorporating the broadcast media within distance education strategies, and most systems in fact have relied on a multi-media approach. Radio and television are relied upon to deliver information in a timely and lively manner, thereby compensating for the print media's relative coldness and lack of flexibility.

Distance teaching has been relied upon most often within Third World countries to increase and in many cases democratize educational opportunity. In a recent review of selected distance learning institutions, Nettleton (1988) notes that the Chinese Radio and Television University currently enrolls over one million students, while Mexico's Telesecundaria, now in its twentieth year, is providing 7th through 9th grade instruction via television, print, and local monitors to 408,000 rural students (Arena, 1988). Furthermore, open universities established in Korea

(1972), Thailand (1978), and Indonesia (1983) have each reported enrollments exceeding 150,000 in the past year.

The proliferation and growth of open learning systems unfortunately has outstripped research comparing their cost-effectiveness with that of traditional institutions. Obviously, they are helping countries respond to demands for higher education fueled by population growth as well as burgeoning enrollments at the primary and secondary school level. With regard to the large Asian distance universities, costs per student have so far proven to be substantially less than those of equivalent, conventional institutions (Nettleton, 1988, Table 9). However, dropout rates have been quite high (e.g., 30 to 50 percent) and student services virtually nonexistent in some instances. Apparently, administrative control and logistical support tend to deteriorate as enrollments increase. Open schools and universities also run the risk of being considered second-class alternatives to established academic institutions. Their faculties are frequently overworked and underpaid, and course demands may rule out any time for research. Furthermore, there are questions surrounding the value and marketability of certificates and diplomas obtained from institutions that some critics perceive (correctly or incorrectly) to be "diploma mills."

Based on pioneering efforts conducted over the past 25 years, distance teaching is emerging as a preferred option for the retaining of classroom teachers in low-income countries. During the 1969–1972 period, over 10,000 unqualified teachers successfully completed retraining courses through radio, correspondence, and residential study in Kenya. Large-scale retraining of teachers has since been attempted in Zimbabwe and in Brazil through the Logos II project, but the results of these efforts have been less well documented. More recently, Nepal, through its Radio Teacher Education Training Project has announced plans to provide certificate-level training to many of the 72,000 teachers who lack formal teacher training of any kind. Such programs acknowledge the fact that the shortage of qualified classroom teachers is one of the major stumbling blocks to improving the quality of primary education in the Third World. As the founding director of the Kenya project concluded some time ago:

The use of correspondence methods is gradually becoming widely accepted as a practical solution to the problem of teacher training and upgrading. Beyond this initial step, there is need to continue providing supporting and advisory services to teachers throughout their careers. In other words, a "system" of continuing education is the one which is likely to produce long-term benefits in the educational development of a country. (Kinyanjui, 1977, p. 177)

Perraton (1984b) has documented the practical advantages of distance training as a form of on-the-job training. This is particularly important in situations where it may be impossible to remove teachers from their schools, either because the teachers themselves do not wish to leave or, as is more likely the case, there is no one available or qualified to replace them. In such circumstances, correspondence, radio, and occasionally television can reach them while they continue working. In Chile, for example, the Ministry of Education joined forces with the National Institute for Distance Education in 1979 to run a course on evaluation methods for the country's primary and secondary teachers. According to an undated report prepared by Chadwick, "a carefully organized, quasi-programmed and self-sufficient text accompanied by weekly television programs for motivation, pacing, and enrichment of content" were the main instructional elements of the program. The course lasted 10 weeks, after which time an achievement test was administered on a nationwide basis. About one-third of all Chilean teachers enrolled in the course. Of that group, 90 percent passed the exam.

Distance education methods are also effective in overcoming the communication handicaps faced by teachers in remote schools. Although problems of sending materials, exchanging correspondence, and receiving radio signals can be severe in remote areas of developing countries, they generally have not prevented rural teachers from participating in retraining programs at a distance. Physical isolation, on the other hand, has been a major impediment to attendance at campus-based programs.

In the final analysis, distance teacher retraining schemes have proven most appealing to planners on financial grounds, even though there have been only a few studies to date documenting the programs' comparative cost-effectiveness (Oliveira & Orivel, 1988; Chale, 1983; Perraton, 1982). As is the case with virtually all media systems, distance teaching is capital intensive. It characteristically demands heavy capital investment in course development and equipment. However, once such initial investments have been made, costs do not rise at anything approaching the rate of enrollment. Thus, the bigger the distance teaching system, the more likely will its costs per student be lower than those incurred within traditional programs. Two caveats must be noted, however. First, if some form of face-to-face instruction or tutoring is included (and experience suggests that they should be), system costs will rise in proportion to the number of students. Also, the addition of television, cassette recorders, or other relatively sophisticated learning technologies can be expected to raise system costs significantly.

How far have distance teaching programs come in solving the Third World's nearly universal problems of teacher shortage and teacher quality? Recent research suggests that training that emphasizes basic skills is more effective (vis a vis student learning) than training that attempts to refine skills at a higher level (Lockheed & Hanushek, 1988). While hard evidence may still be lacking to support such conclusions and the policies they imply, ministries of education throughout the developing world are voting with their pocketbooks. They evidently have concluded that distance teaching systems incorporating one or more broadcast media are a cost-effective and practical means for achieving both enrollment and quality improvement objectives.

CONCLUSIONS

Educational broadcasting continues to play significant roles within Third World nations because radio, television, and associated cassette technologies offer planners hope and, in some cases, proven means for increasing access to education and for upgrading the quality of instruction. The media are not panaceas. They have not provoked the "learning revolutions" foreseen by succeeding generations of technology enthusiasts. Their effectiveness rests with how well they are designed, deployed, and ultimately used within specific contexts. As Wilbur Schramm, Tony Bates, and other distinguished observers of the field have noted repeatedly, differences *within* media outweigh differences *between* media in terms of cost-effectiveness. In other words, well-designed radio instruction is likely to be more cost-effective than poorly designed television teaching, just as good lectures will be more effective than poorly made filmstrips or recordings.

The hallmark of educational broadcasting is its distributive power, the ability to reach a large number of learners wherever they may be living, working, or already studying. By the same token, the mass media can address people's educational needs and aspirations at different stages in their lives. It is this attribute more than any other that accounts for the exponential, worldwide growth of distance teaching programs in recent years. Employers and workers also recognize the value of distance in-service training programs that allow people to upgrade job skills without having to abandon temporarily their work or home responsibilities.

Historically, mass-mediated instruction has been capital intensive, perhaps too much so given the tendency of many radio and television projects to break down at the local level for lack of reinforcing human communication and follow-up. The clear need to restrain recurrent costs has too frequently led administrators to cut back on ancillary learning materials and services. This is a false economy if learners then have nowhere to turn for remedial help and encouragement.

If educational broadcasts are to keep students motivated and raise their achievement levels over time, it is imperative that they provide demonstrably superior instruction. With few shining examples, this has not generally been the case in low-income nations. School broadcasts often have not been adequately integrated with ongoing instructional activities. Pedantic, "talking head" production techniques have bored students, limited learning, and eventually driven teachers to switch off their sets. Needed are fresh and carefully derived production formats that maintain learners' interest and elicit active responses on a continuing basis.

The promise of educational broadcasting to broaden access to education and to increase its effectiveness remains largely unfulfilled for the combination of pedagogical, institutional, and economic reasons highlighted in this chapter. To fulfill such ambitious goals in the future, the following challenges must be met:

1. *The challenge of building multi-media learning systems.* To be effective, the mass media must not be promoted as flashy add-ons or as stand-alone alternatives to traditional forms of instruction. They work best and have the most positive ripple effects when they are introduced within a coherent cluster or system of innovative policies and practices.

2. *The challenge of maintaining local support.* Experience from a large number of projects reveals that classroom teachers tend to lose interest in broadcast instruction over time. Inflexible transmission schedules and poor program quality are often to blame for this phenomenon. Also at fault may be classroom teachers' sense of inferiority, perceived loss of control, and diminished professional efficacy in the face of new media. Such feelings can and should be counteracted by aggressive feedback strategies that involve teachers on a continuing basis in the program review and revision process. The addition of cassette recorders has increased teachers' independence and control in some instances, but such technologies do not constitute a complete solution to the problem and they are still beyond the financial means of most Third World nations at the present time.

3. *The challenge of institutionalizing successful demonstration projects.* How can educational systems absorb and maintain programs once their pilot phases have ended and outside advisors have departed? Historically, "going to scale" has presented almost insurmountable obstacles to many of the most successful demonstration projects. For this reason, one must question the wisdom of investing so much in such projects in the first place. Establishment of innovative programs as autonomous units outside the normal chains of command is an expedient but misguided strategy in most instances. In the future, territorial and budget battles within educational institutions and between these institutions and other participating agencies (such as national broadcasting organization) should be resolved at the beginning and not the end of pilot programs.

4. *The challenge of meeting recurrent costs.* Given the scarce resource constraints confronting Third World governments, the cost of continuing even the most popular and apparently effective pilot projects may be insurmountable without new sources of support. For this reason, media planners and evaluators must monitor continuously each element of their programs to ensure that it is contributing its share to the achievement of system goals. At the same time, new sources of private and community support must be cultivated.

Such sources have been identified within most distance teaching projects where the comparative advantages of mediated instruction are perceived to be great, and where learners have been willing to assume some of the financial burden.

5. *The challenge of diffusing exemplary program series and formats.* The advent of satellite communication and cassette recorders now makes it possible to share programs both on real time as well as on a delayed basis. This creates opportunities for Third World educators at various levels to exchange ideas and to participate in training activities on a national and even international scale. By the same token, instructional programs can be shared more widely, although cultural and linguistic differences will continue to limit the scale and utility of such exchanges, particularly at the primary and secondary school levels. Cross-cultural adaptation and use of successful program concepts and formats make much more sense. When carefully designed and monitored, such technology transfers will enable Third World educators to benefit from successful experience elsewhere and, perhaps just as importantly, stimulate more effective uses of broadcast media within their own systems.

REFERENCES

Academy for Educational Development. (1988). Update on interactive radio instruction activities. In *Development communication report* (Special Issue). Washington, D.C.: Clearinghouse on Development Communication.

Anzalone, S. (1987). *Using instructional hardware for primary education in developing countries: A review of the literature.* Cambridge, MA: Harvard University, BRIDGES Project.

Arena, E. (1988, April). *Mexican telesecundaria system: A cost analysis.* Discussion paper, World Bank seminar on Educational Technology, Washington, D.C.

Arnove, R. F. (Ed.) (1976). *Educational television: Policy critique and guide for developing countries.* New York: Praeger.

Bates, A. W. (1984). *Broadcasting in education: An evaluation.* London: Constable.

Bates, A. W. (1987). Media in distance education. In J. Jenkins (Ed.), *Commonwealth co-operation in open learning: Background papers.* London: The Commonwealth Secretariat, 1988.

Carnoy, M. (1976). The economic costs and return to educational television. In R. F. Arnove (Ed.), *Educational television: A policy critique and guide for developing countries.* New York: Praeger.

Carnoy, M., & Levin, H. M. (1975). Evaluation of educational media: Some issues. In D. T. Jamison (Ed.), *Instructional science.* Amsterdam: Elsevier Scientific Publishing Co.

Chadwick, C. (unpublished). *Use of distance education methodology for in-service teacher training.* Arlington, VA: Institute for International Research, Clearinghouse on Development Communication.

Chale, E. M. (1983). Teaching and training in Tanzania. Unpublished doctoral dissertation, University of London.

Coombs, P. (1968). *The world educational crisis: A systems analysis.* New York: Oxford University Press.

Emery, M. (1985). Another exciting revolution? A rejoinder to Kupisiewicz and White. *Prospects, 15* (4), 493–509.

Friend, J., Searle, B., & Suppes, P. (Eds.). (1980). *Radio mathematics in Nicaragua.* Stanford, CA: Stanford University.

Goulet, D. (1977). *The uncertain promise: Value conflicts in technology transfer.* New York: Overseas Development Council.

Grant, S. (1977). *Administrative history of out-of-school television in the Ivory Coast.* Washington, D.C.: Academy for Educational Development.

Hawkridge, D., & Robinson, J. (1982). *Organizing educational broadcasting.* Paris: United Nations Educational, Scientific, and Cultural Organization (UNESCO).

Hudson, H. E. (1984). *When telephones reach the village: The role of telecommunications in rural development.* Norwood, NJ: Ablex.

Imhoof, M., & Christensen, P. (Eds.) (1986). *Teaching English by Radio: Interactive radio in Kenya.* Washington, D.C.: Academy for Educational Development.

Jamison, D., & McAnany, E. (1978). *Radio for education and development.* Beverly Hills, CA: Sage.

Kaye, A. (1976). The Ivory Coast Educational Television Project. In R. Arnove (Ed.), *Educational television: A policy critique and guide for developing countries* (pp. 140–179). New York: Praeger.

Kemmerer, F., & Wagner, A. P. (1986, June). Limits on the use of educational technology in developing countries. Paper presented at the International Conference on Economics of Education, "Tackling the New Policy Issues," Dijon, France.

Kinyanjui, P. E. (1977). In-service training of teachers through radio and correspondence in Kenya. In P. L. Spain, D. T. Jamison, & E. G. McAnany (Eds.), *Radio for education and development: Case studies.* Washington: The World Bank.

Lenglet, F., McAnany, E. G., & Grant, S. (1979). Educational television in the Ivory Coast. In A. Melmed (Ed.), *The organization and management of distance media systems: Some new directions.* Palo Alto, CA: EDUTEL.

Lerner, D., & Schramm, W. L., (Eds.). (1967). *Communication and change in the developing countries.* Honolulu: East-West Center Press.

Lockheed, M., & Hanushek, E. (1988). Improving educational efficiency in developing countries: What do we know? *Compare, 18* (1), 21–38.

Lyle, J. (1982). Since 1967: The original case studies reviewed. In D. Hawkridge & J. Robinson, *Organizing educational broadcasting.* Paris: United Nations Educational, Scientific, and Cultural Organization (UNESCO).

Mayo, J., Hornik, R. C., & McAnany, E. (1976). *Educational reform with television: The El Salvador experience.* Stanford, CA: Stanford University.

Nettleton, G. (1988). *Uses and costs of educational technology for distance education in developing countries: A review of the recent literature.* A Review Paper. Population and Human Resources Department. Washington, D.C.: The World Bank.

O'Brien, R. C. (1976). *Professionalism in broadcasting: Issues of international dependence.* Sussex, England: Institute of Development Studies.

Oliveira, J., & Orivel, F. (1988, April). *Training teachers at a distance: The case of*

Oliveira, J., & Orivel, F. (1988, April). *Training teachers at a distance: The case of Logos II in Brazil*. Discussion paper, World Bank seminar on Educational Technology, Washington, D.C.

Perraton, H. (Ed.). (1982). *Alternative routes to formal education: Distance teaching for school equivalency*. Baltimore, MD: Johns Hopkins University Press.

Perraton, H. (1984a). *The scope of distance teaching: Alternative routes to formal education*. Baltimore, MD: Johns Hopkins University.

Perraton, H. (1984b). *Training teachers at a distance*. London: The Commonwealth Secretariat.

Reiser, R. A., & Gagne, R. M. (1983). *Selecting media for instruction*. Englewood Cliffs, NJ: Educational Technology Publications.

Romiszowski, A. J. (1974). *Selection and use of instructional media*. London: Kegan Paul.

Samarajiva, R., & Shields, P. (In Press). Telecommunications in the Third World: Value choices in resource allocation. In S. B. Lundstedt (Ed.), *Telecommunication, values, and the public interest*.

Schramm, W., Coombs, P., Kahnert, F., & Lyle, J. (1967). *The new media: Memo to educational planners*. Paris: UNESCO.

Schramm, W., Nelson, L. M., & Betham, M. T. (1981). *Bold experiment: The story of educational television in American Samoa*. Stanford, CA: Stanford University Press.

Searle, B. (1985). Evaluation of three interactive radio projects. *Development Communication Report, 49*. Washington, D.C.: Clearinghouse on Development Communications.

United Nations Educational, Scientific, and Cultural Organization (UNESCO). (1985, 1987). *Statistical yearbook*. Paris: UNESCO.

Walberg, H. J. (1984). Synthesis of research on teaching. In M. C. Wittrock (Ed.), *Handbook of research on teaching*. Washington, D.C.: American Educational Research Association.

Webster, F., & Robins, K. (1986). *Information technology: A Luddite analysis*. Norwood, NJ: Ablex.

Selected Bibliography

This bibliography provides a selected listing of reference material of particular relevance to educational development in international settings. Emphasis was on published items appearing since 1980. More complete bibliographic listings are available at the conclusion of each chapter.

Academy for Educational Development. (1988). Update on interactive radio instruction activities. In *Development communication report* (Special Issue). Washington, D.C.: Clearinghouse on Development Communication.

Ad Hoc Committee on the Use of Microcomputers in Developing Countries. (1986). *Microcomputers and their applications for developing countries*. Boulder, CO: Westview Press.

Andrews, D. H., & Goodson, L. A. (1980). A comparative analysis of models of instructional design. *Journal of Instructional Development*, 3(4), 2–16.

Anzalone, S. (1987). *Using instructional hardware for primary education in developing countries: A review of the literature*. Cambridge, MA: Harvard University, BRIDGES Project.

Armitage, J., Batista, J., Harbison, R. W., Holsinger, D. B., & Helio, R. (1986). *School quality and achievement in rural Brazil*. Washington, D.C.: The World Bank, Education and Training Department.

Arriagada, A. (1981). *Determinants of sixth grade student achievement in Colombia*. Unpublished manuscript, The World Bank, Education Department, Washington, D.C.

Arriagada, A. (1983). *Determinants of sixth grade achievement in Peru*. Unpublished manuscript, The World Bank, Education Department, Washington, D.C.

Ashton, P. T., & Webb, R. B. (1986). *Making a difference: Teachers' sense of efficacy and student achievement*. New York: Longman.

Asia Development Bank. (1987). *Distance education in Asia and the Pacific.* (2 vols.). Manila: Author.

Bae, H. (1987). *A cross-national study of teachers' conceptions of effective teaching.* Unpublished doctoral dissertation, School of Education, State University of New York at Albany.

Balderston, J., Wilson, A., Freire, M., & Simonen, M. (1981). *Malnourished children of the rural poor.* Boston: Auburn House.

Barr, R., & Dreeben, R. (1983). *How schools work.* Chicago: University of Chicago Press.

Bass, R. K., & Dills, C. R. (Eds.). (1984). *Instructional development: The state of the art, II.* Dubuque, IW: Kendall Hunt.

Bates, A. W. (1982). Options for delivery media. In H. Perraton (Ed.), *Alternative routes to formal education.* Baltimore, MD: Johns Hopkins University.

Bates, A. W. (1984). *Broadcasting in education: An evaluation.* London: Constable.

Bates, A. W. (1988). Media in distance education. In J. Jenkins (Ed.), *Commonwealth co-operation in open learning; Background papers.* London: The Commonwealth Secretariat.

Baum, W. C., & Tolbert, S. M. (1985). *Investing in development: Lessons of World Bank experience.* New York: Oxford University Press.

Becker, H. (1988). *The impact of computer use on children's learning: What research has shown and what it has not shown.* Baltimore: Johns Hopkins University, Center for Educational Research on Elementary and Middle Schools.

Berman, P. (1981). Educational change: An implementation paradigm. In R. Lehming & M. Kane (Eds.), *Improving schools: Using what we know* (pp. 253–286). Beverly Hills, CA: Sage.

Bhola, H. (1984). *Campaigning for literacy.* Paris: United Nations Educational, Scientific, and Cultural Organization (UNESCO).

Block, C. (1985). Interactive radio and educational development. *Development Communication Report, 49.*

Boothroyd, R. A., & Chapman, D. W. (1987). Gender differences and achievement in Liberian primary school children. *International Journal of Educational Development, 7*(2), 99–105.

Branson, R. K. (1988). Why schools can't improve: The upper limit hypothesis. *Journal of Instructional Development, 10,* 27–32.

Brodman, J. (1985). *Microcomputer adoption in developing countries: Old management styles and new information systems, a case study of microcomputer adoption in Kenya and Indonesia.* Cambridge, MA: Harvard Institute for International Development.

Burchfield, S. (1986). *Improving energy data collection and analysis in developing countries: A comparative study in Uganda, Liberia, and Sudan.* Washington, D.C.: United States Agency for International Development, Bureau for Africa.

Carron, G., & Bordia, A. (Eds.). (1985). *Issues in planning and implementing national literacy programmes.* Paris: UNESCO, International Institute for Educational Planning.

Chale, E. M. (1983). Teaching and training in Tanzania. Unpublished doctoral dissertation, University of London.

Chambers, R. (1981). Rapid rural appraisal: Rationale and repertoire. *Public Administration and Development, 1,* 95–106.

Chapman, D. W. (1983). Career satisfaction of teachers. *Educational Research Quarterly, 7*(3), 40–50.

Chapman, D. W. (1989, March). Education data quality in Nepal. Paper presented at the annual meeting of the American Educational Research Association, San Francisco.

Chapman, D. W., & Boothroyd, R. A. (1988). Evaluation dilemmas: Conducting evaluation studies in developing countries. *Evaluation and Program Planning, 11,* 37–42.

Chapman, D. W., & Boothroyd, R. A. (1988). Threats to data quality in developing country settings. *Comparative Education Review, 32*(4), 416–429.

Chapman, D. W., & Carrier, C. A. (1989, March). *The dimensions of teacher concern about adopting an innovation: The case of Liberian primary school teachers.* Paper presented at the annual meeting of the American Educational Research Association, San Francisco.

Chapman, D. W., & Hutcheson, S. M. (1982). Attrition from teaching careers: A discriminant analysis. *American Educational Research Journal, 19,* 93–105.

Chapman, D. W., & Kelly, E. F. (1981). A comparison of the dimensions used by Iranian and American students in rating instruction. *International Review of Education, 27,* 41–60.

Chapman, D. W., & Windham, D. M. (1986). *The evaluation of efficiency in educational development activities.* Tallahassee: Florida State University, Improving the Efficiency of Educational Systems Project.

Christensen, P. (1985). The Radio Language Arts Project: Adapting the Radio Mathematics Model. *Development Communication Report, 49.*

Cieutat, V. J. (1983). *Planning and managing an education sector assessment.* Washington, D.C.: U.S. Agency for International Development.

Clark, R. (1983). Reconsidering research on learning from media. *Review of Educational Research, 53*(4), 445–459.

Claveria, O. B. (1982). *Report on the implementation of the IMPACT experiment—universal primary education (IDS).* Dhaka, Bangladesh: Institute for International Research.

Coombs, P. H. (1985). *The world crisis in education.* New York: Oxford University Press.

Coombs, P. H. & Hallak, J. (1987). *Cost analysis in education.* Washington, D.C.: The World Bank.

Cousins, J. B., & Leithwood, K. A. (1986). Current empirical research on evaluation utilization. *Review of Educational Research, 56*(3), 331–364.

Cummings, W. K. (1986). *Low-cost primary education: Implementing an innovation in six nations.* Ottawa, Canada: International Development Research Centre.

Darling-Hammond, L. (1984). *Beyond the commission reports: The coming crisis in teaching.* Santa Monica, CA: The Rand Corporation.

Department of Education. (1986). Beginning teacher assistance program: What are the competencies that teachers will be expected to demonstrate? Richmond, VA: Department of Education, Division of Professional Development.

Dhungana, M., & Butterworth, B. (1988). Status report: Education management information systems research initiative in Nepal. Tallahassee: Florida State University, Improving the Efficiency of Education Systems Project.

Dick, W., & Carey, L. (1985). *The systematic design of instruction* (2nd ed.). Dallas, TX: Scott, Foresman.

Dreeben, R., & Thomas, J. A. (Eds.). (1980). *The analysis of educational productivity, vol. I: Issues in microanalysis.* Cambridge, MA: Ballinger.

Eckblad, G. (1981). Assimilation resistance and affective responses in problem solving. *Scandinavian Journal of Psychology, 22,* 1–16.

Eckblad, G. (1981). *Scheme theory: A conceptual framework for cognitive-motivational processes.* London: Academic Press.

Eicher, J. C., Hawkridge, D., McAnany, E., Mariet, F., & Orivel, F. (1982). *The economics of new educational media: Overview and synthesis.* Paris: United Nations Educational, Scientific, and Cultural Organization (UNESCO).

Everhart, R. (1983). *Reading, writing, and resistance.* Boston: Routledge.

Friend, J. (1985). Classroom uses of the computer: A retrospective view with implications for developing nations. Washington, D.C.: The World Bank, Education and Training Series.

Friend, J. (1985). A model for interactive radio lessons: The Radio Mathematics Project. *Development Communication Report, 49.*

Friend, J., Galda, K., & Searle, B. (1986). From Nicaragua to Thailand: Adapting interactive radio instruction. *Development Communications Report, 52.*

Friend, J., Searle, B., & Suppes, P. (Eds.). (1980). *Radio mathematics in Nicaragua.* Stanford, CA: Stanford University.

Fuller, B. (1985). *Raising school quality in developing countries: What investments boost learning?* Washington, D.C.: The World Bank, Education and Training Series, No. 2.

Fuller, B. (1986). Defining school quality. In J. Hannaway & M. Lockheed (Eds.), *The contributions of the social sciences to educational policy and practice: 1965–1985* (pp. 33–70). Berkeley, CA: McCutchan.

Fuller, B. (1986). Is primary school quality eroding in the Third World? *Comparative Education Review, 30,* 491–502.

Fuller, B. (1987). What school factors raise achievement in the Third World? *Review of Educational Research, 57*(3), 255–292.

Gaal, A. H., & Burchfield, S. (1988). *Education management information systems research initiative in Somalia: Status report.* Tallahassee: Florida State University, Improving the Efficiency of Education Systems Project.

Gagne, R. M. (Ed.). (1987). *Instructional technology: Foundations.* Hillsdale, NJ: Erlbaum.

Gagne, R., Briggs, L., & Wager, W. (1988). *Principles of instructional design* (3rd ed.). New York: Holt, Rinehart, & Winston.

Government of Botswana. (1983). *Botswana education and human resources sector assessment* (Report). Gaborone: Ministry of Education and Tallahassee: Florida State University, Improving the Efficiency of Education Systems Project.

Government of Indonesia. (1986). *Indonesia education and human resources sector assessment* (Report). Jakarta: Ministry of Education and Culture and Tallahassee: Florida State University, Improving the Efficiency of Education Systems Project.

Government of Liberia. (1986). *The feasibility of integrating programmed learning with conventional instruction in Liberian primary education* (Report). Monrovia: Ministry of Education and Tallahassee: Florida State University, Improving the Efficiency of Education Systems Project.

Government of Liberia. (1988). *Liberia education and human resources sector assessment* (Report). Monrovia: Ministry of Education and Ministry of Planning and Tallahassee: Florida State University, Improving the Efficiency of Education Systems Project.

Government of Nepal. (1988). *Nepal education and human resources sector assessment* (Report). Kathmandu: Ministry of Education and Culture and Tallahassee: Florida State University, Improving the Efficiency of Education Systems Project.

Government of Somalia. (1983). *Somalia education and human resources sector assessment* (Report). Mogadishu: Ministry of National Planning and Tallahassee: Florida State University, Improving the Efficiency of Education Systems Project.

Government of Somalia. (1984). *Somalia civil service study* (Report). Mogadishu: Ministry of Labor and Tallahassee: Florida State University, Improving the Efficiency of Education Systems Project.

Government of the Yemen Arab Republic. (1985). *Yemen education and human resources sector assessment* (Report). Sana'a: Ministry of Education and Tallahassee: Florida State University, Improving the Efficiency of Education Systems Project.

Harrison, G. V., & Morgan, R. M. (1982). *An evaluation of the Improved Efficiency of Learning Project.* Monrovia, Liberia: U.S. Agency for International Development.

Hartley, J. (1985). *Designing instructional text* (2nd ed.). New York: Nichols.

Hartley, M., & Swanson, E. (1984). *Achievement and wastage: An analysis of the retention of basic skills in primary education.* Draft manuscript, The World Bank, Washington, D.C.

Hatry, H. P., & Greiner, J. M. (1985). *Issues and case studies in teacher incentive plans.* Washington, D.C.: The Urban Institute Press.

Haugen, E., McClure, J. D., & Thomson, D. (Eds.). (1981). *Minority languages today.* Edinburgh, Scotland: Edinburgh University Press.

Hawkridge, D., & Robinson, J. (1982). *Organizing educational broadcasting.* Paris: United Nations Educational, Scientific, and Cultural Organization (UNESCO).

Heinich, R., Molenda, M., & Russell, J. D. (1985). *Instructional media: And the new technologies of instruction* (2nd ed.). New York: John Wiley.

Heyneman, S., & Jamison, D. (1980). Student learning in Uganda: Textbook availability and other factors. *Comparative Education Review, 24,* 206–220.

Heyneman, S., Jamison, D., & Montenegro, X. (1983). Textbooks in the Philippines: Evaluation of the pedagogical impact of the nationwide investment. *Education Evaluation and Policy Analysis, 6*(2), 139–150.

Heyneman, S., & Loxley, W. (1983). The effect of primary-school quality on academic achievement across twenty-nine high- and low-income countries. *American Journal of Sociology, 88,* 1162–1194.

Holloway, S. D., & Hess, R. D. (1985). Mothers' and teachers' attributions about children's math performance. In I. E. Sigal (Ed.), *Parental belief systems: Psychological consequences for children* (pp. 177–199). Hillsdale, NJ: Erlbaum.

Hord, S. M., & Hall, G. E. (1986, April). *Institutionalization of innovations: Knowing when you have it and when you don't.* Paper presented at the annual meeting of the American Educational Research Association, San Francisco.

Hudson, H. E. (1984). *When telephones reach the village: The role of telecommunications in rural development.* Norwood, NJ: Ablex.

Imboden, N. (1980). *Managing information for rural development projects.* Paris, France: Organization for Economic Co-Operation and Development.

Imhoof, M. (1985). Interactive radio in the classroom: Ten years of proven success. *Development Communication Report, 49.*

Imhoof, M., & Christensen, P. (Eds.). (1986). *Teaching English by radio: Interactive radio in Kenya.* Washington, D.C.: Academy for Educational Development.

Improving the Efficiency of Education Systems (IEES) Project. (1985). *Enhancement of school quality in Somalia.* Tallahassee: Florida State University, IEES Educational Efficiency Clearinghouse.

Improving the Efficiency of Education Systems (IEES) Project. (1988). *Somalia country plan.* Tallahassee: Florida State University, IEES Educational Efficiency Clearinghouse.

Jamison, D. T., & Lockheed, M. E. (1985). *Participation in schooling: Determinants and learning outcomes in Nepal.* Washington, D.C.: The World Bank, Education and Training Department.

Jamison, D., Searle, B., Galda, K., & Heyneman, S. (1981). Improving elementary mathematics education in Nicaragua: An experimental study of the impact of textbooks and radio on achievement. *Journal of Educational Psychology, 73*(4), 556–567.

Jenkins, J. (1988). *Commonwealth co-operation in open learning: Background papers.* London: The Commonwealth Secretariat.

Joyce, B., & Weil, M. (1986). *Models of teaching.* (3rd ed.). Engelwood Cliffs, NJ: Prentice-Hall.

Kachru, B. B. (Ed.). (1982). *The other tongue: English across cultures.* Urbana: University of Illinois Press.

Karweit, N. (1985). Should we lengthen the school term? *Educational Researcher, 14*(6), 9–15.

Kaufman, R. A. (1988). *Planning educational systems.* Lancaster, PA: Technomic.

Kelly, E. (1984). *Horse races, time trials, and evaluation designs: Implications for future evaluations of the Improved Efficiency of Learning Project.* Albany, NY: State University of New York at Albany, School of Education.

Kelly, E. (1984). *Preliminary report no. II—overall test results.* Albany, NY: State University of New York at Albany, School of Education.

Kemmerer, F. (1988, November). *The use of information in inducing, tracking, and monitoring change.* Paper presented at the World Bank and U.S. Agency for International Development Conference on Education Policy Adjustment: "Raising School Quality and Efficiency," Washington, D.C.

Kemmerer, F., & Wagner, A. (1986, June). *The limits of the use of educational technology in developing countries.* Paper presentation at the International Conference on Economics of Education: "Tackling New Policy Issues," Dijon, France.

Kroonenberg, P. M., & Snyder, C. W., Jr. (In Press). Individual differences in assimilation resistance and affective responses in problem solving. *Multivariate Behavioral Research*.

Laponce, J. A. (1987). *Languages and their territories*. Toronto, Canada: University of Toronto Press.

Lareau, A. (1987). Social class differences in family–school relationships: The importance of cultural capital. *Sociology of Education, 60*, 73–85.

Leinhardt, G. (1980). Modeling and measuring education treatments in evaluation. *Review of Educational Research, 50*(3), 393–420.

Leithwood, K., & Montgomery, D. (1982). The role of the elementary school principal in program improvement. *Review of Educational Research, 52*, 309–339.

Levin, H. M. (1983). *Cost-effectiveness: A primer*. Beverly Hills, CA: Sage Publications.

Lockheed, M., Vail, S., & Fuller, B. (1986). How textbooks affect achievement in developing countries: Evidence from Thailand. *Educational Evaluation and Policy Analysis, 8*, 379–392.

Lockheed, M. E., & Hanushek, E. (1987). *Improving the efficiency of education in developing countries: Review of the evidence* (Discussion Paper, EDT 77). Washington, D.C.: The World Bank.

Lockheed, M. E., & Hanushek, E. (1988). Improving educational efficiency in developing countries: What do we know? *Compare, 18*(1), 21–38.

Mayo, J., & Hornik, R. C. (1981). *Evaluation and research in the planning, development, and support of media-based education*. Paris, France: International Institute for Educational Planning.

McAnany, E., Oliveira, J., Orivel, F., & Stone, J. (1983). Distance education: Evaluating new approaches in education for developing countries. *Evaluation in Education, 6*, 289–376.

Messec, J. (1986). *Soomaali-English English-Soomaali technical term dictionary of economics*. Tallahassee: Florida State University, Improving the Efficiency of Education Systems Project.

Meyer, J. (1987). Implications of an institutional view of education. In M. Halinan (Ed.), *The social organization of schools* (pp. 157–175). New York: Plenum.

Michael, R. (1982). "Measuring the non-monetary benefits of education. In W. W. Geske & T. Geske, (Eds.), *Financing education: Overcoming inefficiency and inequity* (pp. 119–149). Urbana: University of Illinois Press.

Montemerlo, M. D., & Tennyson, M. E. (1976). Instructional systems development: Conceptual analysis and comprehensive biography (NAVTRAEQUIPCEN-257). Orlando, FL: Naval Training Equipment Center.

Murnane, R. J., & Cohen, D. K. (1986). Merit pay and the evaluation problem: Why most merit pay plans fail and a few survive. *Harvard Educational Review, 56*(1), 1–17.

Nelson, H. (Ed.). (1981). *Somalia: A country study*. Washington, D.C.: U.S. Government Printing Office.

Nettleton, G. (1988). *Uses and costs of educational technology for distance education in developing countries: A review of the recent literature* (Review Paper). Washington, D.C.: The World Bank, Population and Human Resources Department.

Nichols, D. G. (1982). Low-cost learning systems: The general concept and some specific examples. *NSPI Journal, 4* (September), 4–8.

Nichols, D. G. (1983). *Handbook of IEL instructional management.* Gbarnga, Liberia: Improved Efficiency of Learning Project.

Nielsen, H. D. (1982). *Analysis of achievement test scores for PAMONG and regular primary schools of Gianyar Bali trimester, 1, 1981–1982.* Jakarta, Indonesia: Department of Education and Culture.

Nielsen, H. D. (1982). *Improving the process of peer group learning in PAMONG primary schools.* Jakarta, Indonesia: Department of Education and Culture.

Nielsen, H. D., & Bernard, D. C. (1983). *Final report: Self-instructional learning system.* Solo, Indonesia: Universitas Sebelas Maret.

Oakes, J. (1982). Classroom social relationships: Exploring the Bowles and Gintis hypothesis. *Sociology of Education, 55,* 197–202.

Oliveira, J., & Orivel, F. (1988, April). *Training teachers at a distance: The case of Logos II in Brazil.* Discussion paper, World Bank seminar on Educational Technology, Washington, D.C.

Ornstein, A. C. (1982). Innovation and change: Yesterday and today. *High School Journal, 65,* 279–286.

Oxford, R., Clark, J., Hermansen, J., Christensen, P., & Imhoff, M. (1986). *Final report: Evaluation of the Kenya Radio Language Arts Project.* Washington, D.C.: Academy for Educational Development.

Pappagianis, G. J., Klees, S. J., & Bickel, R. (1982). Toward a political economy of educational innovation. *Review of Educational Research, 52,* 245–290.

Pasigna, A. L. (1985). Success story: Liberia's Improved Efficiency of Learning Project. *NSPI Journal, 24*(9), 7–8.

Pasigna, A. L. (In Press). *A post-hoc analysis of "low-cost" learning systems.*

Perraton, H. (Ed.). (1982). *Alternative routes to formal education: Distance teaching for school equivalency.* Baltimore, MD: Johns Hopkins University Press.

Perraton, H. (1984). *Training teachers at a distance.* London: The Commonwealth Secretariat.

Perry, Lord Walter, & Rumble, G. (1987). *A short guide to distance education.* Cambridge, MA: The International Extension College.

Postlethwaite, T. N. (1987). Comparative educational achievement research: Can it be improved? *Comparative Education Review, 31*(1), 150–158.

Postlethwaite, T., & Thomas, R. (Eds.). (1980). *Schooling in the ASEAN Region: Primary and secondary education in Indonesia, Malaysia, the Philippines, Singapore, and Thailand.* Oxford: Pergamon Press.

Pravica, S. S., & McLean, L. D. (1983). The effects of principal participation in curriculum and implementation: Support from an evaluation of a new mathematics curriculum. *The Alberta Journal of Educational Research, 29,* 46–53.

Prophet, R. B. (1987, September). Rhetoric and reality in science curriculum development in Botswana. Paper presented at the British Education Research Association Meeting, Manchester, UK.

Prophet, R. (1988). *Rhetoric and reality in science curriculum development in Botswana.* Gaborone: University of Botswana. Mimeo.

Psacharopoulos, G. (1985). Returns to education: A further international comparison. *Journal of Human Resources, 20*(4), 584–604.

Psacharopoulos, G., & Loxley, W. (1986). *Diversified secondary education and development.* London: Oxford University Press.

Psacharopoulos, G., & Woodhall, M. (1985). *Education for development: An analysis of investment choices.* New York: Oxford University Press.

Reiser, R. A., & Gagne, R. M. (1983). *Selecting media for instruction.* Englewood Cliffs, NJ: Educational Technology Publications.

Rogers, E. M. (1983). *Diffusion of innovations* (3rd ed.). New York: The Free Press.

Romiszowski, A. J. (1984). *Producing instructional systems: Lesson planning for individualized and group learning activities.* London: Nichols.

Rosenblum, S., & Louis, K. S. (1981). *Stability and change.* New York: Plenum.

Rosenholtz, S. J., & Smylie, M. A. (1984). Teacher compensation and career ladders. *The Elementary School Journal, 85*(2), 149–166.

Ross, A. S. (1984). Practical problems associated with program evaluation in Third World countries. *Evaluation and Program Planning, 7,* 211–218.

Rutter, M. (1983). School effects on pupil progress: Research findings and policy implications. *Child Development, 54,* 1–29.

Scheirer, M. A., & Rezmovic, E. L. (1983). Measuring the degree of program implementation: A methodological review. *Evaluation Review, 7*(5), 599–633.

Schramm, W., Nelson, L. M., & Betham, M. T. (1981). *Bold experiment: The story of educational television in American Samoa.* Stanford, CA: Stanford University.

Schweda-Nicholson, N. (Ed.). (1986). *Languages in the international perspective.* Norwood, NJ: Ablex.

Scotton, C. M. (1982). Learning lingua francas and socioeconomic integration: Evidence from Africa. In R. Cooper (Ed.), *Language spread: Studies in diffusion and social change.* Bloomington: Indiana University Press.

Searle, B. (1985). *General operational review of textbooks.* Washington, D.C.: The World Bank, Education and Training Series.

Searle, B., & Galda, K. (1980). Measuring of the effect of radio mathematics lessons on student achievement. In J. Friend, B. Searle, & P. Suppes (Eds.), *Radio mathematics in Nicaragua.* Stanford, CA: Stanford University.

Sembiring, R., & Livingstone, I. (1981). *National assessment of the quality of Indonesian education.* Jakarta: Ministry of Education and Culture.

Sepulveda-Stuardo, M. A., & Farrell, J. P. (1983). The use of textbooks by teachers and students in learning and teaching (World Bank Staff Working Paper No. 530). Washington, D.C.: The World Bank.

Shin, S. H., Chang, S. W., & Park, K. S. (1984). *Study of impact of E-M Project of Korean education.* Seoul: Korean Educational Development Institute.

Simon, H. A. (1981). *The sciences of the artificial.* Cambridge, MA: The MIT Press.

Smith, M. E. (Ed.). (1986). *Introduction to performance technology.* Washington, D.C.: National Society for Performance and Instruction.

Smyth, J. (1987). *Somalia: Preparation mission report.* Paris, France: Office of the Assistant Director-General. Mimeo.

Snyder, C. W., Jr., & Nagel, J. (1986). *The struggle continues: World Bank and African Development Bank investments in Liberian educational development (1972–1985).* McLean, VA: Institute for International Research.

Snyder, C. W., Jr., & Nagel, J. (1988). *Indicators of quality in Botswana primary education.* Tallahassee, FL: Learning Systems Institute.

Stevenson, H. W., Stigler, J. W., Lucker, G. W., Lee, S., Hsu, C. C., & Kitamura, S. (1987). Classroom behavior and achievement of Japanese, Chinese, and American children. In R. Glasser (Ed.), *Advances in Instructional Psychology* (Vol. 3, pp. 153–204). Hillsdale, NJ: Erlbaum.

Strudwick, J. (1986). A proposal for research in strengthening local education capacity: Indonesia and Botswana. Tallahassee: Florida State University, Improving the Efficiency of Education Systems Project.

Thiagarajan, S. (1980). *Protocol packages.* Englewood Cliffs, NJ: Educational Technology Publications.

Thiagarajan, S. (1983). *A report on the IEL Materials Cost Reduction project.* Gbarnga, Liberia: The Improved Efficiency of Learning Project.

Thiagarajan, S. (1984). *Appropriate educational technology for developing nations: Low cost learning systems.* Bloomington, IN: Institute for International Research.

Thiagarajan, S. (1985). *Factors that contribute to inefficiencies in primary schools in developing nations: A survey of the literature* (Project Report for USAID Honduras No. 522–9105). Washington, D.C.: United States Agency for International Development.

Thiagarajan, S. (1985). *Instructional system design for improved learning.* Gabarone, Botswana: Institute for Educational Research.

Thiagarajan, S. (1988). *Belize's Posterized Programmed Teaching Technology Project: An interim evaluation report.* Bloomington, IN: Institute for International Research, Inc.

Thiagarajan, S., & Kemmerer, F. (1987). *How to improve teacher incentive systems.* Tallahassee: Florida State University, Improving the Efficiency of Educational Systems Project.

Thiagarajan, S., & Pasigna, A. L. (1985). *Final contractor's report: Improved Efficiency of Learning (IEL) Project* (Final Report to the U.S. Agency for International Development, Contract No. AID/AFR–C–1494). McLean, VA: Institute for International Research.

Thias, H., & Carnoy, M. (1973). *Cost benefit analysis in education: A case study of Kenya.* Baltimore, MD: Johns Hopkins Press.

Thomas, J. A., & Kemmerer, F. (1983). *Money, time, and learning* (Final Report to the National Institute of Education, Contract No. 400–77–0094). Chicago, IL: University of Chicago.

Tornatzky, L. G., Fergus, E. O., Avellar, J. W., Fairweather, G. W., & Fleischer, M. (1980). *Innovation and social process: A national experiment in implementing social technology.* Elmsford, NY: Pergamon Press.

Tyler, L. E. (1983). *Thinking creatively.* San Francisco, CA: Jossey-Bass.

United Nations Educational, Scientific, and Cultural Organization (UNESCO). (1985, 1987). *Statistical Yearbook.* Paris: UNESCO.

Verspoor, A. M. (1986). Textbooks as instruments for the improvement of the quality of education. (World Bank Discussion Paper, EDT 50). Washington, D.C.: The World Bank.

Verspoor, A. M., & Leno, J. L. (1986). Improving teaching: A key to successful educational change (World Bank Discussion Paper, EDT 50). Washington, D.C.: The World Bank.

Walberg, H. J. (1984). Synthesis of research on teaching. In M. C. Wittrock (Ed.), *Handbook of research on teaching*. Washington, D.C.: American Educational Research Association.

Waugh, R. F., & Punch, F. F. (1987). Teacher receptivity to systemwide change in the implementation stage. *Review of Educational Research, 57*(3), 237–254.

Weiner, B. (1983). Some methodological pitfalls in attributional research. *Journal of Educational Psychology, 75*, 530–543.

Wellman, L. (1987). *Factors relating to the implementation of the New York state curriculum for English as a second language in secondary schools*. Unpublished doctoral dissertation, School of Education, State University of New York at Albany.

Windham, D. M. (1983, September). *Cost estimates of the revised Improved Efficiency of Learning (IEL) Project* (Supplemental Report to the IEL Cost Analysis Project). Monrovia: Ministry of Education.

Windham, D. M. (1983, January). *Cost issues in the Liberian Improved Efficiency of Learning (IEL) Project* (Report No. 1). Monrovia: Ministry of Education.

Windham, D. M. (1983, March). *Internal economies in the Liberian Improved Efficiency of Learning (IEL) Project* (Report No. 2). Monrovia: Ministry of Education.

Windham, D. M. (1983, June). *The relative cost-effectiveness of the Liberian Improved Efficiency of Learning (IEL) Project* (Report No. 3). Monrovia: Ministry of Education.

Windham, D. M. (1986). *Internal efficiency and the African school*. Washington, D.C.: The World Bank.

Windham, D. M. (1988). Effectiveness indicators in the economic analysis of educational activities. *International Journal of Educational Research, 12* (6), 575–665.

Windham, D. M. (1988). *Indicators of educational effectiveness and efficiency*. Tallahassee: Florida State University, Improving the Efficiency of Education Systems Project.

Witherell, R. A., Morgan, R. M., Yoon, H. W., Kim, S. U., & Lee, C. J. (1981). *Korean elementary-middle school project* (AID Evaluation Special Study No. 5, Working Paper No. 530). Washington, D.C.: U.S. Agency for International Development.

Wolfson, N., & Manes, J. (Eds.). (1985). *Language of inequality*. Berlin: Mouton.

Wooster, J. (1986). *The effect of three variables on teacher implementation of a centrally imposed curriculum*. Unpublished doctoral dissertation, State University of New York at Albany.

World Bank. (1988). *Education in Sub-Saharan Africa: Policies for adjustment revitalization, and expansion*. Washington, D.C.: The World Bank.

Index

About the Contributors

CAROL A. CARRIER is Professor of Instructional Design in the Department of Curriculum and Instruction and Assistant Vice-President for Academic Affairs at the University of Minnesota. She is coauthor of *Teacher Development* and her research has appeared in the *American Educational Research Journal*, *Journal of Educational Research*, *Journal of Instructional Development*, and *Contemporary Educational Psychology*. She has delivered technical assistance and technology training in Europe, Africa, and the Middle East.

DAVID W. CHAPMAN is Associate Professor of Education at the State University of New York at Albany where he teaches program evaluation in the Department of Educational Theory and Practice. He is coauthor of *The Evaluation of Educational Efficiency: Constraints, Issues, and Policies* (with Douglas M. Windham). His research on educational improvement has appeared in the *American Educational Research Journal*, the *International Journal of Educational Development*, *Educational Evaluation and Policy Analysis*, and the *Comparative Education Review*. In addition to his research and work in educational improvement in the United States, he has worked in technical assistance activities in over 13 developing countries.

JOAN M. CLAFFEY is engaged in education research and planning as a private contractor. Since 1987 she has been a consultant to the Agency for International Development (AID), the International Labour Organization, and the World Bank. From 1982 to 1987 Claffey served as project officer with AID's Bureau for Science and Technology, Office of Education, where she developed and managed a multi-country project to improve the efficiency of education systems. Claffey has led education sector assessments and project design efforts in Botswana, Liberia, and Somalia, and has provided technical assistance in more than a dozen additional countries in Africa, Asia, the Near East, and the Caribbean. From 1976 she was Director of Michigan State University's Non-Formal Education Center.

BRUCE FULLER is a project officer with the Bureau of Science and Technology, Office of Education, of the United States Agency for International Development. He previously was a researcher with the World Bank. His recent research has appeared in the *Review of Educational Research*, the *Comparative Education Review*, and the *Sociology of Education*.

FRANCES KEMMERER is an Assistant Professor in the Department of Educational Administration and Policy Studies at the State University of New York at Albany. She also serves as Institutional Coordinator at the University at Albany for the USAID funded Improving the Efficiency of Education Systems Project. Her specialty is the allocation of resources within systems and schools.

JOHN K. MAYO is Director of the Center for International Studies and Professor of Communication at Florida State University. He has directed research and development projects on educational broadcasting and on the transfer of communication technology in Mexico, El Salvador, Peru, the Dominican Republic, Thailand, and Nepal.

JERRY L. MESSEC is Assistant Director for Research and Information Management for the Improving the Efficiency of Educational Systems (IEES) Project in the Learning Systems Institute at Florida State University. Messec specialized in Middle Eastern Studies at the University of Chicago and Far Eastern Studies at the University of California at Berkeley. He currently assists educational systems in Africa, the Middle East, and Asia in policy research and the design of information systems.

ROBERT M. MORGAN is Professor of Educational Research and Director of the Learning Systems Institute at the Florida State University in Tallahassee, Florida. He was Director at the Korean Elementary-Middle School project and is the Principal Investigator of the Improved Efficiency of Educational Systems (IEES) project referred to in his chapter. An experimental psychologist, he has been active in instructional systems design work since its inception.

CONRAD WESLEY SNYDER, JR., is Research Associate with the Learning Systems Institute at Florida State University where he serves as Project Coordinator for the Junior Secondary Education Improvement Project in Botswana. He is coeditor of *Research Methods for Multimode Data Analysis* published by Praeger (1984) and coauthor of *Architecture for Progress* and *The Struggle Continues*. He currently is coauthoring a text on *Understanding Human Action Through Experimentation*. Over the last 16 years he has spent 7 years in educational development projects in Africa: Botswana, Lesotho, Liberia, Malawi, and Swaziland.

SIVASAILAM THIAGARAJAN is Vice-President of the Institute for International Research. His specialization is instructional systems design for developing nations. Thiagarajan has over 30 years of experience in development assistance and has worked in both recipient and provider agencies. He has managed large-scale instructional development projects in developing countries, including the Improved Efficiency of Learning Project in Liberia.

DOUGLAS M. WINDHAM is Professor of Education Administration and Policy Studies and Professor of Public Policy at the State University of New York at Albany. A specialist in the economics of education, he has published extensively on the issues of higher education finance in developed countries and on fiscal policy and macro-education planning in developing nations. His most recent publications include, *Indicators of Educational Effectiveness and Efficiency* and *The Evaluation of Educational Efficiency: Constraints, Issues, and Policies* (with David W. Chapman).